THE MODEL
AIRCRAFT
HANDBOOK

THE MODEL
AIRCRAFT
HANDBOOK

revised by

Howard G. McEntee

British edition edited by Ron Moulton

ROBERT HALE · LONDON

This book is based on *The Model Aircraft Handbook*
by William Winter.

Acknowledgment with thanks is made to the following
for the use of illustrations in this book: Aristo-Craft
Distinctive Miniatures; Estes Industries; Model
Aeronautical Press Ltd.; Sturdi-Built Model Mfg.;
Victor Stanzel & Co.; World Engines, Inc.; Doug McHard;
Marcus Norman; Ron Moulton; Frank Zaic; and Model &
Allied Publications Ltd., publishers of *Aeromodeller*, and
Radio Control Models & Electronics.

ISBN 0 7091 8767 X

Printed in Great Britain by
St Edmundsbury Press
Bury St Edmunds, Suffolk
and bound by Hunter & Foulis

Dedicated to my wife Elinor,
who labored long and hard
over proofreading
and typing the text

CONTENTS

ILLUSTRATIONS

1

TYPES OF MODELS

The rapid developments in electronics, plastics and adhesives have had
their influence on model aircraft. Whereas the highly detailed true-to-
scale model was once a problem child for both construction and actual
flight, it has now become commonplace. In the same way, we now have
helicopter models capable of doing all the things we expect of the full-
scale "choppers", and gliders up to one quarter full size which can soar
for hours on end. The world record for this category is twenty-eight
hours, limited only by the demands on the pilot and the batteries for the
radio-control system! Materials such as balsa wood, tissue and silks
have given way in some cases to expanded polyurethane plastic, film
polymers and thermoplastic coverings. We use carbon fibre for reinforcement, epoxy for mouldings and cyanoacrylates for instant joints in
assembly.

All these changes are sophisticated reflections of our scientific pro-
gress into the 1980s, and to a large degree they overtake the basics
which should concern the reader of this book. They belong to the kit-box
or ready-to-operate type of model off the shelf from the specialist shop
and require amazingly little (apart from money) for the purchaser to get
them into the air.

That is not to say these latest designs and types make model aircraft
easier to operate. On the contrary, the very speed with which they
enable the enthusiastic "modeller" to reach the flying field is frequently

counter-productive, because in the process, the newcomer is not given the opportunity to understand the most basic needs for success.

This book is intended to meet the demand for such information and takes the reader through all the types of model in order to provide a good understanding of the whys and wherefores.

The first flying model planes were apparently built many centuries ago, though the details are lost in antiquity. However, positive records and sketches of "helicopters" flown at the beginning of the nineteenth century have been found. Early experimenters used steam, compressed-air, and even gun powder engines in their efforts to develop successful flying machines. Twisted or stretched rubber bands were utilized in the smaller models.

By the time the Wright brothers flew successfully at Kitty Hawk in 1903, model airplanes (known in those days as "*aero*planes") had been on the market for many years. And model-plane kit and supply concerns were active in the United States at least by 1909, as is proved by their catalogs.

The astonishing aviation developments of World War I spurred model aviation to quite an extent, but with the New York to Paris flight of Charles Lindbergh in 1927 the field literally exploded. Since that day the ranks of aeromodelers have increased yearly, through good times and bad. So has the number of manufacturers who supply them, to the point that there are hundreds in this field, whose total gross is as much as 40 million dollars per year.

A tremendous distribution system caters to the hobbyist's needs. Almost any fair-sized town has at least one store carrying model supplies. Often retailers run hobby departments which confine their stock solely to model supplies and perhaps hobby-craft materials. The hobby dealer can supply balsa and other needed light woods, cement, covering materials, wire, and other components for assembling original designs. His shelves are crammed with all manner of kits for flying and display models, many with parts so fully prefabricated that even the awkward enthusiast can produce a successful model. He stocks engines from the tiny Cox .02—which weighs only .8 ounce complete with fuel tank and diminutive 4-inch propeller and is so small that some model builders wear it on a tie clasp—up to the one-pound .60 monsters, many of which produce over one horsepower. He carries a wide variety of propellers in countless sizes and shapes, fuel from half a dozen makers in cans from ½ pint to a gallon, glow plugs, tanks, and so on.

If the modeler doesn't see what he wants in a local hobby shop—and no such shop can stock *everything* marketed in this field today—he can

Fig. 1-1.   Types of Models

3

generally order it by mail. Concerns throughout the country specialize in mail-order selling and generally offer complete catalogs to choose from.

Not only does a good dealer have a comprehensive stock; he is able to suggest a choice of kits and parts suited to the age, pocketbook, and ability of any buyer. By starting with the simpler and less expensive models, the budding builder is able to complete and fly them successfully. His interest is heightened, and he goes on to more complex projects, which may be more interesting, more difficult, and more rewarding when they too are completed successfully.

Many youngsters become interested in model aviation or rocketry these days by building one or more of the highly detailed plastic model kits which are stocked by hobby and toy shops in almost infinite variety. The models produced from these kits, many of which are scaled down from real planes or from plans supplied by aircraft manufacturers, cannot fly; many, however, have movable parts such as rotating props, control surfaces, sliding cockpit covers, or even working bomb drops. In addition, some plastic planes can actually fly. The simplest are fairly small models designed to fly at the end of thin wires or cords and powered by the smaller glow-plug engines. Most of these are miniature versions of full-size planes and come ready to fly; some are remarkably accurate copies. In recent years, it has even become possible to obtain all-plastic planes with as much as a 6-foot span, to be flown via radio control. For those who want smaller, simpler, and less expensive planes, several kinds in a span range of 30 to 40 inches come with all radio and propulsion equipment installed. They are ready to fly as soon as wings are attached, batteries are put in the plane and transmitter, and the fuel tank is filled.

Flying planes can also be built right from the raw materials, using frameworks of balsa, covered with thin paper, silk, or other light fabrics. Some manufacturers supply complete lines of model-plane accessories as well; some go even further and produce the engines to power them. Engines of reliable makes may be had in the smaller sizes (.02 to .049 cubic-inch displacement) for under $20; the highly developed and intricate .60 engines used in large radio-control planes can cost $150 and more.

Jet engines have been quite successful in model planes. The most practical type is based on the original Jetex engine. This uses pellets of solid chemical fuel, burns quietly and with no flame, and can propel properly designed planes very well. The fuel is ignited by a fuse, and the power plant might be considered a specialized form of rocket. Larger and much heavier model planes designed around the Dynajet engine (and various imported versions of the same principle) have power plants exactly like those of the World War II buzz bombs. These jet engines are some 18 inches long, burn plain gasoline, and have driven control-line speed planes to over 180 mph actual. Diminutive turbojet engines are also said to have flown reasonably small model planes. Larger jets of this type are built and run just like the huge turbojets flying today, but these are high-priced, require expensive accessories (such as high-speed electric starters), and are somewhat beyond the scope of this book.

The purpose of this book is to provide an orderly plan of action, a guide, not for the expert, but for the average fan who continually seeks to add to his knowledge. His aim is to build better-looking and better-flying models. The beginner, too, will profit by gaining an appreciation of technique in design, construction, and flying methods. The modeler who has made a start, but lacks years of practice, will learn from the experience of others in designing, building, and flying. A picture is given of current practices, theories, and technique. Things the author knows the average builder will ask about are set forth in planned order, making this book a handy reference work. In brief, the author has hoped to pass on much that is known to the expert, but not known to most hobbyists.

The beginner and the inexperienced hobbyist are urged to start at the beginning and not to put the cart before the horse, as too many do today, by building a gas-powered model without first amassing the all-important experience to be gained in making simpler types such as the glider.

A simple glider can be assembled in minutes, using sheet balsa for wings and tail and a hard balsa strip for the body. It can be launched by hand, thrown into the air like a ball. Well-made, hand-launched gliders have flown out of sight! Increased a little in size and sometimes fitted with a paper-covered wood framework, a hand-launched glider can be flown like a regular sailplane by means of a towline. Looping a cord around a wire hook fastened into the bottom of the fuselage, the builder tows his miniature sailplane aloft by running with it as he would with a kite. As altitude is gained, the cord drops off, and the glider is on its own.

A small all-balsa glider with a stick fuselage can be equipped with a propeller and a rubber-band motor by fitting one end of the stick with a wire hook for holding the rubber and the other end with a special fixture, called a propeller hanger or thrust bearing. This little model can be made to climb and turn like a real airplane. By fitting a pair of small wheels close to the nose of the stick (using a wire axle bent to fit around the stick), we can enable the plane to take off from the ground and to built-up framework, covered with light tissue. Provided he does not try to advance too rapidly, such construction, aided by the remarkable kits now on the market, is really not difficult. With a propeller driven by a twisted rubber band, a kit for a plane of 30-inch wing span may cost a dollar or two. Dope and cement add a bit more, of course. When the builder graduates to even a small glow engine the price jumps to perhaps $8 to $10, including engine, fuel, starting battery, and other accessories required. Not all this money must be spent at once, however, as the hobbyist can buy the plane kit and build it, then obtain the engine and the more costly parts when it is finished.

Since flying sites are becoming harder to locate, especially in urban areas, it is often necessary to stick to control-line models when the builder graduates to glow-engine power. These may be flown in small areas, and they don't "fly away." Kits for simple types, scale models, speed planes, and so on, are available. These planes may run from as small as 10-inch span to 4 feet or more. They may fly on the end of very thin 35-foot-long wires (or dacron cords) or on 70-foot-long and much heavier wires. Every movement of the plane is in direct response to a control handle in the flier's hand. With practice he can make a plane do loops, overhead 8's, inverted flight, and so on.

Solid scale exhibition models are an interesting project. Modelers used to build many of these from balsa and other soft woods, but the field is now dominated by the plastic scale kits already mentioned.

Flying scale planes are fascinating, and many kits are available for both rubber and glow-engine types. The rubber types range in size from 15-inch to 50-inch span, the glow ones from perhaps 24 inches up.

Glow-engine free-flight planes are quite popular in areas where there are large enough fields to fly them. They are not, of course, for the urban modeler, though some cities allow flying them in certain park areas. Engines of .049 displacement allow fine fliers to be built with wing areas of around 150 to 250 square inches.

By far the fastest expanding branch of model aviation today is radio control. Tremendous strides have been made in recent years in radio equipment, which for the simplest types is low in cost, light, and compact. A very good flier can be produced with as little as 12-inch wing span and weighing perhaps 3 ounces; such a model, despite its very land on its wheels at the end of the flight.

A surprising amount of knowledge may be obtained from flying such a simple craft. If the principles of balance, trim, launching, and so on are well learned, the modeler is ready to go to the next step: planes powered with small glow engines. He may also wish to advance to a

Most unusual of all models are ornithopters— crankshaft and rods actuate wings which feature flexible trailing edges

Helicopters vary greatly in design — successful both indoor and out — proponents claim great possibilities

Autogiro models with non-powered vanes have had most success indoors— very difficult to adjust

  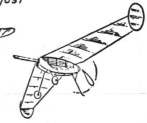

Many early models were pushers — some rudderless— all had positive incidence in front elevator — slight negative incidence in wing

Early champs in speed and duration were twin pushers — used long powerful motors — props rotated in opposite directions — sometimes equipped with landing gear

Tailless or flying wing types obtain stability by sweepback and decreased incidence in wing tips — designs vary greatly

Rubber-powered racing models have flown over 60 m.p.h. — generally use low pitch hardwood propeller with wing area cut to a minimum

Tandem models also vary greatly in design— wings are sometimes equal in area — fuselage contains two rubber motors with torque neutralized

Amphibian models can operate off water or, with wheels extended, from the ground— most frequently are twin-motored

Fig. 1-2. Freaks, Old-Timers, and Experimental Types

7

elementary equipment (just rudder control) is not for the novice, however, as it will be fast and tricky to control. More practical beginner models are available in 30- to 40-inch span; and, of course, there are the 5- to 6-foot-span stunters which weigh 6 to 8 pounds, will do anything full-size planes will do, and can cost as much as £200-£250 to complete.

Model rocketry is a rather recent development, spurred by the excitement created when the original Sputnik circled the earth in the fifties. There are now half a dozen concerns in this country that offer a wide variety of rocket kits, engines, fuels, and accessories. All these rockets use solid fuel, and all are designed for utmost safety. Ignition is by electricity; no tricky and unreliable fuses are utilized. Rather than crashing to earth after each flight, the rockets are brought down softly via parachute. Model rocketeers fly multistage jobs, rockets with camera pay loads, and rockets with folding wings that glide to earth after the engine is exhausted.

There is little risk of boredom in model aviation or model rocketry. Should a hobbyist tire of conventional model planes, for example, he can always try helicopters or an ornithopter (a model that flaps its wings for propulsion) or he can shift to radio control or to rockets. His ambition is his sole limitation!

2

AERODYNAMICS
AND PROPORTIONS

It is customary in books of this kind to begin with an airfoil and to show how it creates lift. However, it is wiser, first, to examine the stability requirements enabling a ship to fly and then relate everything else to these requirements. A fresh approach is necessary if control-line planes are to be considered simultaneously with free-flight planes. It is obvious that a machine that is tethered on control wires will have radically different requirements from one that is not captive.

Any airplane whose movements are not artificially restricted as they are on control lines is free to climb or dive, to roll to right or left, to turn to the right or left, or to combine varying amounts of any of these three movements for an infinite number of maneuvers. An aircraft rotates about three different axes. First, for our discussion purpose, is the vertical or directional axis about which the machine turns. This directional or vertical axis pierces the plane from top to bottom through the machine's center of gravity, or CG. A weather vane has a directional or vertical axis. Revolving on this axis, either a weather vane or a plane can be pointed. In the weather vane, most of the side area is distributed behind the axis so that the force of the wind causes the vane to point into the wind. By use of a vertical tail area, the modeler similarly is able to control his plane about its vertical axis. Without the vertical tail, his machine would twist and tumble to the ground.

The CG can be found by suspending the model by a string from its top center line somewhere forward toward the nose and extending the line indicated by the cord across the fuselage with a pencil. Then, by hanging the model from another point, also along its top center line, and by repeating the process, the designer marks the intersection of the two pencil lines. This is the location of the CG.

A second axis pierces the plane from nose to tail, also through the CG. It is called the lateral axis. The craft rolls about the axis. Perhaps you have seen a spit in a restaurant or at a barbecue. Whatever is to be cooked is pierced with the spit and then rotated slowly above an open fire. The spit is a perfect example of a lateral axis. Call this axis anything you want—rolling axis or sideways axis—so long as you fix its existence in your mind.

The third axis pierces the plane from wing tip to wing tip, again through the CG. The plane dives or climbs around this spanwise axis; when the nose goes up, the tail goes down, and vice versa. Sounds like a seesaw, doesn't it? And that is what this axis is. Keeping this seesaw balanced is the toughest job the model designer has.

You cannot see or feel these axes, but they are there just the same. The designer's problem is to stop or limit to a controllable degree the undesirable movements of his plane around them. What are the principal things he can do to obtain such stability? To begin with the vertical or directional axis, he utilizes a proper amount of vertical tail area, and possibly offset thrust (to right or left) to assist only when absolutely necessary. Dihedral or uptilted wings hold the plane steady on its rolling or lengthwise axis. A stabilizer or horizontal tail surface, perhaps assisted by an offset thrust line (downthrust), prevents uncontrollable climbs or dives. All these things must be approximately correct in size and amount

Successful gas model must have inherent stability about its axes: 1. Directionally (vertical axis), 2. Longitudinally (lateral axis), and 3. Laterally (longitudinal axis)

Fig. 2-1.   Stability Axes

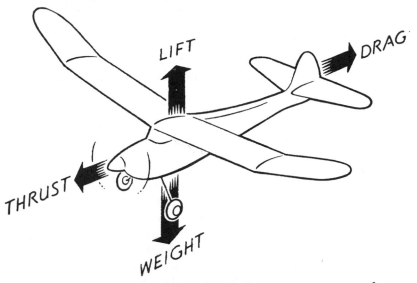

In level flight, principal forces are equal:
THRUST, forward through thrust line, vs.
DRAG, rearward through line of resistance;
LIFT, upward through center of lift, vs.
WEIGHT, downward through center of gravity

Fig. 2-2. Forces Acting upon the Model

or the designer creates worse instability. For an example, an excessively large lifting type of stabilizer will make a fast free-flight gas plane nose down when it picks up speed under high power, or in a dive.

Let's consider briefly the control-line model because of its special requirements. Like any airplane, the control-liner has three control axes. However, the lines that hold such a machine captive, limiting its flight path to a circle around the flier, prevent its turning right or left. As long as the flier maintains control, the plane will not turn away from him to fly out of the circle or toward him to come inside the circle. The control wires replace the function of the vertical tail. Proof of this is seen in speed planes which generally have no vertical tail areas, this surface being omitted to reduce drag. While most control-line models do have vertical tails, their main purpose (aside from esthetics) is to assure that the plane is steered toward the outside of the circle, to keep the line taut. On some the rudder is turned a bit outward; on others the entire vertical surface has a slight outward angle: the trailing edge is farther outboard of the fuselage center line than is the leading edge. On stunt planes this outward angling operates the same way, whether the plane is upright or inverted. There are other ways to produce this pull on the

11

lines, however, and basically, a control-line model really needs no vertical tail.

Nor does the control-line designer need concern himself with the lateral or rolling axis that pierces the plane from nose to tail. The control wires are connected to a bell crank inside the fuselage, or on the wing near the fuselage, and extend toward the flier through a fixed guide attached to the wing near the tip. The wires prevent the plane from dropping a wing tip and rolling either away from or toward the flier (assuming he keeps the lines taut through good flying technique). The wires therefore take the place of dihedral wings. Only in the case of the spanwise axis about which an airplane dives or climbs does the control-line craft have any special requirement, and even that is not exacting. Some horizontal tail surface is necessary, but the amount is not critical, provided it does not become unduly small. The movable elevators which the pilot manipulates with his control handle provide any correction for accidental departures of the plane from stable level flight. Here is another interesting difference between the free-flight and the control-line craft. The former must resist, on its own, any tendency to rotate undesirably about any of its three axes. The control plane, on the other hand, has elevators which enable the flier to force the plane to rotate about its wing-tip or spanwise axis. It is these controlled movements—and the controlled recoveries from them—that create stunt maneuvers. The only stability requirement is that the plane be able to maintain level flight.

With this knowledge of the stability requirements of both free-flying and control-line types, the ins and outs of airplane design will not prove confusing.

An understanding of elemental aerodynamics is necessary before tackling design. Essentially, flight is attained by means of a wing that is drawn through the air to generate lift (the force that keeps the plane aloft); tail surfaces consisting of a fin and rudder (vertical surface) and a stabilizer and elevator (horizontal surface) that exert a continual leverage to hold the plane on a true flight path, as the feathered tail of an arrow; and a propeller, or airscrew, that screws its way forward through the air, pulling or pushing the plane and developing sufficient thrust (propulsive energy) to overcome the drag (air resistance) created by the plane's forward speed.

Lift is generated, first, because of the airfoil (wing-rib or wing cross-section shape) and, second, because of the angle of attack (inclination or angular setting of the wing), the latter being nothing but the tilting up of the leading edge of the wing. (A kite flies because of its angle of attack to the wind that impinges upon its surface.) Most of the lift at ordinary angles of attack results from the airfoil shape. Inclining the wing to the wind stream does boost lift, but it also increases drag, so much so, as more and more angle is imparted to the wing, that drag increases out of all proportion to lift, thereby destroying efficiency. Thus, for any given airfoil shape, there is a certain best angular setting for the wing, usually between 2 and 6 degrees positive. The flat sheet-balsa wings on a small rubber-powered model or on a small glider, lacking any wing-rib shape, must get their lift from a small positive angle of attack. Such models automatically seek the necessary angle of flight to develop lift.

Most of the airfoil's lift is created by the passage of air over the highly curved top surface. This stream of air, because it must travel a greater distance than the air stream passing beneath the wing, accelerates or stretches out, thus reducing air pressure immediately above the wing, forming a partial vacuum. This differential of air pressure—that is, less pressure above the wing and more pressure below—is the source of lift. Roughly two-thirds of the total lift is due to the upper surface of the wing and only one-third to the lower surface when placed at ordinary angles of attack.

Airfoils vary greatly in appearance. Some are curved, or cambered, on top and flat on bottom; others are cambered on top and undercambered on the bottom. Still others are cambered convexly on both top and bottom, along the lines of a streamlined object, depending for lift on a slight angle of attack. Generally speaking, the thicker the airfoil, the greater the lift and drag; the thinner the airfoil, the less the lift and the greater the speed (owing to less drag). Thus, load-carrying planes of the bomber or transport type have very thick wings.

Racers and fighter planes have thinner wings. So it must be with your models. A slow, high-lift model, such as the older type of radio-

UNDERCAMBER   CONVEX BOTTOM

FLAT BOTTOM   FLAT

Fig. 2-3.   Airfoil Types

controlled plane, often had quite thick wings, since it had to carry relatively heavy loads of equipment and batteries and did not travel at very high speeds. Hand-launched gliders have almost flat wings; they are light and travel fast, especially on the launch. High-lift wings have a greater drag. Airfoils must be selected carefully for the purpose the plane is to fulfill. The key to the problem of airfoil selection is a factor called the "lift-drag ratio." Lift-drag ratio is nothing more than the relation between the amount of lift and the amount of drag created per square foot of wing area at any given angle of attack. It is a measure of efficiency expressed simply, for example, as 16 to 1, or 22 to 1. The ratio becomes lower, hence less efficient, if the angle of attack is increased beyond certain limits. Comparing a number of airfoils at a like angle of attack, the designer uses known lift-drag ratios as a means of selecting the particular airfoil best suited for his purpose. If, for example, a high-lift airfoil is required, the designer segregates a group of airfoils fulfilling the requirements. Then, by means of their lift-drag ratios he compares them and eliminates them one by one, until he has the most efficient airfoil for the purpose. Naturally, the airfoil having the highest lift-drag ratio is his choice. The less drag the better, because drag means more power required and hence less duration. Fortunately, no research is required to determine the best model airfoils; it has all been done for you. However, even though there are hundreds of suitable airfoils from which to choose, true model experimenters still try to develop better ones. Some popular airfoils are illustrated in this chapter.

Charts are obtainable to assist in analyzing airfoil sections. These charts plot curves showing the lift coefficients (an offhand indication of relative amounts of lift) at each degree of angle of attack. The charts do the same for drag and for the lift-drag ratio. If a speed model is involved, the builder will select a section that has minimum drag at zero degrees attack (or other chosen angle), provided lift is also developed and a good lift-drag ratio is maintained. For free flight, he would like a high lift-drag ratio and the angular setting necessary to obtain efficiency. A really clever designer would consider the size of the lift coefficient at the same time he considered the lift-drag ratio.

While airfoil charts usually indicate the best airfoil for the job, "scale effect" (see page 18) sometimes plays an upsetting role. Some airfoil sections that look like world-beaters on paper prove to be duds on model airplanes. The list of everyday sections that will work successfully is rather well known. It includes sections that are very old and others that are of recent vintage.

The most famous airfoil section is the Clark Y. It is a good all-round section for modeling, though it has limitations in full-scale practice. Of

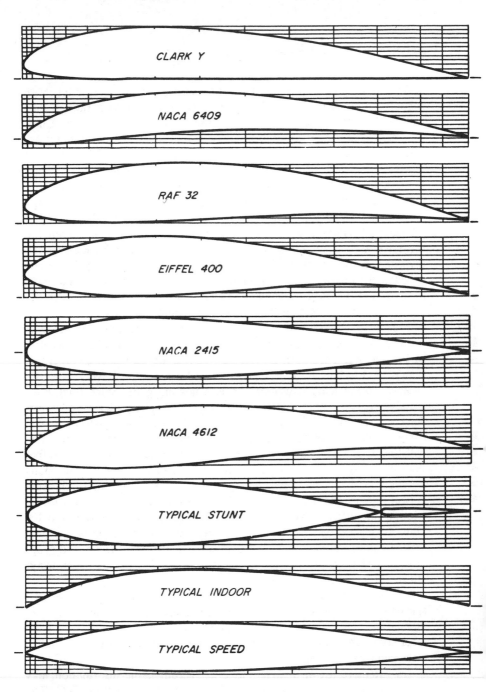

Fig. 2-4.　Popular Airfoil Sections

moderate thickness, it compromises lift and drag so that it applies well
to all free-flight models, although it rarely excels on any. Its flat bottom

15

makes the wing easy to build. The Clark Y is good for sport ships, both rubber and glow. It is good for sport radio planes as well, though they will fly faster than with some of the popular thicker sections. The Clark Y is also used widely for stabilizers, where lifting tails in free flight are required.

Three airfoils that have been very popular in free-flight rubber planes (especially in Wakefield contest planes, where the rules specify a minimum weight and a maximum wing area, leading to rather high loading) are the RAF32 (British), the Eiffel 400 (French), and the NACA 6409 (American). The latter is still quite popular in free-flight (often abbreviated to FF) rubber and gas, though the experts all have their special favorites, many modified from standard wing sections, some strictly original. Airfoils go in and out of favor like clothing fashions, and you'll hear of "thin Clark Y," Benedek, Lindner, Eppler, and so on—and the following year someone will discover some new ones!

Free-flight gas rules used to specify a certain wing area for use with a stated engine size, but in recent years this restriction has been modified to include just engine size in each FF category. Present competition planes tend to climb almost vertically under the urge of very powerful engines, so the main consideration is a floating glide. Since thick wing sections increase drag considerably, thus preventing maximum climb, wing sections have been getting thinner. For ease of construction and covering, many successful designs now utilize flat-bottom sections. You will find wing sections getting sharper at the leading edge, too, rather than the fairly rounded shape of one like the Clark Y. Actually, many a builder probably needlessly goes to extremes to copy one of the successful full-size plane foils, when what he actually achieves on his model wing is far different. What with sag of covering between ribs and the "bumps" caused by ribs, spars, and other wing structural parts, the final section can be quite altered. The only wings that retain their airfoil properly are those completely covered with sheet balsa or the foam wings utilized in some radio-control planes.

Wings on control-line (also commonly called U-control, or just UC) speed planes are generally very thin (some are shaped from thin sheet metal) and often symmetrical or nearly so. Speed planes are one of the most specialized categories, and here again the designers tend to utilize their own ideas of wing sections.

An extensive list of airfoils and other aerodynamic information may be had from the Superintendent of Documents, Washington, D.C. The government reports available from this source are very low in cost.

The amount of lift developed by any wing section is affected by the planform (top view of the wing outline) and by the aspect ratio (rela-

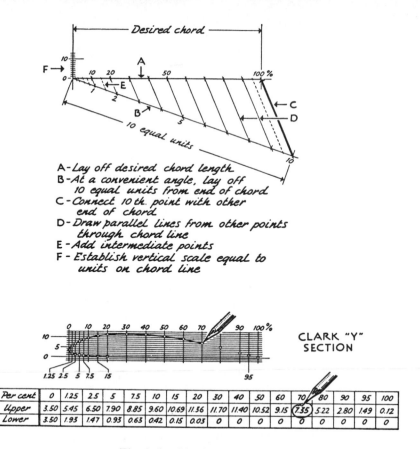

A - Lay off desired chord length
B - At a convenient angle, lay off 10 equal units from end of chord
C - Connect 10th. point with other end of chord
D - Draw parallel lines from other points through chord line
E - Add intermediate points
F - Establish vertical scale equal to units on chord line

CLARK "Y" SECTION

Per cent	0	1.25	2.5	5	7.5	10	15	20	30	40	50	60	70	80	90	95	100
Upper	3.50	5.45	6.50	7.90	8.85	9.60	10.69	11.36	11.70	11.40	10.52	9.15	7.35	5.22	2.80	1.49	0.12
Lower	3.50	1.93	1.47	0.93	0.63	0.42	0.15	0.03	0	0	0	0	0	0	0	0	0

Fig. 2-5.   Plotting an Airfoil

tion between wing length, or span, and wing width, or chord). Aspect ratio is span divided by chord; thus, a 36-inch span divided by a 6-inch chord equals 6 ($36 \div 6 = 6$), or an aspect ratio of 6:1, often just stated as an aspect ratio of six. The planform may be rectangular, tapered, elliptical, or a combination of the three. Both tapered and elliptical planforms are considered to improve efficiency, but in view of the consistent success of plain rectangular wings, it is doubtful if the added difficulties of plotting and cutting a set of wing ribs for tapered or elliptical wings is warranted.

Aspect ratio, however, is much more important than planform. High aspect ratios in real planes mean added efficiency. The narrower the chord, the less the induced drag. In moving forward, a wing disturbs an area of surrounding air. This can be visualized by drawing a wing rib and then setting apart the points of the compass to the same measurement as the length of the rib, scribing a circle with the trailing edge of the rib as the center. The area of the circle indicates the amount of induced drag. The bigger the rib, the bigger the circle, and hence the

17

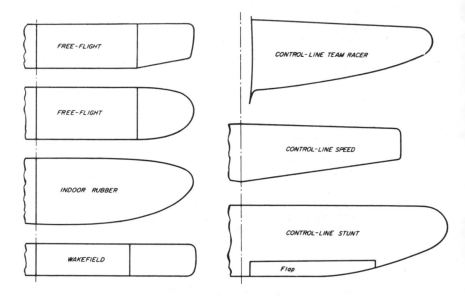

Fig. 2-6. Representative Wing Planforms

greater the induced drag. High-performance sailplanes have extremely high aspect ratios, sometimes in excess of 20:1. For structural reasons, the aspect ratios for transports and bombers usually don't exceed 10:1. Racers and fighters may have ratios of less than 6:1.

Total drag of an airplane includes induced drag, mentioned above, and parasite drag, coming from parts exposed to the air stream, such as wheels, struts, tail, and so on. Included in parasite drag is skin friction, caused by the rubbing of the air stream against the plane's surfaces. This explains the elaborate curves on some model fuselages used to stream-line the plane's surface area and hence to cut down drag.

Unfortunately, a foolproof application of real plane practice to models cannot be made accurately in this case. A 6-inch-wide model wing moving at 15 mph does not have a proportionate amount of lift and drag to a real plane wing, which may be many feet wide and traveling at 300 mph or more. This is due to the fact that an infinitely smaller number of air molecules pass over our model wing at its slow speed than pass over the high-speed plane wing. A factor called Reynolds number is used to express the difference in reaction between, for example, a certain airfoil on a full-size plane wing as against the same airfoil on a wing of model size. Unfortunately, there is a vast difference between the two —one reason it does not pay to strive too hard to duplicate exactly the full-size foil. A science termed low-speed aerodynamics has been employed to determine the best airfoils for *model* purposes and in model sizes, with little regard to what is best for full-size planes. This is really

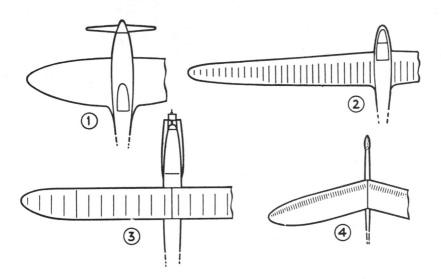

1. Control-line model   2. Sailplane
3. Rubber model   4. Hand-launched glider

Fig. 2-7.   Variations in Aspect Ratio

a matter for the expert modelers; when the reader reaches that category he will perhaps wish to delve into such work. We must start somewhere, however, and the full-size airfoils *are* a reasonable starting point. The larger the model wing's chord, the closer it approaches a true proportion to the real plane. Thus, while high aspect ratios admittedly improve efficiency, model designers compromise between having the largest wing rib (low aspect ratio) for a favorable scale effect and a high aspect ratio for efficiency. And so, although model records have been made with wings of as high as 18:1 and as low as 4:1 aspect ratios, the average is about 10:1 for rubber-powered outdoor models and 6½:1 for gas models. So much for the wing, how it generates lift, its varying airfoil sections, its shape and proportions.

Maximum airfoil efficiency is not so important in control-line models, except possibly in the case of the speed designs. Generally, aspect ratios are rather low for control-line planes. Stunt designs require the maximum possible wing area, which has led in some cases to wings that look like barn doors. In an effort to trim such huge wings to more pleasing appearance, while still retaining lots of area, stunt control-line designers are going in for much more graceful contours and outlines nowadays; in fact some of these planes are extremely attractive despite their disproportionately large wings. Stunt wings range from about 3:1 to 5:1 in aspect ratio, and most have rather generous taper on at least one edge, plus graceful curves to mask the large area.

19

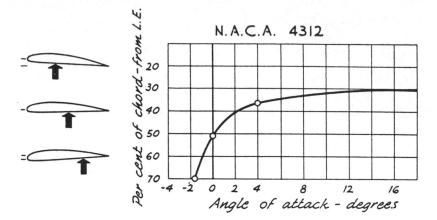

Fig. 2-8.   Center-of-Pressure Movement

While stability is not a great problem in control-line models, it is, of course, paramount for free flight. This is still another reason for wings of relatively high aspect ratio. For maximum inherent stability, the distance the center of pressure (really, the center of lift) moves forward on the wing with an increase in angle of attack must be kept to a minimum. Usually, this CP travel, as it is called, is expressed in a percentage of the chord of the wing. The lower the aspect ratio, the wider the chord, and hence the greater the CP travel. Since the movement of the CP forward of the CG, or center of gravity, creates a larger nose-up or tail-heavy condition, leading to a possible stall, it is important to minimize the CP travel. This can be controlled by avoiding low aspect ratios and airfoils whose graphs indicate a relatively large CP movement.

The wing alone is too unstable for flight by itself. The technical explanation of this is that the CP shifts not only forward toward the leading edge with an increase in angle of attack but backward toward the trailing edge with decreased attack. This movement of the CP is greater with increase in depth of the airfoil, high-lift airfoils usually having a much greater CP travel. Glide a wing from your hand, and it will twirl edge over edge to the ground. Ordinarily, at zero angle of attack, the CP is located at approximately 30 per cent of the wing chord back from the leading edge. Plainly, a stabilizing force is required.

This is provided by a stabilizer, or horizontal tail, that exerts a powerful pressure or leverage not only to keep the wing at its proper angle but to restore the wing to that angle when the plane dives or stalls. Stabilizer area, shape, cross section, angular setting, and position on the plane all vary according to the particular design. The area, for example, must be greater when the distance between the wing and tail is short-

20

ened, giving a smaller tail moment arm (the distance through which a force is exerted, as in a lever); the area will be less when the distance is increased, giving a greater tail moment arm. The usual range of stabilizer area in free-flight planes is from 30 per cent to 50 per cent of the wing area.

The observant reader may recall that some extremely long free-flight designs have large stabilizer areas. This interesting exception to the rule is found in very high-powered free-flight contest machines which use rather high pylons, or fins above the fuselage, to support the wings. The high power provides great forward speed, even in the climb. Because of the stress on long glides and soaring ability, these machines also have large wing areas. Since lift is influenced by area and the square of the speed, tremendous excess lift is created while the engine is running. Therefore, the designer depends on a large lifting type of stabilizer which also increases its lift greatly at high speed and thus prevents the wing from looping or stalling the plane. Why doesn't such a plane dive during the glide, when the forward speed is lowered? The answer is that the CG of the plane is positioned far back, as much as 75 to 100 per cent of the wing chord measured from the leading edge. With a nonlifting tail, the CG would be farther forward, although the plane then would stall under power. (When a 50 per cent tail having a lifting cross section cannot prevent loops, the designer removes some of the angle of attack from the wing to reduce its lift at high speed and moves back the CG.)

Tail moment arm is generally considered the distance between the midpoint of the wing chord and the midpoint of the stabilizer chord. On the average model this tail moment arm is usually one-half the wing span. For example, on a 40-inch wing span a tail moment arm of one-half the span would equal 20 inches. On gas models this tail moment arm is sometimes as small as two-fifths of the span. Tow-launched model sailplanes have moment arms as small as one-third and even one-fourth of the span. Racing models approach the other extreme, having tail moment arms as great as two-thirds to three-quarters of the span. A "square" control-line model is one with equal span and length.

Some builders prefer to think of the distance between midpoints of the wing and stabilizer in terms of wing chord. This is fairly standard in radio-control designs. In the usual stunt radio-control plane, this distance runs from two to three chords. Stunt planes must go through their maneuvers very steadily to gain top competition points, and a long tail moment promotes such stability. On the other hand, these planes must accomplish rather violent maneuvers, and too much stability prevents this or requires excessive control-surface movement. Thus, as in most other aerodynamic matters, a reasonable compromise is essential.

Fig. 2-9.   Typical Stabilizer Sections

Stabilizer cross sections may be flat, streamlined (often termed "symmetrical," when the top and bottom curvatures are equal), or even cambered like an airfoil to develop lift. Flat tails are suited to small models, but if made from balsa sheet, they tend to warp when made too large. Many control-line planes utilize flat stabs; those on speed models are often of thin plywood. Flat stabs are also fairly common on radio-control planes, but in this case they are built up. As we have already pointed out, airfoil section, or lifting, stabs are usual on free-flight competition planes. The symmetrical-sectioned stabilizer comes into use when plane size dictates a more rigid and warp-free structure. This section is used on sport and flying scale gas and radio models where the CG is forward and where none of the load is to be carried by the stabilizer. This is why you see symmetrical-sectioned stabilizers on sport gassies but never on a pylon plane. The lifting stabilizer must be utilized with high-performance pylons, with cabin jobs where the profile of the cabin is such that the wing is rather highly located, and wherever the CG falls farther rearward on the wing chord than 50 per cent of the width of the wing. The lifting-type stabilizer is a must on any high-performance rubber model, owing to the great excess of power at the beginning of the flight (here it does the same job as it does for a fast-flying pylon) and because of the natural rearward position of the CG. The CG can fall behind the wing, on account of the length of the heavy rubber within the fuselage. This, of course, throws some of the weight-carrying burden on the stabilizer.

For maximum stability the wing is usually given a greater angle of attack (built into the structure of the model) than the stabilizer. The difference is generally 2 to 4 degrees. The explanation is this: at moderate angles of attack the airflow over the upper surface of the wing is smooth and unbroken. But as the angle of attack is increased, the airflow no longer follows the contour of the rib section, but breaks away from the surface nearer and nearer the leading edge, until at last air just boils turbulently over the wing, destroying lift. This condition occurs after an angle of attack of approximately 16 degrees has been reached. It is called the "stalling point" or "burble point." Now, if the tail is set at a lesser angle of attack, it will continue to lift after the wing has stalled and consequently tend to restore the plane to a level flight position. Although you cannot see this corrective force at work, it resists the wing's increasing its angle of attack and therefore resists any approach to a stall. The usual arrangement is to set the stabilizer

22

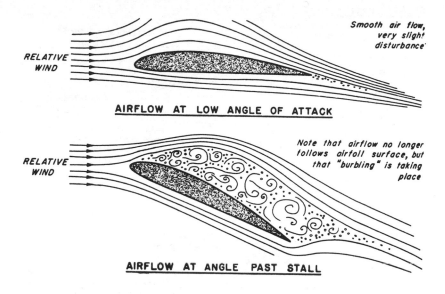

Fig. 2-10.   Angle-of-Attack Effects

at zero degrees and the wing at whatever angle of attack is found necessary to fly the ship. However, this angular difference between wing and tail must not be too large. If it is, the high power of a gas engine or a heavy rubber motor will either loop the model or carry it into a series of vicious power stalls. The term "angle of incidence" is often seen. Incidence is defined as the angular setting of the wing with respect to some arbitrary line fore and aft through the fuselage. Sometimes the thrust line is used; in other cases this line is simply one drawn lengthwise on the fuselage (often as a matter of convenience in drawing the fuselage outline). Angle of incidence should not be confused with angle of attack (which is the angle at which the wing travels through the air), though it is possible for the two to be the same.

Planes can fly with no apparent angular difference between wing and tail; in fact this setup is quite standard with modern radio-control stunt planes. Such planes thus have no inherent stability in the pitch direction (that is, up or down), and none is wanted. Radio equipment is now reliable enough so that these planes must be "flown" all the time; if left to their own devices they generally are soon headed straight downward! But with this lack of built-in stability, they do not take much control-surface movement to perform the required maneuvers; in other words, the inherent stability of the plane is not continually "fighting" the control movements signaled by the pilot. Such planes are said to have neutral stability: they go where they are pointed. Since free-flight planes are not controlled by a ground pilot, they must have built-in stability. To make them easier to fly for the less experi-

23

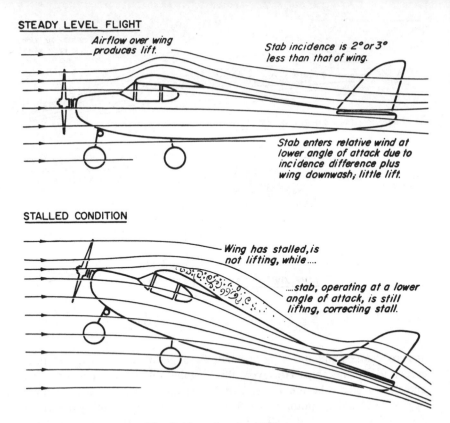

STEADY LEVEL FLIGHT

Airflow over wing produces lift.

Stab incidence is 2° or 3° less than that of wing.

Stab enters relative wind at lower angle of attack due to incidence difference plus wing downwash; little lift.

STALLED CONDITION

Wing has stalled, is not lifting, while....

....stab, operating at a lower angle of attack, is still lifting, correcting stall.

Fig. 2-11.   Angular Difference

enced pilots, sport radio-control planes also have built-in pitch stability; that is, there is enough angular difference between wing and stabilizer so the plane will bring itself back to level flight if it is put in a climb or dive and the controls are then neutralized. Because control-line stunt planes must also do all sorts of maneuvers, often flying as much inverted as upright, again we find the zero-zero setup in wing and stabilizer.

One sometimes hears the term *décalage* in aerodynamics. This is simply the angular difference between wing and stabilizer. Thus the control-line and radio-control stunters noted above have zero *décalage,* while sport radio and most free-flight planes have several degrees, possibly as much as six.

Stabilizers have many shapes. Aspect ratios in free-flight planes range around 4:1, and shapes are generally rectangular, possibly with a bit of taper on leading or trailing edges or both. Corners are often rounded, ends slanted one way or the other, to relieve the "barn-door look" and give a bit of individuality. As with wings, an elliptical planform is possibly the most efficient, but it is also much more time-consuming to build.

24

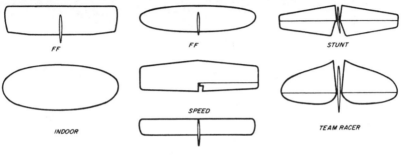

FF

FF

STUNT

INDOOR

SPEED

TEAM RACER

WAKEFIELD

Fig. 2-12. Representative Tail Planforms

However, the stabilizers on indoor rubber duration models are usually elliptical, as are the wings.

Nowadays you often can see free-flight power models with the stabilizer set at quite a spanwise angle from horizonal; in other words, one tip is much higher than the other. While this might look like sloppy construction or stabilizer attachment, it is really for a very important reason. The tilted stabilizer controls the amount of turn in the glide. Modern power duration models, both engine and rubber, climb very steeply—some practically vertically. Under these conditions, the stab tilt hasn't much effect, but when the plane settles into a steady glide, it is forced into the desired turn by stabilizer tilt. The plane will turn toward the side with the higher stabilizer tip. Tilt angles run from 1 to 6 degrees or so. This method of controlling glide turn is also seen in other duration models which travel at high speed under power, but are expected to level off into a long flat glide; included are Jetex models and hand-launched gliders (the latter are "powered" aloft by a tremendous heavy thrust from a modeler's strong right arm!).

"Rudders" is a term which often includes both the vertical fin and the area to the rear of it (hinged on some types of models—radio-control, for example). They vary a great deal in shape, but generally have aspect ratios of 1:1 to 2:1. While there may be a "best" shape for rudders, and many experts have strong preferences, it is here that the designer can often really express himself, since rudders of most reasonable shapes seem to work alike.

Rudder area on gas models ranges from 4 per cent to 10 per cent of the wing area. The former figure is possible on some pylon planes, but cabin types require from 7 or 8 per cent up. On rubber models, rudder area is somewhat larger, say, 16 to 18 per cent. The nearer the wing, the more rudder area is required, and vice versa. Sometimes twin rudders are used. It is claimed that such an arrangement improves the efficiency of the stabilizer by reducing tip loss, especially at high angles of attack. The area of *each* twin rudder is roughly equal to 65 per cent of the required single-rudder area.

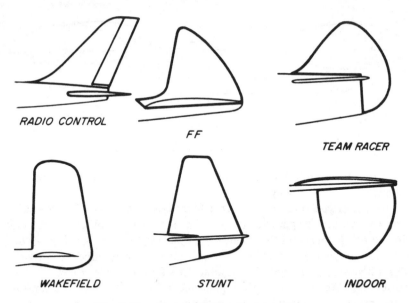

RADIO CONTROL

FF

TEAM RACER

WAKEFIELD

STUNT

INDOOR

Fig. 2-13. Representative Rudder Shapes

The horizontal tail, or stabilizer, controls the upsetting diving and zooming forces; the rudder, or vertical tail, holds the airplane on a steady heading, controlling left or right turning forces. The one remaining requirement for inherent stability is lateral (rolling) control of the airplane. For example, if a wing dips, some quality of the ship's design must function automatically to bring the wing back into position.

Lateral control is accomplished by upturning, or uptilting, the sides of the wings from the center line toward the tips. This is known as "dihedral." Dihedral takes a number of forms. It may appear as a shallow V when the wing is viewed from the front, each side of the wing slanting upward to the tip. Or it may be polyhedral with a number of distinct breaks, or increasing changes in dihedral toward the wing tips. Visualize the shallow V with each side of the letter bending sharply upward again approximately halfway toward the tip. Elliptical dihedral is the most efficient, but it is also the most difficult to build. Polyhedral is the most popular. The correct amount of dihedral is essential and varies with the vertical location of the wing on the model. Low-wing installations, for instance, require a greater dihedral angle than do high wings. Parasol wings need least of all. Minimum dihedral seems to be about 1 inch for every foot of wing span, although 1½ to 2 inches per foot of span are recommended to insure stability. High-powered models —contest jobs, for example, especially gas jobs with relatively short

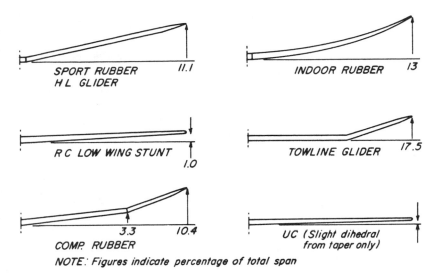

SPORT RUBBER
H L GLIDER   11.1

INDOOR RUBBER   13

R C LOW WING STUNT   1.0

TOWLINE GLIDER   17.5

3.3   10.4
COMP. RUBBER

UC (Slight dihedral
from taper only)

NOTE: Figures indicate percentage of total span

Fig. 2-14.   Representative FF Dihedral Angles

wings—use as high as 3 inches of dihedral for each foot of span. This should be the maximum needed for a low-wing gas design. About 2½ inches of dihedral per span foot seems adequate for most models.

Early radio models were developed from free-flight gas designs and had just as much dihedral, but the modern trend is to less and less dihedral for radio-control designs, particularly the competition stunters. For the same reason they have little or no *décalage:* the designers seek neutral stability, not a plane that will "fight" the controls. With a full set of controls (rudder, elevator, and ailerons) it has been found entirely feasible to fly radio jobs with a perfectly flat wing: zero dihedral. You often see scale radio-control planes, copies of the full-size craft that had zero dihedral, which are quite stable in the air, thanks to advanced radio gear and a good pilot. Sport radio jobs, of course, generally do have some dihedral, just as they generally have some *décalage;* they are thus easily flyable by pilots who are less than expert.

Control-line planes seldom have dihedral. They just don't need it, as the guiding lines supply all the lateral stability that is required.

Power affects lateral or rolling stability. The propeller is nothing but a rotating wing developing thrust as its lift. The propeller blades create their own resistance in turning, causing torque, a force that tends to rotate the model in the opposite direction to the turning propeller. If the propeller turns counterclockwise, the torque rotates the model clockwise, and vice versa. The higher the power, the greater the torque. You may have noticed that with the usual right-hand propeller on your model,

27

flight under power tends to be in left-hand circles with the left wing tip low. Since dihedral prevents flying one wing low, it can be seen that the greater the torque, the greater the amount of dihedral required for stability. Among free-flying types, dihedral ranges from as little as 1 or 2 degrees on a radio-control model to as much as 12 degrees on a Wakefield type where a propeller of perhaps 20 inches or more in diameter compels some all-out compensation for the resulting great torque. How does dihedral work? While there are a number of interpretations of its action, the correct answer is that dihedral serves to decrease the angle of attack of the higher wing tip when the plane begins to slip in a turn. At the same time the effective angle of attack in the lower wing tip is increased. The result is to add lift to the wing tip that has dropped earthward and to subtract lift from the tip that has rolled skyward; the ship will be rolled upright.

The more the dihedral used, the less efficient the plane. Dihedral sacrifices lift. For example, if the two wing panels were to be given 90 degrees dihedral—measured between a flat surface on which the wing rests and the wing tip—both wing tips would meet in an upright position overhead. Naturally, there would be no lift, and the plane could not fly. The designer therefore is grudging in his use of dihedral because of its cost in terms of lift. He is forced, however, to allow enough dihedral to guarantee safe flight. He also knows that he must allow for windy weather. A plane that flies smoothly on a calm day may not have sufficient dihedral for a breezy day when it will develop a spiral power dive into the ground.

Still another valuable function of dihedral, particularly in polyhedral form, is to roll upright at the top of a loop any model that accidentally gets into an inverted position through too much power while in a tail-heavy trim condition.

The explanation of why low wings require more dihedral and high wings less dihedral reveals a cardinal principle of stability. This is aptly called "pendulum stability," which, as the name indicates, means that the lower the CG (center of weight) relative to the CP (center of wing lift), the greater the inherent stability of the airplane. Let's suppose a parasol model gets into a one-wing-low position. Then its weight, acting through the plane's CG, tends to swing back to a vertical line running from the plane's CP to the earth in the same manner as the pendulum in a grandfather clock swings. This is one reason that most free-flight types have high wings. You can see that a plane with the CG (the center of weight) located above the CP (the center of wing lift) could not be stable, for if it were tipped, the weight and lift centers would tend to reverse. Low-wing models thus have greater dihedral in order to raise the CP closer to the CG, or even above the latter. Again, modern radio-control planes are an exception; here the pilot's skill takes the place of dihedral. Similarly, in control-line planes the lines eliminate need for dihedral.

For a maximum stability, it is desirable to concentrate weight as much as possible. Weight should also be kept as close as possible to the CG. A 1-ounce object that is 6 inches away from the CG has double the effect of an object of the same weight that is 3 inches away. Such an object—let's say the engine—resists sudden movements, but also acquires an inertia or tendency to keep moving, once displaced. Thus if the plane should be forced to turn unexpectedly, the weight of the engine would tend to continue in the same direction despite the corrective force of dihedral or other features of the design. Similarly, a heavily built tail structure is a disadvantage; so are unusually heavy wings, especially when the tips are far from the CG. Extremely long structures, as in long-moment-arm fuselages, or very high-aspect-ratio wings, tend to place weights far from the CG. Contest fliers know that the nose of a free-flight gas plane should be short. Sometimes the propeller is located below the leading edge of a parasol wing, or even behind that edge. There is only one exception to the rule of minimizing the distance between weights and the CG. This is the desirability of placing weighty objects as low as possible—like the batteries on a radio model, especially in sport radio designs. By placing the objects low, the CG position itself is lowered with respect to the airplane. The lower CG enhances pendulum stability, within reasonable limits, of course.

One often hears the term "spiral instability." This is generally considered to be caused by a combination of design defects, and its result is the "spiral dive," when the model follows a twisting high-speed path into the ground. Some observers will call a spiral dive a "spin," but the two are widely different. For one thing, free-flight planes very seldom get into true spins. In a spin the lifting surfaces are completely stalled, and the plane rotates about an axis running more or less vertically through the fuselage near the propeller. In a spiral dive, a plane is definitely still "flying"—that is, the wings are lifting; but the stability factors of the plane are such that it is not restored to the desired level or gently circling flight path. It is generally felt that too little dihedral and/or too much rudder area (plus vertical area on the side of the fuselage to the rear of the wing) are strong contributors. As the plane tilts sideways, perhaps due to a wind gust, it starts a side slip. The dihedral is not sufficient to level the wings quickly. As the plane slips sideways

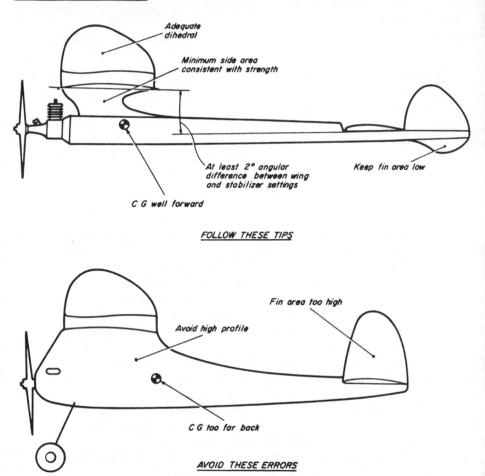

Fig. 2-15.   Insuring Spiral Stability

the overly large rudder tends to swing the tail in a manner to further tighten the turn. These effects build up, strengthened by the added speed of the plane as it noses downward; it is always observed that a plane in a spiral dive tends to "tighten up": to turn in smaller circles and travel at constantly increasing speed.

Another factor is the force from the twisting propeller slip stream, which can impinge on the vertical side surfaces of the model—the wing pylon, if any, the fuselage side, the rudder. This slip-stream effect can be such as to increase spiral instability. To lessen this tendency, the pylon area can be reduced (though not so much as to weaken it structurally), the rudder area can be reduced, or a single rudder may be replaced by a pair of tip rudders of smaller area. Or perhaps part of the rudder area can be shifted beneath the fuselage. Since rubber-powered

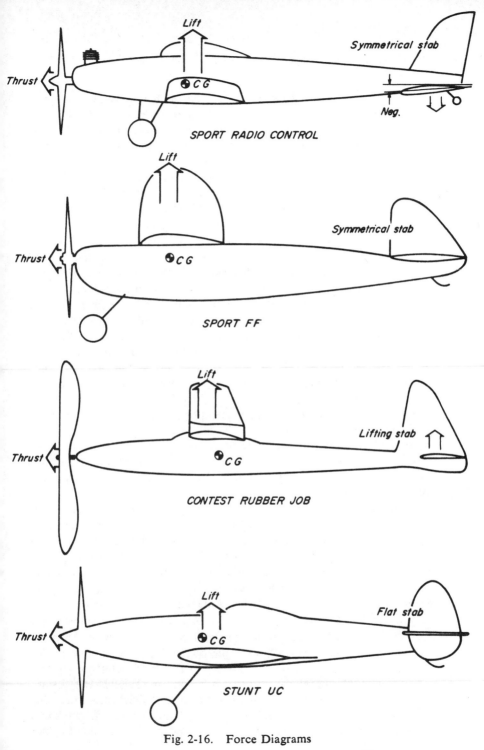

Fig. 2-16.   Force Diagrams

31

planes generally have much larger propellers than gas-powered ones, and the slip stream for such large props is therefore more "diffused" over the fuselage, it is not so great a problem in spiral diving. It is often found that increased angular difference between wing and stabilizer (a greater *décalage*) will help, as this produces greater longitudinal stability.

One cannot go too far in the matter of greater dihedral and less rudder area, however, as the plane is then apt to fly with its tail "wagging," or in a sense wallowing through the air. This is also termed "Dutch roll."

Present competition rules for free-flight gas models specify only engine size. The designer is thus free to make his plane large—which would limit the climb due to weight and drag, but would give a very floating glide—or to make it rather small for the engine size. Here we would have a skyrocket climb, but not as good a glide. Which way to go depends a lot on the weather conditions in which the plane is most likely to fly. The big floater could be upset more easily by gusty weather, and it would probably be blown downwind faster in the glide; offsetting the latter is the fact that it could probably be kept in sight longer. All these factors are weighed by the experienced competition free-flight designer; he often carries two planes, one for windy conditions, one for calm.

Since the competition rules may possibly change each year, the budding model designer would do well to check with the Society of Model Aeronautical Engineers (Kimberley House, Vaughan Way, Leicester, Tel: 0533 58500). Most model contests are sanctioned by the Society, and all entrants must be Society members. As such, they are kept advised of proposed and actual rules changes.

Competition events come and go, year by year. Some which have been quite popular in the past die out for one reason or another (team racing is a good example), then are reinstated in modified form. Others are dropped for lack of sponsorship. PAA-Load was at one time quite a popular free-flight event, based on a special type of glow-engine plane which had to carry a "payload"; as you may realize from the name, the event was originally set up by Pan American Airways, which offered very fine prizes for this event at large meets. When this sponsorship ceased, the event declined, though several other forms of model-plane "weight lifting" were tried. After being out of the rules completely for several years, two similar events appear in the 1968 rules on a provisional status; this means the events will be run unofficially, and if sufficient interest is aroused, they will be added to the official rules in coming years. Payload Gas requires ROG (rise off ground) take-off, maximum 15-second engine run, plane wing span of not over 36 inches. Engines must not exceed .025 cubic inch. The plane must carry a 1-ounce payload of certain specified dimensions, and total plane weight with this load must be at least 5 ounces, and no more than 100 ounces. The Payload Cargo event has the same engine and weight requirements, but wing spans up to 48 inches are allowed, and the maximum engine run is 20 seconds. Payload Gas scoring is based on total elapsed time of three scoring flights; in Payload Cargo, the score is the total gross weight carried on three official flights. These specifications bring some unusual design problems with them, and it will be interesting to see if sufficient modelers rise to the challenge to have the events changed to official status.

Rubber-powered ships differ slightly from gas models in design. The nose moment arm is greater, ranging, on the average, from one-fourth to one-third of the wing span. The longer nose results from the fact that the rubber motor, the heaviest part of the model, compels the location of the wing to be at approximately the midpoint of the rubber for satisfactory balance. If the wing is placed farther forward, stalling results. Aspect ratio on rubber models averages about 10:1. Propellers are larger in proportion than on gas models, their average diameter being one-third the plane's wing span. Rudder area is greater because of the larger propeller and the long nose area forward of the CG.

Aerodynamics plays an important part in the design of planes other than free-flight gas or rubber. Control-line speed designs place emphasis on minimum drag and maximum efficiency; yet they must be stable in flight or the flier could never keep them on a steady path. Control-line stunt requires maximum lift for minimum weight, ability to turn extremely sharply, to fly stably inverted as well as upright. Radio control has its own special problems, depending on the particular category involved. Indoor models stress superlight weight, plus flight efficiency.

The prospective designer in any of the current model-plane fields must check on the latest trends in his chosen branch, select those that appeal to him, and make innovations of his own to improve performance. There are many fine books on model design, plus the model magazines and other sources where current technique may be studied. The best place of all is on the flying field, observing the planes and fliers in action and asking judicious questions.

3

PREPARATION OF WORKING DRAWINGS

When a modeler purchases a kit, he receives as part of it a working drawing. Sometimes these drawings are in considerable detail, while in other kits they are very simple. It all depends on the model to be built and the degree of prefabrication.

Suppose a modeler wishes to produce an enlarged copy of a plan found in an aviation periodical. Plans that are not full-size generally have a scale indicated: they may be ½ inch to the foot (the small drawing will show a ½-inch line length for each foot of length on the full-size plane), or perhaps ¼ inch, ³⁄₁₆ inch, or ⅛ inch to the foot. Often a bar scale will be found on the plane to indicate scaled-up equivalents of the small-plan measurements.

You must first decide to what size you wish to enlarge the small plan. Perhaps the plan you have found shows the plane with an actual wing span of 4 inches, but you wish to produce a model of this plane with 24-inch span. The small plan will then have to be enlarged six times. You must therefore multiply every dimension by six to get your working plans. Because most model-plane plans are too large to go in model magazines full-size, they are virtually always reduced in size. Here we might find a scale of something like ¼ inch to 1 inch specified. This indicates that the plan is one-quarter full size; you must enlarge it four times to get up to the original model size. Or, you might see just a bar scale along some edge of the plan. In most cases the scale will show from zero to 12 inches, and by measuring any 1-inch division you can see immediately what the scale happens to be.

Generally, model-plane plans are drawn to rather even scales, such as ¼ or ⅛ inch to the foot. If the scale is something like $\frac{5}{32}$ inch to the foot, however, you have a real task ahead. A draftsman's rule with its various scales can be helpful, and so is a table of decimal equivalents of fractions. Thus, $\frac{5}{32}$ inch equals .15625 inch, but you seldom need to go to such extremes of accuracy.

Decimals are most helpful to enlarge plans regardless of the scale involved, for they are so much easier to multiply than fractions. Thus, if you wish to enlarge a small plan to produce a model of 30-inch span, you just figure how many times some main dimension (such as the wing span) must be multiplied to give you 30 inches. Then multiply all other dimensions, as you measure them on the small plan in centimeters or millimeters, by the same factor. A slide rule will speed this multiplication. Proportional dividers (see fig. 3–1) are also very handy for enlarging or reducing plans, though they are only useful for dimensions up to a maximum of perhaps 8 inches.

Enlarging plans is easy if you know how to go about it. Do you have trouble drawing the long sweeping bottom curve of a fuselage? Then pin a square strip of balsa, properly curved, on the drawing and trace its outline with pencil. Or is it the intricate curve of a wing tip that bothers you? Just draw a screen of horizontal and vertical lines over the curve in question on the small plan, spacing the lines ⅛ inch, ¼ inch, or ½ inch apart, depending on the scale. Make a similar screen or grid over the full-scale working drawing, but space the lines a full inch apart. Then count off squares on the small plan to find points of intersection of the curve and the screen lines; repeat the count on the large plan, and mark all intersection points. With a freehand motion, lightly sketch in the curve, going over it heavily when it takes on a satisfactory appearance. A draftsman's French curve or a ship's curve is ideal for drawing model plans.

Suppose we draw up a hypothetical full-size working drawing. The fuselage is usually the first thing to be constructed, so we'll start there. The simplest procedure is to draw a reference line lengthwise through the small plan's fuselage side view; then, at regular intervals, draw cross lines at right angles—at crosspiece stations if given, otherwise spaced ½ inch or 1 inch apart, depending on the size of the original drawing. Another reference line is drawn on the blank paper to start the full-size

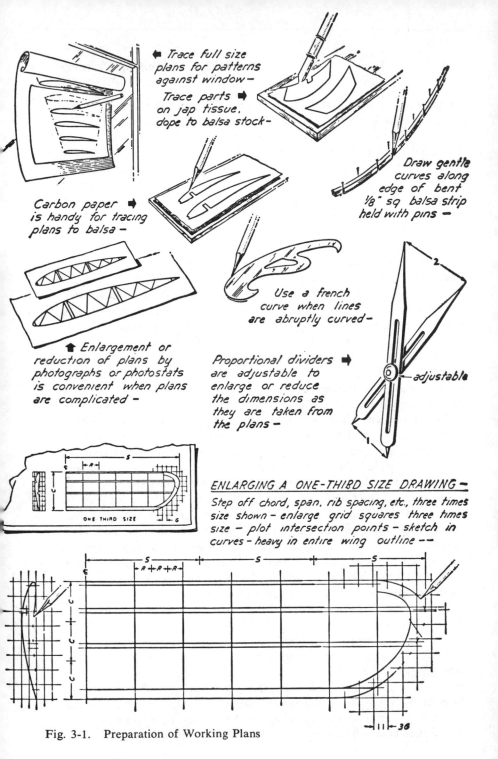

Trace full size plans for patterns against window —

Trace parts → on jap tissue, dope to balsa stock —

Draw gentle curves along edge of bent ⅛" sq balsa strip held with pins —

Carbon paper → is handy for tracing plans to balsa —

Use a french curve when lines are abruptly curved —

↑ Enlargement or reduction of plans by photographs or photostats is convenient when plans are complicated —

Proportional dividers → are adjustable to enlarge or reduce the dimensions as they are taken from the plans —

— adjustable

ENLARGING A ONE-THIRD SIZE DRAWING —
Step off chord, span, rib spacing, etc., three times size shown — enlarge grid squares three times size — plot intersection points — sketch in curves — heavy in entire wing outline —

ONE THIRD SIZE

Fig. 3-1.   Preparation of Working Plans

36

working plan. Then, if the large plan is to be four times the small one, for example, the vertical cross lines are spaced 2 inches or 4 inches apart on the reference line, depending on the line spacing used on the small plan. The idea is to measure each cross line out from the reference line to both top and bottom fuselage edges, then multiply these measurements the required number of times to achieve full scale, transferring each measurement in turn to the proper cross line on the large working plan. After all these fuselage outline points have been found, pin a strip of balsa on the indicated shape and draw in the final outline.

It's a lengthy job, but not too difficult. Depending on the drafting tools or similar equipment available to the individual builder, the work can be simplified greatly. A large drawing board, a T-square, a triangle, and a French curve are indispensable to anyone who does much model designing. These drawing tools not only speed up a tedious job, but also insure accuracy. Along with the divider mentioned before, a pantograph (an automatic device that draws plans to any desired proportion when a pointer is moved over the outlines of a small plan to be enlarged) can also be purchased reasonably at an art-supply store.

However, any accurately squared flat object (sheet metal, for instance) will substitute in a pinch for both T-square and triangle. Even a scrap of plain white paper will substitute for dividers. Just place the margin of the paper over the part on the plan to be enlarged; mark the dimensions with two pencil dots; then transfer the paper to the full-scale plan; and measure off the two pencil marks as many times as required. Another clever trick is to make a cardboard copy—really a scaled-down ruler— of the bar scale found on the small plan. By using this special ruler for measuring various parts of the small plan and transferring these measurements to the identical figure on an ordinary rule, the builder obtains full-scale dimensions almost as fast as he can measure them.

Wings of constant chord are scaled up easily by using the leading and trailing edges as reference lines. Rib spacing is measured off along one wing edge, and rib lines are drawn in at the indicated positions. Curved tips, stabilizers, and rudders are enlarged by making the screen of squares already described. Tapered wings are scaled up by drawing a rectangle around the small wing to be enlarged, the long side being the span, the short side the maximum chord. Still working with the small plan, the builder draws lines through the leading and trailing edges, extending them until they intersect one side of the reference rectangle. Then it is a simple matter to measure back from the front or leading edge of the rectangle to the point of intersection of the small wing's leading edge, multiplying and transferring the new measurement to a full-size rectangle drawn on

Preparation of Working Drawings

BY SUPERIMPOSING THE TIP RIB OVER THE CENTER RIB, INTERMEDIATE RIBS CAN BE DRAWN IN. NOTE SEVERAL LINES DRAWN AT RIGHT ANGLES TO THE CAMBER LINES TO AID IN DIVISION OF SPACE BETWEEN ROOT AND TIP RIBS.

FOR SECTIONS WITH A FLAT LOWER CAMBER, THE METHOD SHOWN BELOW IS BEST. DIVIDE "x" & "Y" INTO EQUAL PARTS (AS MANY PARTS AS THERE ARE RIBS).

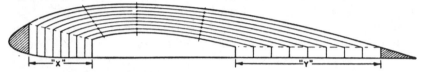

BY DRAWING A SEMI-SYMETRICAL TIP RIB OVER THE ROOT SECTION AS SHOWN BELOW, RIBS MAY BE DRAWN IN WHICH TAPER FROM AN UNDERCAMBERED AIRFOIL AT CENTER OF WING TO A STREAMLINED SECTION AT THE TIPS.

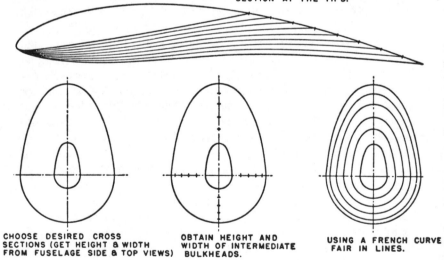

CHOOSE DESIRED CROSS SECTIONS (GET HEIGHT & WIDTH FROM FUSELAGE SIDE & TOP VIEWS)

OBTAIN HEIGHT AND WIDTH OF INTERMEDIATE BULKHEADS.

USING A FRENCH CURVE FAIR IN LINES.

Fig. 3-2.   Tapering Ribs and Bulkheads

the working-plan sheet. The distance between the leading- and trailing-edge intersection points with the side of the small rectangle is, in turn, multiplied and transferred to the large plan. Then the leading and trailing edge reference lines are filled in, followed by rib lines.

Sometimes only half a wing is given with a full-size plan. A simple trick in drawing up the missing half is to trace the given half on thin tissue, then invert the tissue and paste it down on the plan, end to end with the half wing already shown. Or the given half-wing plan may be rubbed with thin oil, making the paper transparent so that the lines can be seen in reverse through the other side. By use of modern commercial copying machines it is also possible to get an enlarged and reversed copy of a drawing or portion thereof. Most model wings, even on small planes, are built in two halves, then joined to obtain the desired center dihedral. Exceptions are free-flight power and glider wings with a flat center section and tip dihedral.

Making patterns, or templates, of fuselage bulkheads or formers and of ribs in a tapered wing is a tough job. Fortunately, practice has evolved accurate methods. These methods are difficult to describe, but they are diagramed clearly.

Full-size plans are awkward affairs, especially when it comes to cutting out parts of a curved wing-tip, rudder, or stabilizer section or of a bulkhead. It is not always practical to work directly on the plan. It is advisable, for instance, to transfer directly to the wood the patterns of curved parts that are to be cut out. A practical way is to trace the part in question on thin tissue and then dope the tissue onto the wood for a cutting guide. Simple, isn't it?

Or, if the builder can place the sheet wood under the section of the plan being used, with carbon paper between, he can trace directly onto the wood the outline of the part to be cut out. Care must be taken to have the wood grain running in the direction indicated on the plan. Resourcefulness always pays dividends.

A wing-rib template is advisable if the wing is of constant chord. Such a template insures that all ribs are both accurate and identical. Trace the given wing section on thin cardboard or, better yet, on thin aluminum.

4

CONSTRUCTION

Since balsa is still the prime construction material for the home builder, though plastic sheet and foam are being used to a growing extent in the ready-to-fly plane field, let's consider this wonderful material for a moment. First, most modelers are aware of the wide variation in weight, or density, and know that for key parts which carry heavy loads (fuselage longerons, wing spars) a fairly heavy stock should be selected. Furthermore, care should be taken to choose strips with straight and uniform grain, no flaws or worm holes. Parts under less stress can be of lighter wood, and it is in this sort of selection that the experienced builder keeps the over-all model weight down, while still assuring ample strength and warp resistance.

The suppliers grade balsa by specifying the weight of a cubic foot of wood; modelers will rarely have a cubic foot to weigh, so some idea of the weight of a "standard sheet" is helpful. Cubic-foot weight varies from about 6 to 16 pounds, and in a good hobby-shop stock you can find practically the whole range. A few balsa suppliers grade weight by color code, the colors appearing on the end of each strip. Unfortunately this practice is not widespread, nor are the codes uniform, so the average modeler must select his wood by feel (weight) and by appearance. Probably the most "standard" size of sheet balsa is $\frac{1}{16}$ inch thick by 3 inches wide and, like practically all balsa, 36 inches long. Light sheets of this size run as low as .375 ounce; medium would be around .7 ounce;

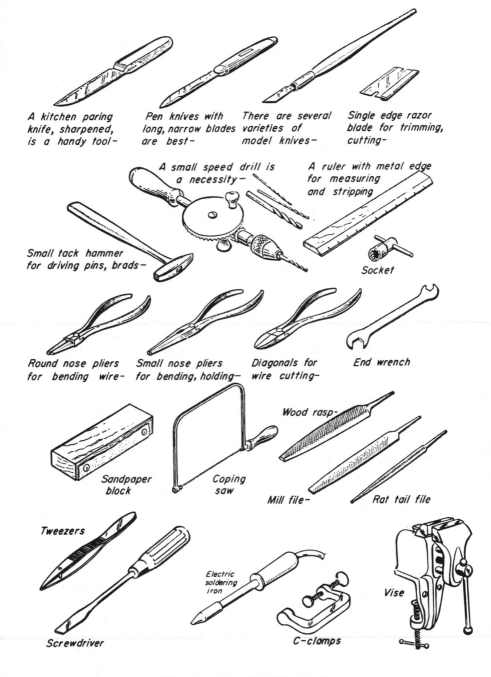

A kitchen paring knife, sharpened, is a handy tool—

Pen knives with long, narrow blades are best—

There are several varieties of model knives—

Single edge razor blade for trimming, cutting—

A small speed drill is a necessity—

A ruler with metal edge for measuring and stripping

Small tack hammer for driving pins, brads—

Socket

Round nose pliers for bending wire—

Small nose pliers for bending, holding—

Diagonals for wire cutting—

End wrench

Sandpaper block

Coping saw

Wood rasp—

Mill file—

Rat tail file

Tweezers

Screwdriver

Electric soldering iron

C-clamps

Vise

Fig. 4-1.   Model-Making Tools

41

heavy as much as 1.25 ounces. The very lightest wood is termed "contest balsa" by some suppliers, since competition fliers often shoot for the least possible weight and make considerable use of such wood. From the weights mentioned, you can easily work out a simple table of wider and narrower sheet and sheet of different thicknesses. Also, strip balsa may be figured the same way: for example, a very soft and light $\frac{1}{8}$-inch-square strip will weigh about .125 ounce for four pieces; the same size in medium weight will be about .225 ounce for four, while in heavy weight the four could total .35 ounce.

Almost as important as weight is the "cut." Since balsa grows like other trees in a series of radial rings, when a log is sawed it may be cut directly across the rings (from the center of the log to outer edge), which is called "quarter grain," or it may be sliced off one side, termed "tangent" cut. And there will be all possible variations between. For some uses in a model plane, it is necessary to have sheet that will bend readily, as for making fuselage tubes or covering wing leading edges and such. For this you want tangent cut; you can identify it by the surface appearance, which shows *only* very narrow dark markings lengthwise of the sheet and no cross markings whatever. Tangent cut is quite bendable in the fingers even when dry; for extreme bends you can wet it and fasten it in the shape you desire, and it will retain this shape when it dries.

Quarter-grain sheet is useful for ribs, fuselage side covering (if no bending across the sheet is required), or bulkheads. This material has the darker lengthwise markings too, but most prominent are various cross-sheet "rays," speckles, and other marks difficult to describe. Such sheet cannot be bent to any extent, even when you wet it.

Between quarter and tangent cut comes a wide variety of cuts known in the trade as "random." An experienced modeler often selects wood for just about *every* part of his model by both weight and cut.

Where more strength than is afforded by balsa is required, various harder woods are available. Spruce is one favorite; it is very straight-grained, fairly uniform in weight, and is often used for wing spars (one thin strip atop the ribs, another along the bottom) and longerons. White pine is utilized for propeller blocks. Very hard woods are employed for engine bearers, particularly in radio-control and control-line models, since they will stand the crushing force of tightened engine-mounting bolts.

Some of the standard sizes of balsa are illustrated in figure 4–2. The vast majority of balsa is cut to 3-foot length, but some suppliers handle 4-foot stock. You can obtain balsa sheet up to 8 inches in width. Some

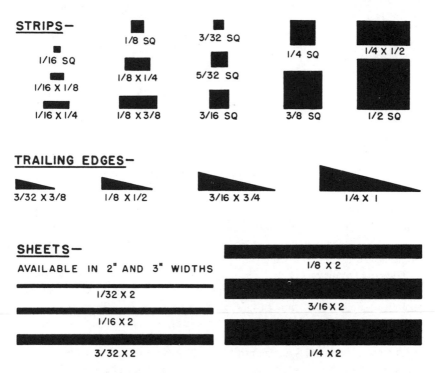

Fig. 4-2. Common Balsa Sizes

suppliers carry special leading-edge shapes, triangular balsa, and other special shapes. Most can supply blocks in a wide variety; these are useful for making cowlings and nose areas of power models, wing tips, tail cones, and the like.

Modelers have a choice of a number of completely different ways to construct wings, tails, fuselages, and other structural parts (see figs. 4–4 and 4–5).

There are multispar wings with six to eight thin spars spaced on both the top and the bottom of the wing, single-spar wings with their balsa-sheeted leading edges, the standard two-spar wings, sparless wings with heavy leading and trailing edges to carry the load, and numerous less important types. Tail surfaces differ in the same manner.

The term "fuselage" refers to the body of the airplane. The most popular fuselage, or body, from the hobbyist's standpoint, is the common box. Such a fuselage most often consists of four longerons or longitudinal members braced by crosspieces. Box fuselages combine simplicity of construction, light weight, and adequate strength.

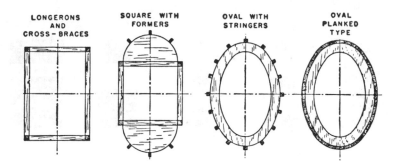

Fig. 4-3.   Four Basic Types of Fuselage Construction

A form or jig made of straight pins holds the wood strips in position while the sides are being built. The completed sides are joined together afterward by means of top and bottom crosspieces precut to their proper lengths.

The first step is to lay the side-view plan of the fuselage on the bench, stretching the paper tight to pull out wrinkles that could hamper construction. Thumbtack the corners of the plan to keep it taut; then cover it with a sheet of wax paper or, even better, Saran wrap. (Wax paper tends to leave a sticky residue where touched by model cement, which dries slowly, whereas Saran is not affected at all by cement. Either covering keeps the wood from being glued fast to the plan and possibly to the table too.) Drive straight pins into the bench along the inside line of both the top and bottom longerons. Curve the longerons around these pins. Tack other pins along the outside of the longerons to hold them in place. Do not pierce the balsa strips with the pins. Now cut to an exact fit all the crosspieces visible on the side view of the plan and glue them in their respective positions. Select for the longerons four pieces of strip balsa that match in hardness and in thickness. If these longerons are not matched, the stronger ones will pull the fuselage out of alignment, either when it is removed from the form or when the two side frames are joined together. Install all the vertical crosspieces first; then follow with the diagonal braces. Cut all the crosspieces to the required size before cementing any of them in place. Construct the two side frames simultaneously, one over the other in the form. This insures identical fuselage sides. To remove the completed parts from the forms, pull out all the pins. Peel off the plastic wrap, and separate the two fuselage halves by sliding a two-edged razor blade between the longerons.

Assembling the two sides is the only difficult operation. First, cut the top and bottom crosspieces to their proper lengths. Attach the widest crosspieces first; then, after the cement has dried, draw together the nose

44

and tail ends of the body as required, finally inserting the remaining crosspieces.

When joining together the side frames, attach four crosspieces, two top and two bottom, at the widest part of the body. To hold them in place temporarily, force four thin straight pins through the sides of the longerons; then, after putting a drop of cement on the end of each crosspiece, stick the crosspieces on the pin points flush with the inside surface of the longerons. Glue all four crosspieces first to one side frame; then attach the other side frame to the loose ends of the crosspieces. If the longerons are very thin, even a fine pin can weaken them. In this case, weights may be utilized to hold the side frames upright on the building surface, while the initial four crosspieces are installed. Some modelers prefer to use this method in any case, so the longerons won't be weakened in the slightest. The weights may be books, blocks of wood or metal, bottles, and so on. Careful checking with a square, as depicted in figure 4–5, should always be done to indicate whether the fuselage is true. As more and more crosspieces are added to the structure, look straight down from the top, to be sure the top and bottom pieces coincide as they should.

Many fuselages require that the forward ends of the longerons be brought closer together than the wider center area. If difficulty is experienced here, a rubber band or two will help hold these ends in alignment.

Typical wood sizes for box-type fuselages are as follows: $\frac{1}{16}$-inch-square balsa for models having a 12- to 18-inch wing span; $\frac{3}{32}$-inch-square for 18- to 24-inch wing spans; $\frac{1}{8}$-inch-square for 24- to 36-inch spans; $\frac{5}{32}$-inch-square for 36- to 48-inch spans; $\frac{3}{16}$-inch-square for 48- to 60-inch spans; and $\frac{1}{4}$-inch-square for spans over 60 inches. Some ships (racers) may have unusually large fuselages in proportion to their wing span and consequently require heavier wood than the sizes tabulated above. A nicely rounded nose, which could be used in connection with a propeller spinner or cone for streamlining, is not too difficult to make. Four pieces of sheet balsa or thin balsa blocks, as the size of your model may require, are glued to each of the four sides of the nose. This solid nosing should be extended back two or three or more crosspiece stations so that the wood can be carved and shaped to flow in with the fuselage outlines, at the same time forming an absolutely rounded nose.

Round and streamlined noses are common on rubber-powered models. On the other hand, many competition free-flight gas models have the fuselage chopped off flat at the front end; this makes for simple construction, and the engine is easily accessible. Most radio-control models have some measure of streamlining at the nose, usually obtained by building it up with balsa blocks, then carving to the desired contours. Since weight is not so important, control-line models (except for the simplest types or those with profile fuselages) are usually made this way too.

Gas-model fuselages of box construction occasionally are covered with sheet-balsa siding rather than paper or silk. Medium hard sheet balsa $\frac{1}{16}$-inch thick is correct for small gas models of 48-inch or so wing span, $\frac{3}{32}$-inch on larger ones.

A second popular system of constructing flat-side fuselages is the sheet-balsa method. This system is simple and sturdy. It is widely used for many types of planes: sport rubber, small and medium-size contest free-flight and towliners, sport free-flight, U-control (the sheet-balsa method is practically universal here), and radio-control. (On larger sizes the wood may be silk-covered for added strength.) First, two identical sides are cut from sheet balsa, to be connected together with sheet-balsa bulkheads (or plywood if called for). The sides may be assembled by the same basic methods that applied to assembling the sides of cross-piece construction. The top and bottom of this fuselage may be sheet as well, or the bottom may be sheet, with the top rounded off with some blocks, formers, and stringers, or bent sheet balsa, perhaps with a cockpit cutout. For rubber and gas free-flight, the sides would be $\frac{1}{32}$- to $\frac{1}{16}$-inch thick for models under 24 inches span; $\frac{1}{16}$-inch thick for 24- to 30-inch spans, $\frac{3}{32}$-inch thick for spans of 36 to 48 inches; and $\frac{1}{8}$-inch thick for still bigger machines.

The bulkheads should be $\frac{1}{16}$-inch thick for free-flight models of approximately 18-inch wing span, $\frac{3}{32}$- to $\frac{1}{8}$-inch thick for an 18-inch to about a 30-inch wing, $\frac{1}{8}$- to $\frac{3}{16}$-inch thick for spans from 48 to 54 inches, and $\frac{1}{4}$ thereafter. Where internal strength is required for attaching wings and landing gears, hard plywood should be substituted for sheet-balsa bulkheads.

Box fuselages of perfectly square cross section are often mounted on edge with one corner beneath the wing, another corner at the bottom of the plane, and one corner on each side. Such a model is known as a "diamond."

Streamlined fuselages are often of so-called *monocoque* or shell construction. They have little internal structure, aside from a few formers, and are either hollowed out from balsa block or built up with many lengthwise stringers cemented to the formers. The final covering can be either paper, silk, or balsa planking.

The hollowed-balsa variety makes the perfect fuselage for smaller models, particularly for scale types with their many different fuselage curvatures. If the balsa is selected carefully for light weight, the over-all

weight will not be excessive. The fuselage is started by cementing together very lightly a pair of blocks. (Just put a few dabs of cement on
the surfaces, so they may be separated easily later.) The blocks should
each be half the final width of the fuselage or a little thicker, to allow
for outer carving. After cementing, shape the outer contours completely
and sand the surface to a smooth finish. Then split along the lightly
cemented center line (which is usually vertical to the finished fuselage)
and hollow out the interior. With a few sharp wood gouges, this is not
as tough a job as it might seem. Thickness of the walls may be judged
by holding the piece up to a bright light and viewing it from the inside.
Since more strength—and usually more weight, at least in rubber models
—is needed near the nose, this area may be left thicker, but the tail area
should be thinned down more to prevent tail-heaviness. The gouges must
be very sharp, to cut the soft wood cleanly. You can use regular car-
penter's gouges or obtain special gouge blades that fit in the model knife
handles found in many hobby shops. After the main carving has been
done, the finishing touches can be put on the interior by sanding first
with rather coarse paper, then with finer grades, wrapped over short
lengths of dowel of large diameter. Finally, a few formers can be fitted
and fastened in by the cut-and-try-it method. It is easiest to make these
in halves and put cement on them at the same time you cement the two
halves of the shell together.

Built-up, streamlined fuselages generally consist of bulkheads (cut to
shape with templates or patterns from hard balsa) and longitudinal
stringers. This construction is ticklish for any but the experienced builder.
The technique is to put the two center side stringers in place on the two
widest adjacent bulkheads, one stringer on the left side and one on the
right. The next step is to draw these stringers together to a point at the
rear, or to a small tail bulkhead or wooden tail plug, according to the
particular plans being used. After this the nose bulkhead is attached,
and all the intermediate bulkheads are inserted in their proper stations.
Then the top and bottom stringers are installed, followed by all the remaining stringers.

Here are a few steps to facilitate construction of bulkheaded fuselages.
Glue a thin strip of wood across each of the wide bulkheads near the
top and bottom. This prevents splitting. Cut all stringer notches first,
using a thin-pointed sliver of a double-edged razor blade. It is possible
to use a single wide keel, made by tracing the bottom curve of the fuselage on sheet balsa and cutting the keel piece about ½ inch or more high.
First mount the widest bulkheads, followed by all the remaining bulkheads and finally the other stringers.

Bulkhead fuselage designs can be simplified by making a primary framework, either a square tube made from four pieces of sheet balsa or a square built-up internal fuselage having longerons and crosspieces or bulkheads, as the case may be, with four formers, one former each for the top, the bottom, and the two sides. Stringers complete the job.

Planked fuselages make beautiful models. Planking consists of thin flat strips laid side by side over the entire fuselage surface. Where planking strips overlap as the fuselage frame narrows down at the ends, each plank must be shaved to a tapering fit as it is glued in place. The finished planking is sanded smooth and then covered with silk. One piece of silk can be wrapped around the entire fuselage without wrinkling simply by stretching the cloth to make difficult bends.

Planking is begun with four planking strips, one over each of the four foundation stringers that are cemented to the outside of the bulkheads. Other planks are added one at a time to the edges of the first four. Do not complete one side of the fuselage first since it may pull out of line owing to the uneven strain. Give the body a quarter turn each time a plank is fastened in place. To speed up the application of cement to the long edges of the planks, try tubes of cement instead of bottles or cans.

Bulkheads are made from $\frac{1}{32}$-, $\frac{1}{16}$-, $\frac{3}{32}$-, and $\frac{1}{8}$-inch sheet balsa. However, $\frac{1}{32}$-inch sheet is a little too flimsy for the average modeler to work without splitting. Balsa $\frac{1}{16}$ inch thick is used for rubber-powered flying scale designs, original designs, and general-contest rubber-powered models having up to 45- to 48-inch wing spans. In rubber-powered models having more than 30-inch wings, two-ply $\frac{1}{32}$-inch sheet balsa is recommended for bulkheads. Sheet balsa $\frac{3}{32}$ inch thick is used for the purpose on the smaller gas planes; $\frac{1}{8}$-inch sheet is used on the larger ones. Since bulkhead or former grain is vertical, these members tend to bend and split in assembly. Cement a light crosspiece across the grain to stop splitting. On gas models, bulkheads need not be cut out for lightness or for the passage of a rubber motor. Stringers are $\frac{1}{16}$ inch square for planes having approximately a 24-inch wing span, $\frac{1}{16} \times \frac{1}{8}$ inch (set on edge) for 24- to 36-inch spans, $\frac{1}{8} \times \frac{1}{4}$ inch or even $\frac{1}{8}$ or $\frac{3}{8}$ inch on 6-foot designs. When a square fuselage is built with the intention of being rounded off or faired to a more streamlined cross section, try balsa strips $\frac{3}{32}$ inch square for the longerons when the wing span is less than 36 inches, $\frac{1}{8}$ inch square for spans of 36 to 48 inches, and $\frac{3}{16}$ or $\frac{1}{4}$ inch square for intermediate and large-size gas jobs, respectively. Planking strips are $\frac{1}{16} \times \frac{1}{4}$ inch; they are $\frac{1}{16} \times \frac{3}{8}$ inch for rubber-powered models and as heavy as $\frac{1}{8} \times \frac{1}{2}$ inch for gas design.

Crutch construction is useful for planes, usually engine-powered, which have fairly deep fuselages. The crutch is simply a pair of fairly sturdy balsa longerons fastened together with a reasonable number of crosspieces and often with hardwood engine bearers cemented to the forward end. The crutch lies horizontally, and fuselage formers are cemented on top and bottom, to be faired in with stringers as required by over-all fuselage contour. An advantage is that the crutch is built flat on the bench, and while it is still there, half-formers are attached for the top (or bottom, as desired). While still on the table, the stingers can be cemented. Thus when you lift the crutch from the table, you have a rather sturdy and rigid assembly which may be quite quickly completed. The crutch side members are usually flat: $\frac{1}{8} \times \frac{1}{4}$ inch cross section for fairly small models, larger for heavier jobs.

Great variation is seen in wings, not only in the number of ribs and spars but in over-all construction. We see single-spar, double-spar, multi-spar, sparless, curved-sheet, and, in the radio-control field, many foam-core wings (usually completely balsa-sheeted). Simple built-up structures are lightest, of course, and are found in small rubber-driven models, both scale and sport. As wings get longer and larger, more spars are generally added. Wings formed from a single curved sheet of balsa are found in many sizes of sport planes; as the size increases, some stiffening along their length is generally required, and most such wings have a few ribs on the underside to preserve the curvature.

Sheeted wings are popular in control-line models (except for stunters, where weight must be kept to a minimum); these are often formed of curved upper and lower sheets, with a few ribs inside. Sheeted wings are also popular on larger radio planes, but here the sheet is usually put on over a complete framework; it adds strength, gives stiffness to resist twisting, and provides a clean aerodynamic surface.

Control-line speed models often have wings contoured from fairly thin sheets of wood harder than balsa; also frequently seen are wings with thin aluminum outer skins, generally attached to a single sturdy center spar.

Hand-launched gliders almost invariably have very thin sheet wings; they must be quite sturdy to withstand the terrific heave some modelers can impart at launching.

The simplest style of wing is that made from thin sheet balsa. The shape is first outlined on the sheet and cut out with a razor blade. Dihedral is imparted by part cutting across the wing center, then cracking it to give the desired angular difference. The center area must receive several coats of cement, and it is wise to reinforce it with a layer of silk applied with the cement. Flat (no-camber) wood wings are practical on models up to approximately 18 inches in span. For wings of less than 12 inches, $\frac{1}{32}$-inch sheet is required; $\frac{1}{16}$-inch sheet is used for wings

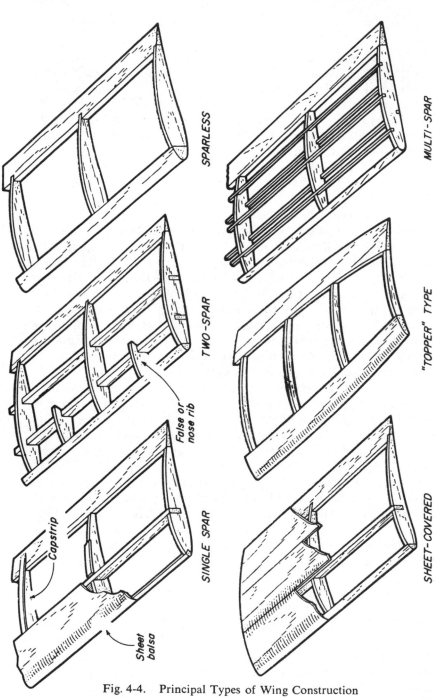

SPARLESS

MULTI-SPAR

TWO-SPAR

"TOPPER" TYPE

False or nose rib

Capstrip

SINGLE SPAR

SHEET-COVERED

Sheet balsa

Fig. 4-4.   Principal Types of Wing Construction

50

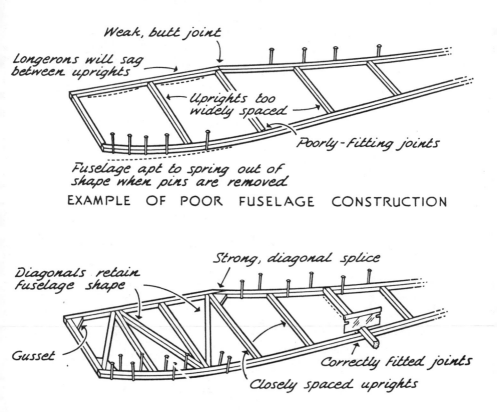

Weak, butt joint

Longerons will sag between uprights

Uprights too widely spaced

Poorly-Fitting joints

Fuselage apt to spring out of shape when pins are removed

EXAMPLE OF POOR FUSELAGE CONSTRUCTION

Diagonals retain fuselage shape

Strong, diagonal splice

Gusset

Correctly fitted joints

Closely spaced uprights

SOUND FUSELAGE CONSTRUCTION

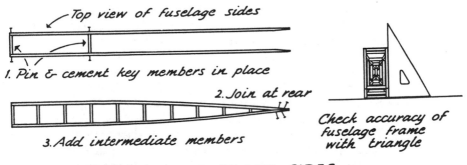

Top view of fuselage sides

1. Pin & cement key members in place

2. Join at rear

3. Add intermediate members

Check accuracy of fuselage frame with triangle

ASSEMBLING FUSELAGE SIDES

Fig. 4-5. Assembling the Fuselage

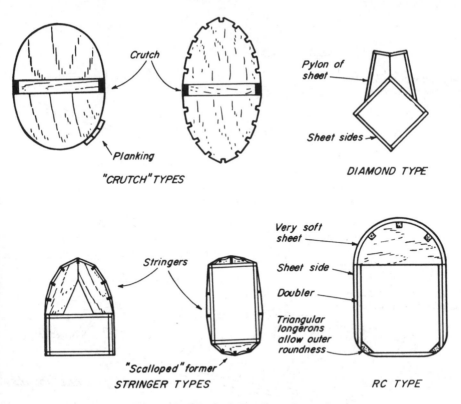

Crutch

Planking

"CRUTCH" TYPES

Pylon of
sheet

Sheet sides

DIAMOND TYPE

Stringers

"Scalloped" former

STRINGER TYPES

Very soft
sheet

Sheet side

Doubler

Triangular
longerons
allow outer
roundness

RC TYPE

Fig. 4-6. Typical Fuselage Cross Sections

ranging between 12 inches and 2 feet in span. These sizes hold true for ordinary hand-launched gliders, all-balsa ROG's (rise-off-ground stick models), and small cabin-type models. Contest hand-launched gliders that are subjected to very high launching stresses make heavier wood imperative. Here $\frac{3}{32}$- to $\frac{1}{8}$-inch sheet balsa is desirable. The wood in this wing must be sanded to an airfoil cross section.

Surprisingly, small planes will fly quite well with just a plain flat wing, even one left blunt at leading and trailing edges. A bit more efficiency may be gained by rounding all edges or by giving the sheet a slight airfoil shape by sanding the front and rear areas, but only on the upper surface.

A much improved all-balsa sheet wing is had if the sheet is given camber, or airfoil shape. Efficiency is improved, since there is less drag for a given amount of lift, and the strength of the span is greatly increased by the curved surface. These wings may be made of the same sheet thickness noted above, for the same sizes of models. They are usually cut in halves; after one half has been cut and shaped to suit the builder (and note that with sheet-balsa wings of any sort you can in-

52

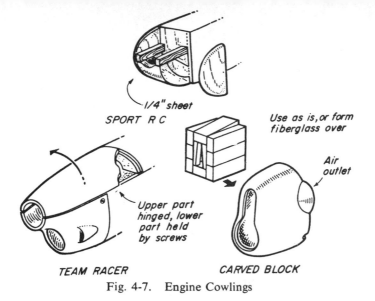

1/4" sheet

SPORT R C

Use as is, or form fiberglass over

Air outlet

Upper part hinged, lower part held by screws

TEAM RACER   CARVED BLOCK

Fig. 4-7.   Engine Cowlings

clude taper, curved wing tips, and so on, just as easily as making a "barn-door" shape), the second can be cut to match exactly. For wings with 12-inch span, a center rib and one halfway out on each side would be ample. An 18-inch wing might need two ribs each side of center. For an 18-inch wing, the chord might be some 2½ inches, and even ⅛-inch camber (which means the highest part of the undercurve would be ⅛ inch higher than the underside of the leading and trailing edges) would be useful, with 3/16 inch about maximum. Cut the ribs to desired airfoil, making the center rib of each half from at least ¼-inch-thick sheet. Dampen the upper surfaces, bend carefully in your fingers to shape (remember, the wood must be picked from the bendable cuts—tangent cut is the best here), and pin to your building board over the ribs to dry. Then you can cement in the ribs. When dry, sand the inner ends to obtain desired dihedral, and cement the halves together. A 1-inch-wide silk reinforcement at the center completes the job.

Any wing made of one sheet of balsa is known as a single-surface wing; one made from two sheets of wood for both a top and a bottom surface is called a double-surface wing.

To make a double-surface all-balsa wing, cut out two wing outlines from sheet wood of the necessary thickness. The bottom piece of sheet balsa (lower surface of the wing) is pinned flat on the bench. The wing ribs (and edges and spars, if any) are then glued to this sheet balsa in their positions as indicated by the plans, after which the top piece of sheet balsa (upper surface of the wing) is bent over the ribs and cemented to them and to the bottom surface at both the leading and trailing edges. Sheet balsa 1/32 inch thick is sufficient for double-surface wings on rubber-powered designs having wing spans of 24 to about 36 inches; $\frac{1}{16}$-inch balsa is used for larger sizes. For free-flight gas models, where power and higher flying speeds make weight of less importance than on rubber-powered models, $\frac{3}{32}$- to $\frac{1}{8}$-inch sheet balsa is suitable for spans of approximately 36 to 60 inches. For U-control use, $\frac{1}{16}$- to $\frac{1}{8}$-inch-thick sheet is best on spans up to 30 inches. Select soft balsa. To prevent nicks or actual breakage in the leading edge, cover the leading edges of all wood wings with a band of covering tissue on small models, silk on the larger ones. The entire surface of a wood wing should be sanded to eliminate as much roughness as possible. A few coats of sanding sealer will fill the pores in the wood and will contribute substantially to cutting down the drag due to skin friction in flight.

Heavier sheet balsa sometimes is used for solid wings on various types of U-control machines, especially team racers and profile trainers. On the team racer, $\frac{1}{4}$-inch hard sheet would be required for a span of 24 inches or so. The same applies to the trainer, except that the work of shaping is tough for a beginner. He would be better off with a prefabricated kit. Trainer wings may run to $\frac{3}{8}$ inch in thickness; they are fully shaped in a kit.

Next to the flat sheet-balsa wing in simplicity is the built-up, paper-covered, single-surface variety exemplified in baby ROG's and small stick models of from 6- to 18-inch wingspread. Such wings are generally of rectangular shape and never have spars. The leading and trailing edges carry the entire load. These wings are assembled from square strips in the same manner as a fuselage side frame. The front and rear edges are pinned to the bench while the crosspieces or ribs are cemented in place. For an 18-inch wing the only crosspieces needed are one at the center line, one at each wing tip, and one halfway out on each wing panel. Dihedral is obtained by cracking the two wing edges at the center line, then cementing the cracks after the tip (or tips if polyhedral or tip dihedral is desired) has been raised to the proper elevation off the bench. The model tissue covering is applied to the top of the wing frame only. *Never* dampen or dope the surface of the tissue on such wings, since the light framework is sure to waɪp. If the tissue is wrinkled to any extent, it may be smoothed with a flatiron before applying. Model-plane dope is amply strong to attach the paper to the framework; cement should not be used; it too will cause warps. The wing may be attached to a plain motor stick by a pair of music-wire clips, one cemented to the leading and one to the trailing edge. Such clips allow the wing to be moved fore and aft for balancing purposes.

The cambered single-surface wing is constructed in the same way as a flat wing with the exception that the curved wing ribs are cut to shape

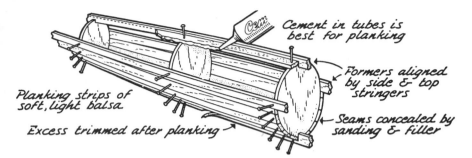

Cement in tubes is best for planking

Formers aligned by side & top stringers

Planking strips of soft, light balsa

Seams concealed by sanding & filler

Excess trimmed after planking

Fig. 4-8.   Fuselage Planking

beforehand from thin sheet balsa. The covering is applied to the top of the wing only and should not be sprayed or doped. Select strips $\frac{1}{16}$ inch square for spans of less than 15 inches, $\frac{3}{32}$ inch square for wings ranging between 15 and 24 inches in span, and $\frac{1}{8}$ inch square for spans between 24 and 30 inches.

Considerably greater efficiency is had on small wings with no center spar, if the ribs are of thin sheet balsa, cambered on top and flat on the bottom, and the wing is papered both top and bottom. Freedom from warping is increased if a thin strip is run spanwise on the ribs at the highest part of the airfoil curve, which is usually one-fourth to one-third back from the leading edge. This piece can be very small: $\frac{1}{16}$ inch square is enough for light wings up to 18 inches or so. With this spar in place, the paper can be tightened (described in chapter 7) with a light spray and even given a light coat of thin dope, and it won't warp if reasonable care is taken.

The single-spar wing is popular on small and medium-size rubber jobs, towliners, and gas free-flight models. On larger wings, there is a tendency for the wing to warp about the single spar. The single spar always should be placed well forward on the chord of the wing, usually at about the one-third-chord position. The spar must be deep to prevent the shrinking of the top-surface covering material from warping the wing upward like a bow. Spar and edge sizes vary widely. On a small wing of, perhaps, 24-inch span, the spar would be $\frac{1}{8} \times \frac{1}{4}$ inch; for 30 to 36 inches of span, $\frac{1}{8} \times \frac{3}{8}$ inch. The leading edge for these two examples would be $\frac{1}{8}$ and $\frac{3}{16}$ inch square, if set on edge with the material fitting into a triangular slot cut in the fronts of the ribs. If the leading edge is set perpendicularly, $\frac{1}{8}$ inch square would suffice for the smaller size, $\frac{1}{8} \times \frac{1}{4}$ inch for the other. These edge sizes, incidentally, hold true when other spar arrangements are used. On very large wings, the edge might be

¼ × ½ inch or even larger. Trailing edges are triangular-cut in standard widths. Use ⅜-inch wide for the 20-inch span, ½-inch wide for 24 inches to 30 inches or so of span, and ¾ for 30 to 54 inches or so of span.

When two spars are employed, the cross section of the material is smaller. Thus, in place of a single spar measuring ¼ × ½ inch, two spars of ³⁄₁₆ × ⅜ inch could be substituted. The combined cross section of the two spars would be greater than that of the one spar. Compare material cross-section areas when computing such substitutions. Sometimes the front spar of a two-spar wing is placed on the bottom surface, but the rear spar is on the top to help prevent warping.

A popular construction, in all wing sizes from small rubber sport planes of perhaps 18-inch span up to big radio models of 6-foot span, is the use of sturdy leading and trailing edges (these can be quite light in the rubber planes, of course, much heavier in the big planes), plus a pair of spars placed above each other at the deepest point of the airfoil. Flat strip is normally used for these spars, set in rib slots with the wide side horizontal. For even greater strength and stiffness—needed only in the larger and heavier planes—"webs" are cemented between (on the rear edge of) the top and bottom spars; the grain of such webs must run vertically.

The first step in constructing a double-surface built-up wing is to cut out all the wing ribs from the proper grade of balsa. Sheet balsa ¹⁄₃₂ inch thick is proper for models of up to 24-inch wing spread, ¹⁄₁₆ for spreads between 24 and 48 inches. Small gas planes require sheet ¹⁄₁₆ inch thick for ribs; intermediate gas designs, ³⁄₃₂ inch thick; and large gas models, ⅛ inch. Magazine plans include a full-size wing-rib pattern. (Kits contain die-cut sheets of wood.) Paste this paper rib on thin stiff cardboard or aluminum, and cut out a template for marking the outlines of the required number of ribs on the sheet balsa. Here is a handy tip for quick, accurate work: pin all the ribs together side by side in a bundle with straight pins. In this way all the ribs can be trimmed and sanded to a uniform outline. The spar notches should never be cut in ribs until they are matched together in this manner. These notches are best cut while the ribs are still pinned together in a stack; then they will all match perfectly, and the spars will drop neatly in place.

The next step in assembling the wing is to pin the spar (or spars, if there is more than one on the underside) and the leading and trailing edges to the building board over the plan. Naturally, if the ribs are undercambered, a bottom spar will not touch the board; it should be supported at the proper height on small blocks of scrap balsa. Drive the pins on either side of the spar, not through it. The ribs are cemented directly

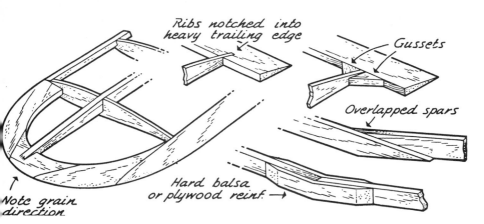

Fig. 4-9.   Wing Structure Details

over the rib stations indicated on the drawings; then come the leading and trailing edges. With undercambered ribs, it may be necessary to jack up the front of the trailing edge with slivers of wood. The curved wing tips are cut to shape from pieces of sheet balsa, generally at least two pieces to a tip. If you use but one piece of sheet balsa for a wing tip, it will warp and twist out of shape on any but the smallest of models. The segments of each tip are butted and cemented together cross-grain to form one piece, which is in turn pinned in place on the wing frame until the cement takes hold.

Sheet balsa used in wing-tip construction varies from $\frac{1}{16}$ inch for 12- to 18-inch spans to $\frac{1}{8}$ inch for 30- to 48-inch spans for rubber-powered models; $\frac{1}{8}$ inch and $\frac{1}{4}$ inch are used for free-flight gas models of intermediate and large sizes. Sheet balsa can be laminated for greater thickness or strength. Squared tips, à la Mustang, may be shaped from soft balsa blocks, hollowed for lightness. Sparless wings, popular in small free-flight gas models and U-control stunt models, depend on their sturdy leading and trailing edges to carry the load. The leading edge is a thick piece of balsa shaped to flow into the rib contour. The trailing edge is carved to a sharp edge. A 40-inch wing for a rubber-powered model calls for approximately a $\frac{1}{2} \times \frac{3}{4}$ inch leading edge and a $\frac{1}{4} \times \frac{3}{4}$ inch trailing edge.

Multispar wings may have all the spars on top, on the underside, or part on each side, and they may all be in the forward half of the wing or distributed over the entire chord.

The multispar wing is assembled flat on the bench like any other built-up wing, except that if undercamber construction is used it cannot be completed until the wing is taken from the form in a semifinished condition and inverted for the finishing touches. First of all, the positions of the spars on the wing ribs determine the procedure in assembly. Since rubber-powered contest-model designs often have undercambered wing ribs, it is probable that most, if not all, of the spars for the bottom surface of the wing will not touch the bench when they are fastened in place in their proper notches cut into the ribs.

To facilitate assembly, therefore, it is advisable to design your model so that at least one bottom spar is located on the deepest bulge on the lower surface of the ribs, insuring that the spar will rest flat on the bench. If this is done, all the ribs can be cemented in position right on the spar. The spar itself can be pinned to the bench. The trailing edge should be shaped and pinned in place before anything else is done. If the ribs are cemented both to the spar and to the trailing edge, they can be held in perfect alignment. The leading edge comes next, followed by all the top spars and finally by the wingtips. Now comes the novel part of the procedure. Remove all the pins from the form and invert the wing. The remaining bottom spars are now glued in place.

For multispar rubber competition-model wings in the 36- to 54-inch sizes, the ribs might be cut from $\frac{1}{16}$-inch sheet balsa; the spars are balsa $\frac{1}{16}$ inch square, the leading edge is $\frac{1}{8}$ inch square set on edge "diamond" fashion, and the trailing edge is $\frac{1}{8} \times \frac{3}{8}$ inch or $\frac{1}{8} \times \frac{1}{2}$ inch triangle stock. Six to eight spars are used, half on the top surface and half on the bottom. Larger gas models may use three to five spars of deep cross section, all placed on the bottom surface or inserted through holes in the ribs. The latter makes for a strong, warp-free structure.

Modelers have several reasons for covering the leading-edge section of their wings with thin sheet balsa. One reason is that a more accurate wing-rib contour can be made with wood than with paper, which usually sags between the ribs. Another reason is to gain sufficient strength to withstand collisions of the leading edges with branches or sharp objects that would cut through the wing. Still another is that the sheet greatly stiffens the wing and also strengthens it.

Except for wings that are completely sheet-covered, the sheeting seldom extends more than halfway back from the leading edge, and often less than this. Many builders prefer to run the sheet back to the highest point on the rib curvature; if the wing is built with top and bottom spars at this point, the sheet can be cemented to them at its rearmost edge. If not, a thin spar, running from tip to tip, should be notched into the ribs at the desired point; this is to terminate the sheet.

For more strength and stiffness (but for somewhat lighter weight than those wings that are fully sheeted top and bottom), the sheeting may be applied to the wing forward area, both top and bottom. Again, strips of

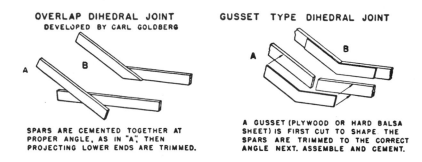

OVERLAP DIHEDRAL JOINT
DEVELOPED BY CARL GOLDBERG

GUSSET TYPE DIHEDRAL JOINT

SPARS ARE CEMENTED TOGETHER AT PROPER ANGLE, AS IN "A", THEN PROJECTING LOWER ENDS ARE TRIMMED.

A GUSSET (PLYWOOD OR HARD BALSA SHEET) IS FIRST CUT TO SHAPE. THE SPARS ARE TRIMMED TO THE CORRECT ANGLE NEXT. ASSEMBLE AND CEMENT.

Fig. 4-10.   Strong Dihedral Joints

some sort are usually employed, to which the rear edges of the sheet are cemented. Going one step further, what is generally termed a "D-spar" wing is obtained with this top and bottom sheeting, generally to one-third of the chord back from the leading edge, and with vertical-grain sheet webs cemented between all ribs, from top to bottom spar. This produces an extremely stiff wing, both as to spanwise bending and to twisting, and is much favored in radio-control planes. Begin construction by assembling the ribs, top and bottom spars, and the leading and trailing edges. While this assembly is still on the building board (the leading edge must have been faired to the same contour as the ribs, of course), dampen the top sheeting and pin it in place; when dry, attach it with slow-drying cement, to give you time to apply cement to the many surfaces. Then invert the wing, level it up, and apply the bottom sheeting. Pin down the ribs right side up on the board once more, and level out most carefully (it is practically impossible to take out any warp or twist you have built in after the webs are in place); then cut the webs to fit between ribs and cement them in.

False ribs can be substituted for sheet-balsa covering of the leading-edge area of planes where the extra stiffness and strength of sheet are not really required. False ribs are nothing but the abbreviated or cut-off noses of the regular ribs. They are cemented in place between spar and leading edge and serve to keep the covering from sagging badly between the full-length ribs.

On large rubber-powered designs and all gas models it is advisable to sink the rear edges of the wing ribs into notches cut in the trailing edges. The notches should be cut about $\frac{1}{16}$ to $\frac{1}{4}$ inch deep, depending on size. Never force tight fits, as warps will result. If the leading edge is wide enough to take notches without excessive weakening, it too may be notched. Many kits come with both leading and trailing edges notched this way, which is a big help to the builder in facilitating fast and accurate wing assembly.

Dihedral imposes some mean problems in making wing-spar joints for gas models. There are two popular methods for reinforcing the spliced spar joints. The builder may slant the ends of the spar sections to butt them together neatly and then "box" the joint by cementing to each of its sides (the front and the rear faces) flat pieces of hard sheet balsa or possibly ply. Or the spar sections can be so placed in each wing panel that their ends will overlap when joined. If surface sheeting is used, the ends of the sheet on each side are also carefully matched and butted together. When the entire sheeting job is complete, silk reinforcement may be added. On the larger radio models, thin fiberglass cloth is often utilized at the dihedral joint, applied with either model cement or, even better, polyester or epoxy cement.

On smaller Half-A free-flight models, a single thickness of ⅛-inch sheet is sturdy enough for the pylon-deck support. For bigger Half-A's, laminate two thicknesses of ⅛-inch sheet. On Class A free-flights, it is advisable to laminate two thicknesses of ³⁄₁₆-inch sheet. Since most pylon planes these days use balsa sheeting on the fuselage, at least back to the trailing edge of the wing, the pylon may be faired firmly into this sheet, to make a neat and strong joint. Needless to say, the pylon must be rugged and completely wobble-free.

Tail surfaces can be considered in almost all instances as small wings. Construction is similar but lighter. Stabilizers with flat cross sections generally consist of one square spar, rectangular edges, and square crosspieces. The leading edges are rounded after assembly, with the trailing edges shaved to a thin edge. Spars and crosspieces vary as follows: ¹⁄₁₆ inch square for 12- to 18-inch wing spans, ⅛ inch square for 24- to 30- or 36-inch spans, ¼ inch square for medium-size gas models. Leading edges for tails are, on the average, of the same thickness as the crosspieces, but twice as wide. For the spar and crosspiece sizes noted above, leading edges would vary from ¹⁄₁₆ × ⅛ inch to ¼ × ½ inch. Trailing edges should be approximately three times as wide as the spar and crosspiece thickness, ranging in the cases cited from ¹⁄₁₆ × ³⁄₁₆ inch to ¼ × ¾ inch. Sometimes, for lightness, stabilizer and rudder crosspieces are of the same depth as the spar but only half as thick. Thus with a ⅛-inch-square spar, ¹⁄₁₆ × ⅛ inch crosspieces would be used. For small rubber models a single sheet of either ¹⁄₃₂- or ¹⁄₁₆-inch balsa serves as a simple tail. Sheet-balsa tails should be quarter-grained; otherwise thin stiffener strips must be glued across the tail to prevent warping.

Streamlined and lifting-type stabilizers may be sparless (just a leading and trailing edge) or may have one or two heavy spars or any number of light spars. Sometimes two thin sheets of balsa are used with ribs placed between. Although lifting-type tails very often are built up with spars and ribs like a wing, they can also be satisfactorily constructed by using one sheet of balsa, curved to an airfoil shape over a single heavy center rib and held at the proper camber by twin rudders cemented to the tips. Sheet $\frac{1}{32}$ inch thick is adequate for small rubber models; $\frac{1}{16}$ inch thick for large rubber ones and small gas models; and $\frac{3}{32}$ inch thick for large gas models.

Rudders, too, have infinite varieties. However, rudders having flat and streamlined cross sections are the most popular. Sheet balsa is most commonly used, $\frac{1}{16}$ inch thick for Half-A size, $\frac{1}{8}$ inch for Class A, and so on. Coat the wood with dope that has been plasticized with about eight drops of caster oil to the ounce of dope. This prevents warping.

Rudders and stabilizers are assembled in a form with straight pins in the same manner as built-up wing frames.

Now let's see how these systems of construction are applied to everyday airplanes, control-line, for instance. In both team racers and stunt models, sheet-sided fuselages are often used. But here there is an innovation. Since such planes take abuse, "doublers" are used. A doubler is an added thickness of material cemented to the inside front of the fuselage side. It usually extends to the rear ends of the engine mounts or to the trailing edge of the wing. In the team racer, it may be sheet balsa. In stunt models it should be plywood. Team models generally are of a shoulder or low-wing layout. Stunters are mid-wing or low-wing. In all cases, slots are cut through the fuselage to match the wing contours. These big cutouts are one reason doublers are needed. Nose impacts due to flying errors are the other reason. Solid wood wings for team ships have been mentioned. Stunt frameworks must be light and tough; hence the use of lightweight built-up wings. These wings usually have a top and bottom spar, such as $\frac{1}{4}$ inch square on a 40-inch span, with wide trailing edge and a D-spar leading edge. This D is formed by covering the front of the wing, both top and bottom, with $\frac{1}{16}$ sheet balsa, with the grain running spanwise. The sheet butts against both top and bottom spars. If vertical-grain pieces of scrap are inserted between the ribs against the rear faces of the spars, truly tremendous strength results.

The speed plane uses a variation of the hollow-block fuselage, plus the solid wing. However, the block fuselage should be in two halves, upper and lower, hollowed to a wall thickness of perhaps $\frac{3}{8}$ inch near the nose. Also, pine should be used, and even this wood is of doubtful strength for lower shells. Hence these shells are cast of magnesium and aluminum. Besides strength, these metal "pans," as they are called, afford a very firm mount for the engine and the control bellcrank (or other mechanism) and assist in engine cooling by radiating heat from the engine, which is firmly bolted to them.

The double-sheeted wing principle might also be used, but the material would be one-piece sheet aluminum, wrapped around a metal spar and flush-riveted along the only seam at the trailing edge. The solid wing would be shaped like that of the team racer, but again pine would be utilized for maximum strength. Also, the leadouts must run through the wing for minimum air resistance, and consequently long grooves are cut in the undersurface of the wing. Metal tubing is placed in the grooves, the leadouts running through the tubing. The grooves are covered over so carefully that close inspection will not reveal them. Tails are flat, solid surfaces; use plywood for speed models, sheet balsa for stunt and team-racer designs. Vertical tails made of plywood will stand less chance of damage in nose-over landing accidents.

Wakefield design hasn't changed much in some years, though the planes now have slimmer fuselages than they used to. Rubber endurance planes of all types generally have very slim fuselages, sometimes in the form of a tube. The rubber motor of most such planes generally terminates about halfway between the wing trailing edge and the stabilizer, and the fuselage to the rear of the rubber attachment can be made much lighter.

5

LANDING GEARS
AND PONTOONS

Landing gears may employ a single wheel, two wheels and a tail skid, or even three wheels in a tricycle arrangement with one wheel on the plane nose and two back under the wing.

Retractable landing gears are sometimes seen on radio-control planes; they may be operated electrically or by pressure from the engine and can, of course, be raised and lowered at the will of the flier. Light retracting landing gears are sometimes also used on sport free-flight rubber and gas models. One reason for using them is to protect the propeller on landing, when it would be subject to breakage. Often just a single wheel on a folding strut is utilized; a dethermalizer fuse can cause it to rise or to lower, as the flier desires.

Landing gears as such are not required on competition free-flight models, either gas or rubber. All rubber models are now hand-launched, but gas ones get a little longer engine run if launched via ROG; actually, all the modeler must do with the usual competition model is to hold it almost vertically, with two projections from the rear of the stabilizer touching the ground. When he releases (which must be done without giving any upward push to the model), the tremendous engine power instantly lifts the plane aloft. This is termed an ROG take-off.

Landing gears are, however, necessary on most types of scale models, and here we normally see either two- or three-wheel arrangements. With two wheels, the scale design often calls for a tiny wheel at the tail of the plane; this may or may not be made steerable in radio planes. On tricycle-style radio models, the nose wheel is most often made steerable.

The lightest arrangement on sport rubber types is a single wheel on a wire strut at the nose and two skids projecting downward from the outer tips of the stabilizer. Such an arrangement is not particularly stable on the ground, of course, especially when propeller torque takes over. Two-wheel gears are really better. The wheels may be placed fairly far forward, to protect the propeller on landings, but a forward location usually leads to "ground-looping" when take-offs are attempted. The only cure for this is to move the wheels back farther. Normally, if they are just under the leading edge of the wing, the plane will successfully ROG, but it will very likely "nose over" on landing, especially if it comes down on grass or weeds. On a tricycle-style plane, the main wheels (the two that are under the wing) are placed a little to the rear of the CG (center of gravity), so that the plane will rest on all three wheels when on the ground. If the main wheels are too far back, it will be difficult to make the plane ROG.

Scale-model landing-gear struts are often made of music wire, with strips of balsa, harder wood, or even metal attached, to make them wider fore and aft, as on a full-size plane. Small rubber scale planes may have struts of hardwood, or even balsa, but the latter are very apt to break. Split bamboo, a material widely used in model building years ago, is fine for landing-gear struts, as it is tough, strong, and resilient and may be given a streamline strut shape. It is sold by some of the large suppliers.

Whatever material is used for the struts, they must be firmly anchored to the fuselage in an area that will withstand the stresses of rough landing. It is usual to strengthen the attachment area with additional gussets, side plates, or other reinforcing pieces. Normally, most strain falls on the rear member of those gears made in the form of a V-strut on each side of the fuselage. This is where landing shocks are concentrated, especially if the wheels hit some obstacle that tends to drive them rearward when landing.

So far, nothing has been said about the U-control models. In this field, landing gears must be extremely rugged, as flexible as possible to absorb blows (and to spring back to shape instantly), and well mounted in the machine. In general, the wire selected should be heavier than on free-flights. For example, a Half-A model would use $\frac{1}{16}$-inch-diameter wire for the landing gear, although its wing span might be 12 to 18 inches. A 2-foot model could well use a $\frac{3}{32}$-inch wire, and a 3- to 4-

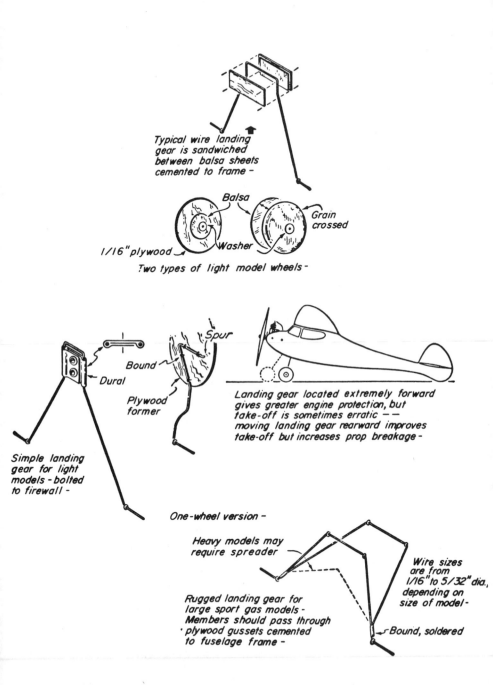

Typical wire landing gear is sandwiched between balsa sheets cemented to frame –

Balsa

Grain crossed

1/16" plywood

Washer

Two types of light model wheels –

Spur

Bound

Dural

Plywood former

Landing gear located extremely forward gives greater engine protection, but take-off is sometimes erratic – – moving landing gear rearward improves take-off but increases prop breakage –

Simple landing gear for light models – bolted to firewall –

One-wheel version –

Heavy models may require spreader

Wire sizes are from 1/16" to 5/32" dia., depending on size of model –

Rugged landing gear for large sport gas models – Members should pass through plywood gussets cemented to fuselage frame –

Bound, soldered

Fig. 5-1.   Landing Gear Design and Construction

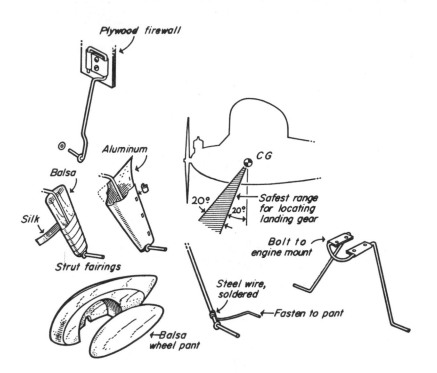

Fig. 5-2.   Sport and RC Landing Gears

foot plane, ⅛-inch wire. In almost all cases, the wire is in one piece, running continuously from wheel to wheel, through the fuselage. It may be attached, free-flight fashion, to a firewall by using heavy strap fittings, or the U-shaped top of the bent landing-gear wire (the part that ordinarily fits into a sandwich mount on most types of planes) can be made extra deep and then bent back at right angles to be fastened in place by strap fittings and bolts. When gears are attached to the wings, the wire may go up to the wing, back to the spar, cross-ship to the other side, and thence down to the other wheel. The portion running along the spar should be well bound and cemented to the wood.

Control-line-plane designers take advantage of any heavy structural members for tying in the landing gear. The familiar hardwood beam mounts in the box-fuselage stunter are ideal for attaching landing-gear wire. The wire may be diverted back along one mount, across to the other, then forward again, and down to the other wheel. The wire should be well bound to the wood. Or a heavy plywood plate should be well glued to the bottom surface of the bearers and a large U, bent in the wire, should be fastened with strap fittings and bolts to the plywood. In

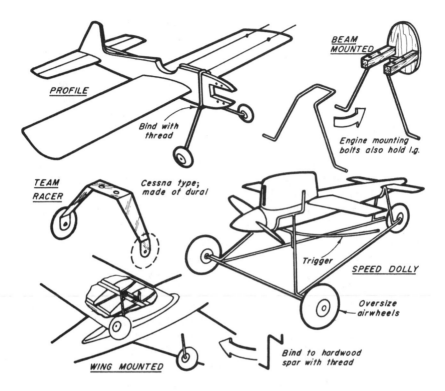

Fig. 5-3. Control-Line Landing Gears

the case of a heavy-profile fuselage, the wire should be bent with a narrow but deep U to fit over the profile. A slight groove at the proper place on each side of the profile will help countersink the wire into the wood. Another style of gear, frequently seen on stunt types, is the dural sheet-metal leg.

Control-line speed models have no wheels or landing gear, but may be either hand-launched or launched ROG from a dolly. The latter is a light framework of music wire, usually with three wheels, which supports the model in a slightly nose-up attitude on the ground. As the plane gathers speed, lift increases sufficiently so that the plane rises off the dolly; some dollies have rather complex arrangements to prevent such lift-off until ample speed and lift have been attained.

Radio-control-plane landing gears generally resemble free-flight and control-line sport-plane ones, but are often quite rugged to stand the repeated landings—sometimes rather rough!—that they must undergo.

Landing Gears and Pontoons

Here, again, music-wire gears are most widespread. Low-wing planes almost always have main wheels of the tricycle gear attached to the wing undersurface, with ply or hardwood inserts to take the strain. Nose gears are usually of the single-leg style and generally have two or three loops in the upper end of the wire, just below the fuselage, to allow the gear to flex on landings without bending or damaging the mounting. Steerable nose wheels are common (on two-wheel-gear planes, the tail wheel is often linked to turn with the rudder, for ground steering), generally driven from the rudder servo.

Sheet-metal landing gears, often seen on the heavier types of model planes (radio and control-line), are constructed from a single piece of one of the harder and tougher grades of aluminum. The metal is usually 1 to 2 inches wide in the area under the fuselage and tapers at the lower ends to around $\frac{1}{4}$ to $\frac{1}{2}$ inch wide, where a machine bolt or other wheel axle is provided. The sheet metal ranges up to $\frac{1}{8}$ inch thick on larger radio planes and is often filed to produce a semistreamlined cross section. Though such gears may be screwed firmly to a ply insert in the fuselage bottom, this allows no rearward "give" to absorb hard landings. Therefore, on radio-control planes, the sheet is often lashed to the fuselage with heavy rubber bands; it will stay put in normal landings, but on a rearward blow it can flex back with no resultant damage.

The larger radio planes nowadays are usually equipped with wheel brakes. The simplest style is the drag brake, which may be no more than a wire or metal strip pressed firmly on the nose wheel. Radio competition today requires several ground maneuvers, one of which is stopping at a mark on the runway. The drag brake will do this, if the pilot is skilled in its use. Much more versatile are controllable brakes, either mechanical or electric. On a tricycle-gear plane, one brake on the nose wheel does a good job, or two may be utilized on the main wheels. On two-wheel planes the latter system is required, of course. Both types have some sort of brake drum attached to the wheel and means of applying drag to the drums. Some radio modelers even find ways to apply a brake selectively on either of the main wheels, or they may be applied together. This helps greatly when taxiing and turning in a wind.

Both mechanical and electric types of brakes are generally operated from the elevator servo, when full-down elevator is signaled. Thus they are seldom energized in normal flight. Electric brakes may be turned on when a switch is triggered by the elevator servo in extreme down position.

Turning to hydro models, there are two types: flying boats and pontoon or float planes. The former have a single boatlike hull, specially shaped for easy take-off and stability when resting or taxiing on the water. Sea wings or sponsons jut from the sides of the hull to hold the ship upright. Sometimes small tip floats are used: pontoons mounted beneath the wing tips to touch the surface of the water whenever the model tilts to one side. Pontoon models may have one, two, or three floats. Several kinds of float arrangement have proved practical. First, there is the familiar two-float scheme as seen on real aircraft. Two long, thin floats are required. These may be of scale or semiscale design. Such arrangements are seen mostly on scale or semiscale sport models where realism is desirable.

Free-flight ROW (rise off water) is no longer a competition event, but when it was, two main float arrangements were popular. In one, there was a single float of moderate size at the nose and two small ones attached to the stabilizer tips. The other popular setup had two smaller floats side by side at the nose and a single one under the tail. These floats were all of abbreviated size and generally had just about enough buoyancy to keep the model afloat and allow it to rise under its own power. Such floats are still useful on sport gas models, but the standard full-size-plane use of two long floats is much more realistic, of course, and also more stable on the water.

The scale type of float follows full-size shape and often has a V-bottom and a rounded top. There is almost always a step near the middle to help the float break free of the water. General shape and details of such floats are seen in figure 5–6. If more buoyancy is required, as for a heavier model, the floats may be made deeper, wider, or both.

On model planes, proper float design is probably a more difficult art than design of the model itself. The designer must know the size of float required for any given size and weight of model. He must know the proportions of the float, how wide it should be, how deep, what angle to make the V-bottom, how far back to locate the step. If the float is not attached to the model at the proper fore-and-aft position and at the proper inclination to the thrust line of the propeller and to the flight path of the airplane, the model may not be able to take off. A discussion of float design by itself would fill a book.

The accompanying table of pontoon dimensions was worked out some years ago, but still offers useful guidance on floats for sport gas planes. For heavier planes, such as radio-control, the floats may be longer as well as larger in cross section.

Blunt or round-nosed floats prevent "digging in." Never use a pointed float. A downward curve or hook incorporated in the float bottom directly in front of the step aids take-off and prevents fore-and-aft rocking during the take-off, known as "porpoising." A small aluminum rudder is required at the rear of each float to prevent circling on the water when

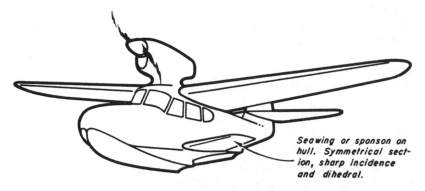

Seawing or sponson on hull. Symmetrical section, sharp incidence and dihedral.

Fig. 5-4.   Flying Boat with Sponsons

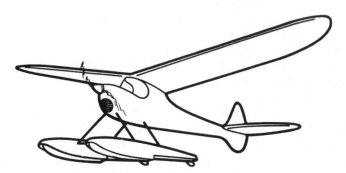

Fig. 5-5.   Twin Float Arrangement

making a take-off run. These aluminum water rudders can be bent for adjustments.

The proper installation of floats on the model is of vital importance. For instance, the float step must lie 2 to 5 per cent ahead of the plane's CG.

For those who don't wish to bother figuring out and building their own floats, there are plastic units on the market that have proved very worth while for radio planes. They are "blow-molded" (by the same process used to make bleach bottles and other large plastic containers) and come in several sizes. These floats are very tough and have proved ideal for flying radio planes off snow. They will even allow nice take-offs and landings on damp grass!

Data on Model Pontoons

(Length of float is equal to 70 per cent of the fuselage length)

Model Length	Model Weight	Float Width	Model Length	Model Weight	Float Width
20 in.	16 oz.	3.37 in.	50 in.	40 oz.	3.50 in.
	18	3.50		45	3.75
	20	3.62		50	4.00
	22	3.87		55	4.25
25 in.	18 oz.	3.25 in.	55 in.	43 oz.	3.50 in.
	21	3.50		48	3.75
	24	3.75		53	4.00
	27	4.00		58	4.25
30 in.	20 oz.	3.25 in.	60 in.	50 oz.	3.62 in.
	24	3.50		55	3.87
	28	3.75		60	4.00
	32	4.00		65	4.12
35 in.	24 oz.	3.25 in.	65 in.	53 oz.	3.62 in.
	28	3.37		58	3.87
	32	3.62		63	4.00
	36	3.87		68	4.12
40 in.	28 oz.	3.25 in.	70 in.	60 oz.	3.62 in.
	33	3.50		66	3.87
	38	3.75		72	4.00
	43	3.87		78	4.12
45 in.	33 oz.	3.37 in.	75 in.	66 oz.	3.62 in.
	38	3.62		74	3.87
	43	3.75		82	4.12
	48	4.00		90	4.37

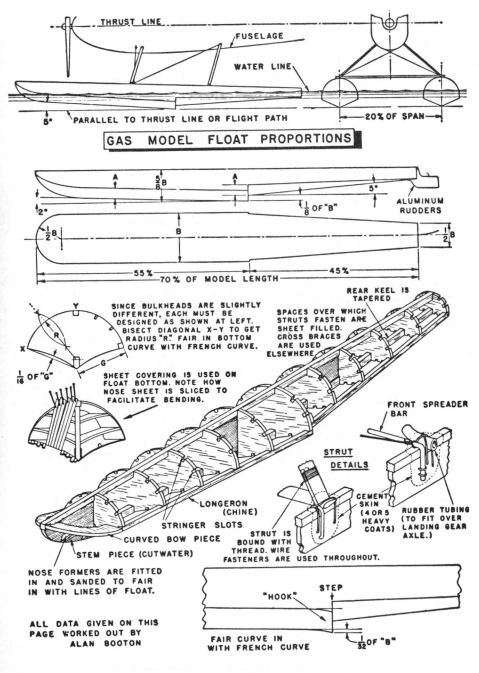

THRUST LINE
FUSELAGE
WATER LINE
PARALLEL TO THRUST LINE OR FLIGHT PATH
5°
20% OF SPAN

GAS MODEL FLOAT PROPORTIONS

A
5/8 B
A
5°
ALUMINUM RUDDERS
1/8 OF "B"
2°
1/2 B
B
B
2
55%
45%
70% OF MODEL LENGTH

SINCE BULKHEADS ARE SLIGHTLY DIFFERENT, EACH MUST BE DESIGNED AS SHOWN AT LEFT. BISECT DIAGONAL X-Y TO GET RADIUS "R." FAIR IN BOTTOM CURVE WITH FRENCH CURVE.

Y
R
X
G
1/16 OF "G"

SHEET COVERING IS USED ON FLOAT BOTTOM. NOTE HOW NOSE SHEET IS SLICED TO FACILITATE BENDING.

REAR KEEL IS TAPERED

SPACES OVER WHICH STRUTS FASTEN ARE SHEET FILLED. CROSS BRACES ARE USED ELSEWHERE.

FRONT SPREADER BAR

STRUT DETAILS

LONGERON (CHINE)
STRINGER SLOTS
CURVED BOW PIECE
STEM PIECE (CUTWATER)

STRUT IS BOUND WITH THREAD. WIRE FASTENERS ARE USED THROUGHOUT.

CEMENT SKIN (4 OR 5 HEAVY COATS)
RUBBER TUBING (TO FIT OVER LANDING GEAR AXLE.)

NOSE FORMERS ARE FITTED IN AND SANDED TO FAIR IN WITH LINES OF FLOAT.

ALL DATA GIVEN ON THIS PAGE WORKED OUT BY ALAN BOOTON

STEP
"HOOK"
FAIR CURVE IN WITH FRENCH CURVE
1/32 OF "B"

Fig. 5-6. Useful Data for Twin Floats

72

On many radio planes converted from wheels to floats, movable rudders are attached to the floats, steerable from the rudder servo. Floats of this type—in fact *any* model-plane floats—should be firmly mounted so they will not shift position on take-off. To save weight, some modelers use flimsy mountings, which often prevent successful ROW take-offs.

Needless to say, maximum effort must be made to waterproof the entire model. Even the *interior* framework of the wing and especially the fuselage ought to have several coats of dope to prevent soaking up moisture. Though a float model makes a perfect water landing, it is not at all unusual for the wind to get under a wing panel and tip the model over. Also, of course, it is not unusual to have a model flip over on its back. Generally the wing structure, if not damaged, will float a light model till you can retrieve it. Heavier radio planes might tend to go deeper into the water. Despite your best efforts, water will probably be found inside the plane after a flying session.

Control-line flying over water is quite spectacular; it naturally requires a dry spot for the pilot to stand on; a small low wharf projecting out toward deep water is fine. Of course, most model seaplanes require only a few inches of water in which to operate. Power must be sufficient for

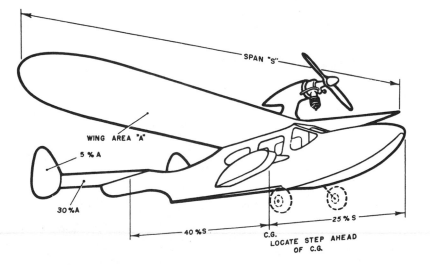

Fig. 5-7. Flying Boat Proportions

the plane to be lifted off the surface before it comes around the circle to the dock; when brought down to the water for a landing, the model will quickly come to rest on the surface.

In colder areas, many modelers equip their planes with skis in the winter and fly from snow. The skis may be made fairly short—perhaps one-fourth the fuselage length—but fairly wide so they won't sink too much in soft snow. Plywood, fiberglass, and metal have been utilized for skis, which are generally pivoted from the same axles that normally hold wheels. To prevent digging in on landing, the skis are normally pulled up at the tip some 10 degrees or so; rubber bands or light springs will do the job, and a cord to the rear of the ski keeps it from tilting up farther than desired.

6

PROPELLERS

For any given model design there is a propeller that will perform better than all others. Rubber-powered models, particularly, require the precise combination of correct propeller diameter (length from tip to tip), pitch (the distance the propeller theoretically will travel forward in one complete revolution, assuming no slippage), and blade area. On gas models, pitch and diameter are the most important factors. The engine manufacturer specifies the required propeller diameters for his engine. Propeller manufacturers turn out such excellent products that very few builders today will take the time and trouble to carve their own gas-model propellers. Still, a few experts trim commercial wood propellers to give what they feel is peak efficiency; control-line speed fliers are among proponents of this practice.

Model builders have evolved a rule-of-thumb technique for choosing propeller specifications for any size and type of rubber-powered model. They have discovered the ratio between pitch and diameter that automatically indicates the blade area for any propeller. Pitch-diameter ratios vary from 1:1 to 2:1. Low-pitch makes for fast climb. Contest endurance-type rubber-powered models use from 1½:1 to 2:1 ratios. A handy fact to bear in mind is that the pitch is always proportional to the thickness of the propeller block. Thus, knowing the diameter and pitch of his required propeller, the designer can figure the width and depth of his block. For rubber power, he knows that the average fuselage endurance model has a propeller diameter equal to approximately 40 per cent of the wing span.

The informed builder, knowing the rough proportions of his block, makes use of a universal layout method. The propeller block is marked into quarters by drawing pencil lines across the widest face. Diagonals are drawn in, running from the ends of the halfway mark on each blade to the opposite corners of the same mark on the other blade (the propeller hub is filled in about $\frac{3}{8}$ inch wide). The propeller tips are tapered in thickness from the halfway mark to the tip, the tip proper being just half the depth of the block at the halfway mark. The hub, likewise, is tapered in thickness to just half the original thickness.

In constructing a prop, select a good block of medium variety, firm and white, with the straightest grain possible and even texture throughout. When you carve a prop from a block that varies in texture, you must lighten the heavier blade by sanding it thinner than the other. This causes an uneven airfoil section. Despite balancing, the prop will still vibrate when turning under power.

After the block has been laid out, drill a hole for the shaft, keeping it as straight as possible. Shape the block by cutting along the outline of the side view first, then the top. When the block is finished, sand the edges and the hub. Carve the tip outline drawn on the top view.

Begin carving by hollowing the rear of the blade first, cambering it about $\frac{3}{16}$ inch at the widest part, fading out as you reach the tip. Excessive camber will not improve performance.

Finish one blade with medium sandpaper; too coarse a paper will leave deep scratches that are very hard to remove. Carve the other blade as much like the first as possible. Uneven blades bring on vibration. The most difficult part to carve is the inside of the blade. Carve as close as you safely may, then use plenty of sandpaper.

When shaving down the front of the blade, be careful not to come too close to the edges. Also watch the thickness of the blade. Thickness should taper from about $\frac{1}{4}$ inch near the hub to $\frac{1}{16}$ inch at the tip. Sand to a smooth, even finish with fine paper, and balance. Use several coats of clear dope, sanding between coats with the finest paper obtainable. These directions apply to diameters of 16 to 20 inches; camber should be decreased for smaller diameters.

For an efficient glide, drag must be reduced to a minimum. The drag of a stalled rubber prop, with its large diameter and great blade area, can be considerable. Freewheeling has been used to reduce this drag in the past; this lets the prop turn like a windmill as the plane glides forward. Most designers feel the drag of a freewheeling propeller is little less than

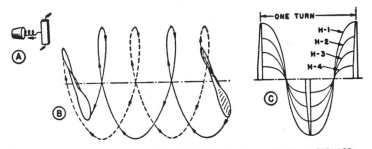

A RADIAL FORCE APPLIED TO A CORKSCREW (A) RESULTS IN A FORWARD MOTION INTO THE CORK. A SIMILAR FORCE APPLIED TO A PROPELLER (B) ALSO RESULTS IN FORWARD MOTION. THIS ACTION IS PLOTTED AS A DIRECT SIDE VIEW (C) TO SHOW HOW THE PATH OF EACH PART OF THE PROP BLADE DEMANDS VARYING PITCH ANGLES (H-1, H-2, ETC.). THIS TYPE OF PROP IS CALLED THE "TRUE PITCH" OR "HELICAL PITCH" TYPE.

Fig. 6-1.   How Propellers Work

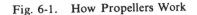

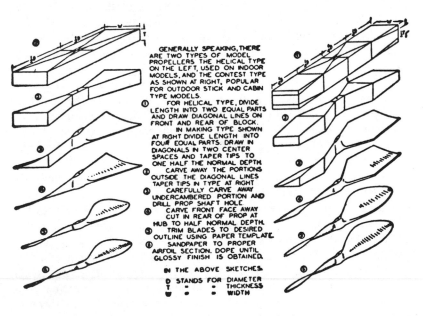

GENERALLY SPEAKING, THERE ARE TWO TYPES OF MODEL PROPELLERS THE HELICAL TYPE ON THE LEFT, USED ON INDOOR MODELS, AND THE CONTEST TYPE AS SHOWN AT RIGHT, POPULAR FOR OUTDOOR STICK AND CABIN TYPE MODELS.

① FOR HELICAL TYPE, DIVIDE LENGTH INTO TWO EQUAL PARTS AND DRAW DIAGONAL LINES ON FRONT AND REAR OF BLOCK. IN MAKING TYPE SHOWN AT RIGHT DIVIDE LENGTH INTO FOUR EQUAL PARTS. DRAW IN DIAGONALS IN TWO CENTER SPACES AND TAPER TIPS TO ONE HALF THE NORMAL DEPTH.

② CARVE AWAY THE PORTIONS OUTSIDE THE DIAGONAL LINES TAPER TIPS IN TYPE AT RIGHT

③ CAREFULLY CARVE AWAY UNDERCAMBERED PORTION AND DRILL PROP SHAFT HOLE.

④ CARVE FRONT FACE AWAY CUT IN REAR OF PROP AT HUB TO HALF NORMAL DEPTH. TRIM BLADES TO DESIRED OUTLINE USING PAPER TEMPLATE.

⑤ SANDPAPER TO PROPER AIRFOIL SECTION. DOPE UNTIL GLOSSY FINISH IS OBTAINED.

IN THE ABOVE SKETCHES

D STANDS FOR DIAMETER
T :   :   THICKNESS
W :   :   WIDTH

Fig. 6-2.   How to Carve Propellers

one that is stopped, and some claim it is lots more! So the folding-blade propeller is now in wide use. The blades are hinged near the hub so they can swing back at right angles against the fuselage sides to present a minimum of frontal area. Centrifugal force holds the blades in position while the rubber motor is unwinding. When the motor has stopped, the air stream blows the blades backward against the fuselage. This arrangement, while superior to freewheeling, has its difficulties. For instance, the propeller must be stopped at one particular position on every flight. If it isn't, the delicate glide adjustments will be thrown out of kilter, and the glide path cannot be controlled properly.

Rubber tensioners have been adopted to control the stopping point of folding propellers. In principle, a coil spring between the propeller and the nose plug, or between the front of the hub and a bent-over right-angle extension of the front end of the shaft, moves the propeller forward as the rubber motor unwinds and loses its tension. A projection, usually an L-shaped piece of music wire formed by a continuation of the shaft rubber hook—see figure 6–3 and the discussion in chapter 10—engages a stop in the rear face of the nose plug. Usually this stop is a wood screw firmly embedded in the wooden plug. When the L-catch strikes the stop, the propeller locks in position and the blades fold back toward the wing. The location of the stop determines the position of the propeller when the blades fold.

Single-blade propellers are quite popular for rubber duration planes, many modelers feeling they are more efficient than the normal two-blade style.

One-blade props require counterweights for balancing. The usual counterweight consists of a lump of solder attached to the end of a short piece of music wire, connected to the propeller hub opposite the single wooden blade. This wire attachment has its end bent at right angles and embedded in the hub. Thread binding and cement prevent it from coming loose. The counterweight is made by pouring molten lead into the empty metal top of a pencil held in a small wood block. The wire attachment piece is held in the pencil top while the lead solidifies.

Wise builders slant their propeller-blade hinges so that the blades fold back and fit flat against the fuselage. The sleekest designs have the nose contoured so that the blades are almost a glove fit against the sides when they are folded. The rubber hook in figure 6–3 (center) snaps open, so the rubber motor can be slipped on, without having to thread it through, strand by strand. The round shape of the hook prevents the rubber from twisting over one side of the hook, which would cause lots of vibration and power loss; an even more certain preventive is the bobbin on the end of the propeller shaft, also seen in figure 6–3 (right). This is usu-

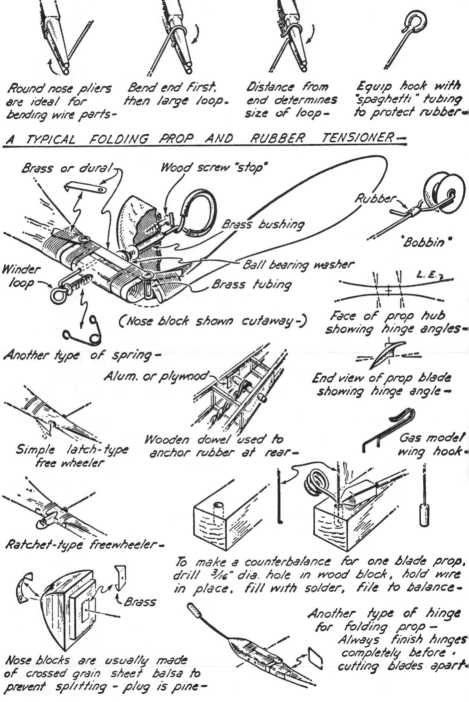

Round nose pliers are ideal for bending wire parts-

Bend end first, then large loop.

Distance from end determines size of loop-

Equip hook with "spaghetti" tubing to protect rubber-

A TYPICAL FOLDING PROP AND RUBBER TENSIONER—

Brass or dural

Wood screw "stop"

Rubber

Brass bushing

'Bobbin'

Winder loop

Ball bearing washer

Brass tubing

(Nose block shown cutaway -)

Face of prop hub showing hinge angles-

L.E.

Another type of spring-

End view of prop blade showing hinge angle-

Alum. or plywood

Simple latch-type free wheeler

Wooden dowel used to anchor rubber at rear-

Gas model wing hook-

Ratchet-type freewheeler-

To make a counterbalance for one blade prop, drill 3/16 dia. hole in wood block, hold wire in place, fill with solder, file to balance-

Brass

Nose blocks are usually made of crossed grain sheet balsa to prevent splitting - plug is pine-

Another type of hinge for folding prop — Always finish hinges completely before cutting blades apart-

Fig. 6-3.   Fittings and Parts

ally of firm plastic, and the rubber strands go around the bobbin center.

When a free-flight gas model hangs on its prop in an almost vertical climb, its actual forward speed is very little, and a low-pitched propeller is at its best. A control-line speed model, on the other hand, requires an unusually high-pitched propeller. Here the propeller is hard put to screw its way forward as fast as the model is traveling.

Propeller pitch for free-flight contest machines should vary according to the type of climb. An almost straight-up flight calls for a lower pitch to enable the engine to exert its power effectively and not dissipate its thrust through slippage. If, on the other hand, the builder favors a wide, circling kind of climb at a comparatively shallow angle, but at a higher flying speed, he should use a slightly higher pitch. Among the Half-A ships there is a tendency to use stock props under any circumstances, with builders favoring 3½ or 4 inches of pitch.

While rubber-driven planes generally utilize wooden propellers, some gas-model fliers prefer props molded from nylon. The main advantage of nylon is toughness, of course; such props are ideal if you fly from rough areas. It is generally considered that wood props are a little more efficient, but it is quite possible to break a blade on almost every landing in fields; thus radio-control fliers who do not normally fly from smooth runways tend to favor nylon props because of the breakage factor.

Manufacturers indicate the pitch and diameter on each propeller by printing them in color on wood props and actually molding them in (and usually printing them also) on nylon types. The makers can supply tables showing a good choice of propellers for practically all types of models, based on engine displacement. These figures are just a starting point, of course; the careful competition flier then varies pitch and diameter a little each way and checks results.

Even though manufacturers hand-balance each wood propeller—and supposedly their molds for the nylon types are accurate enough so the result will be in perfect balance—it is still quite possible to buy a propeller that is rather badly out of balance. This can cause severe vibration—enough in some cases to tear the engine out of its mounts. Such vibration can have serious effects in radio-control planes, leading to servo damage (the receiver is normally wrapped in foam rubber, hence is spared the worst of such vibration) and other troubles. The only answer is to check each new propeller for balance when you get it home in your shop. A very rough balance check may be performed by poking a screw driver through the shaft hole; if this shows one blade heavier than the other (the heavy one will, dip downward, of course) your pro-

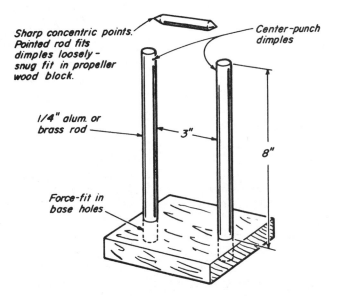

Sharp concentric points.
Pointed rod fits
dimples loosely -
snug fit in propeller
wood block.

Center-punch
dimples

1/4" alum. or
brass rod

3"

8"

Force-fit in
base holes

Fig. 6-4.   Prop Balancer

peller is *really* in need of balancing. One way to do this is to put a close-fitting, smooth-surfaced rod through the hole—it should be a snug fit—and set this "axle" on a pair of parallel knife edges. If care is taken to level the knife edges (razor blades will do nicely), you can check balance quite precisely.

A balancer that does not have to be leveled and will accurately check the balance of even tiny 3-inch nylon propellers is sketched in figure 6–4. The shafts to support the propellers again should be a snug fit in the holes; the shaft ends are turned accurately to a point, with roughly a 45- to 60-degree taper (this is done best in a lathe, but with care you can do an acceptable job in a drill press or even a hand drill clamped to the bench, using flat files to rough out the point and progressively finer emery paper to smooth and polish it). The shafts may be of soft brass or aluminum; they turn very little and won't wear, but the points must be protected from damage. They should be polished as smoothly as possible. The shafts rest in "dimples" made in the supports (brass or aluminum is also fine here) with a sharp center punch; the indentations do not have to be very deep. The shafts should be of such length that they fit into the dimples (the supports are flexible enough to be sprung apart slightly to slip the shaft point in) with a little end play; there should be *no* binding.

Balancing is simply a matter of slipping a propeller on a shaft of correct diameter, checking for the heavy blade, then sanding till balance is achieved. Sanding should be done near the tips, where a tiny amount of material removed will be detectable. Nylon is tough to sand, but keep at it—you can get it off! Use fine sandpaper to finish the surface.

In general U-control practice, selection of the propeller is comparatively simple. The diameter is known. While pitches are given in the tables provided by prop manufacturers, the correct pitch for a given plane may vary according to the weight and drag of the machine itself. Too low a pitch will produce plenty of engine noise but a very poor forward speed, the plane seeming to hang with a very small margin of reserve speed. Too high a pitch will hinder take-off and hold down rpm's noticeably.

Propellers for indoor models are notable for their large diameter (about half the wing span) and large blade area. Needless to say, they must be featherweight, since weight reduces flight endurance. Indoor-model propellers are sometimes carved from soft balsa (which weighs about 4 pounds per cubic foot) to a paper-thin state, tapering from $\frac{1}{16}$ inch at the hub to $\frac{1}{64}$ at the tip. More often these propellers are built up like a wing, the edges being bent from a continuous piece of $\frac{1}{32}$-inch sheet balsa with very thin ribs cut from $\frac{1}{64}$-inch sheet. Built-up propellers are covered with microfilm.

Radio-control plane propellers vary according to engine size. Here again, it often helps to alter length and pitch a bit from whatever might be specified, to see what is optimum for a certain plane. Three-blade nylon propellers are sometimes fitted to radio planes in place of the more common two-blade variety; this may be done to increase clearance between blade tips and the ground. It is generally felt that the equivalent to a 2-blader of specific diameter is 1 inch less diameter in a 3-blade; for example, an 11-inch diameter $\times$ 6-inch pitch double-blade propeller is roughly equivalent to a 10 $\times$ 6 with three blades.

7

COVERING

Covering materials vary according to the type and size of models. (See figure 7–1 for tools and materials used in covering.) Naturally the smaller and lighter planes require very light covering, while the large radio models utilize heavy grades of model silk and nylon, or perhaps some of the newer Mylar-type coverings; or they may be covered entirely with sheets of soft balsa. Light grades of Japanese tissue (which comes in numerous colors) or Silkspan are utilized on small rubber planes. Paper covering actually comes in numerous grades; the Japanese tissue is generally lightest, followed by Silkspan (but there are several grades of this), and bamboo paper is fairly heavy but very strong. Lightweight tissue is used on small gas models, too; large gas models may have silk on the fuselage, paper on wings and tail.

Wet-or-dry paper is very useful; it may be used dry, like ordinary tissue, or can be soaked in water, wrung out, and placed on the framework. Where streamlined fuselages or difficult curved fillets are to be covered, wet covering saves a lot of headaches. Ordinary model tissues will wrinkle when covering double curvatures. Wet papers can be stretched with the greatest of ease around almost impossible curves. Clear dope is used as the paper adhesive; it will stick to the paper despite its wetness.

When using the wet method, it is advisable to dope those portions of the framework which will be in contact with the covering material.

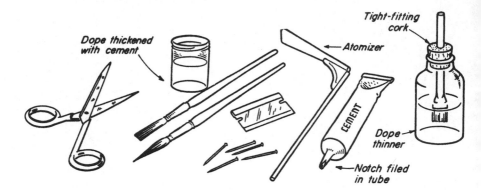

Fig. 7-1. Tools and Materials for Covering

This is good practice whether the plane is to be covered wet or dry because it insures a firm contact of material and framework, minimizes damage from tears, and greatly adds to the strength of the structure. Also, it is difficult to fix any covering to untreated wood because the dope for fixing the material tends to soak into the wood. In the use of wet covering, there is a further advantage in first doping the wood surface. Not only will the covering adhere better; its moisture cannot cause the wide, thin trailing edges of the wings to warp or bow.

Silk is a very strong covering, but is not generally used on smaller free-flight planes because of its weight. Also, when it contracts after being doped, it can seriously warp light structures. Although silk itself is quite light, a considerable amount—and weight—of dope is required to seal the pores and produce a smooth surface. For larger planes, where this added weight is less important, the increased strength of silk is well worth while. Furthermore, silk will easily go over tricky multiple contours, which would require much piecing, even with wet paper. Silk may be applied either wet or dry; if applied wet, it will shrink to some extent as it dries and thus produce a drumtight covering without wrinkles. Dope further tightens the silk, unless the dope is heavily plasticized.

Nylon is even stronger than silk and may be obtained in light grades suitable for model purposes. It does not shrink much when it dries, nor as much as silk when doped. More care must be used, therefore, to eliminate wrinkles when it is being applied.

There are several combinations of silk and nylon fibers which are preferred by many builders. Some of these special materials seem to be heavier than silk, but due to their extremely close weave, they take less dope to seal; thus final covering weight may actually end up less.

If the fuselage is square, the job is easy. Four pieces of covering

84

material are used: one for each side of the body, one for the top, and one for the bottom. The covering can be applied to the outside edges of the frame and shrunk tight by spraying with water. Or the paper, or whatever material is being used, may be fixed to every crosspiece or structural part touching the covering. In either case, the covering is started at the nose of the fuselage, the material being stretched and held tight while it is attached to the rear crosspiece or rudder post. Following this, the covering is doped to one longeron and finally to the other longeron, while the paper is made as tight as possible without wrinkling. All wrinkles should be worked out with the finger tips before the edges of the paper dry to the wood. The dope used for the adhesive is brushed onto the wood surface of the longerons and crosspieces. Where the edges of the covering touch the doped framework, the covering should be rubbed into a firm contact with the wood. The two fuselage sides are covered first, then the top and bottom.

Silk and nylon, because of their weave, can be stretched in any direction to pull out wrinkles. On a covering of silk, nylon, or wet-or-dry paper, clear dope (not thinned or colored) serves as a good adhesive. Final finishing is done with thinned dope.

Streamlined fuselages of all kinds may be covered with strips of tissue. The strips are made as wide as possible without causing wrinkles. Again, silk or nylon may be applied in large sheets. Any faired or streamlined fuselage should have the surfaces of all bulkheads sanded away in a shallow curve between all stringers. The covering should not touch the bulkheads, but should rest on the stringers only, except, of course, at the very nose and tail of the fuselage.

Silk and nylon will require many more coats of dope than paper will for an airtight surface. A wing that is not thoroughly doped actually develops a leakage of air pressure from the bottom surface through to the top. While paper on very light models may be sealed satisfactorily with one or two coats of very thin dope (the dope also serves to flatten the "fuzz" on the surface of some papers), cloth covering will require many more coats. The first coat is the trickiest to apply to silk or nylon, as the dope can go right through the rather open weave and collect in blobs on the underside. This produces a messy job, adds unwanted weight, and can result in uneven tightening. There are several ways to avoid this. For one, use a fairly stiff brush with just a little dope on the ends of the bristles, and rub lightly across the surface with the brush held vertically. The idea is simply to close the cloth pores, not to apply a heavy dope coat. Fairly thick dope is best; if too thin it will sink through to the underside. It may take several coats applied this way to close the pores fully. When they are

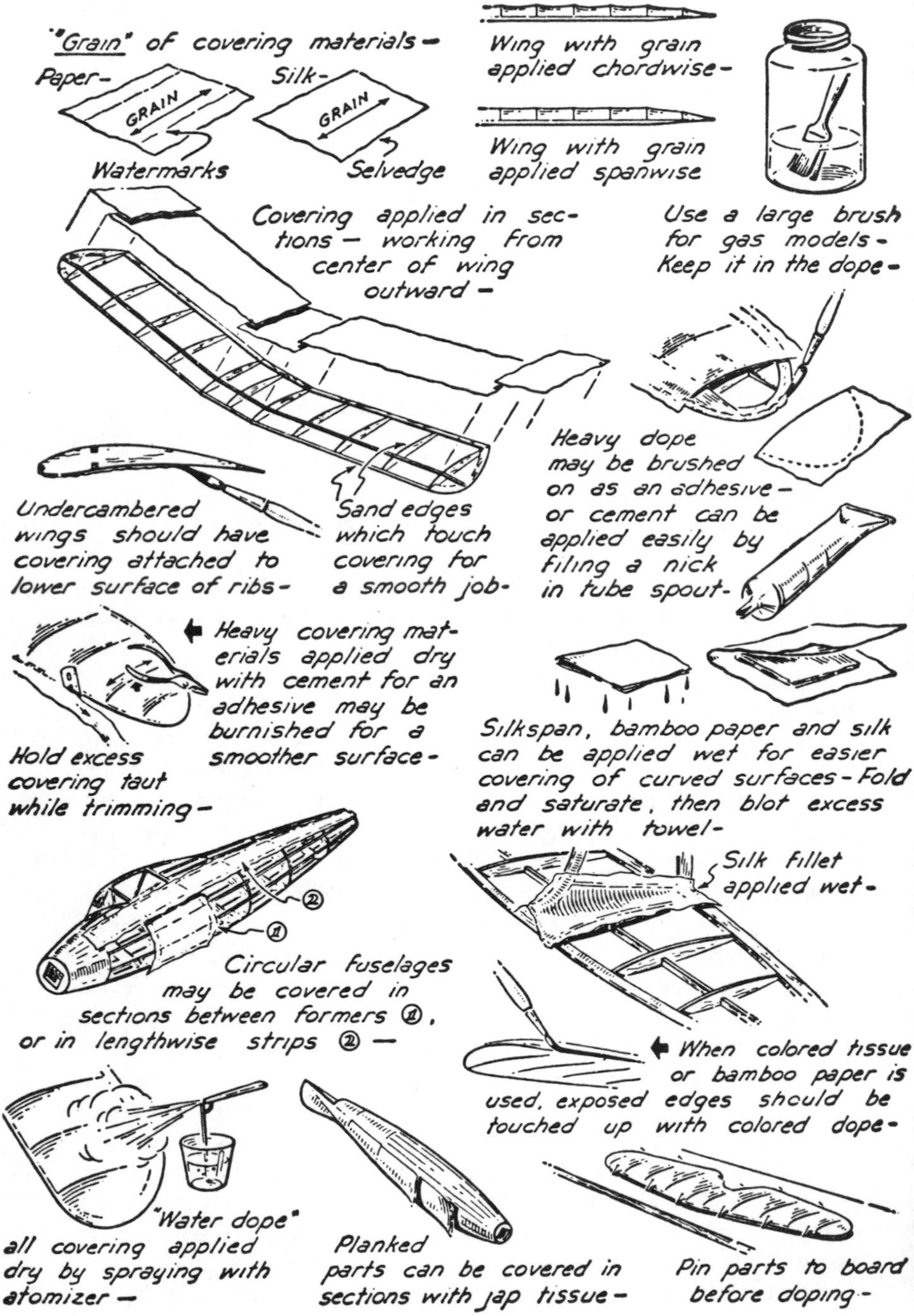

"Grain" of covering materials —

Paper —

GRAIN

Watermarks

Silk —

GRAIN

Selvedge

Wing with grain applied chordwise —

Wing with grain applied spanwise

Covering applied in sections — working from center of wing outward —

Use a large brush for gas models — Keep it in the dope —

Undercambered wings should have covering attached to lower surface of ribs —

Sand edges which touch covering for a smooth job —

Heavy dope may be brushed on as an adhesive — or cement can be applied easily by filing a nick in tube spout —

Heavy covering materials applied dry with cement for an adhesive may be burnished for a smoother surface —

Hold excess covering taut while trimming —

Silkspan, bamboo paper and silk can be applied wet for easier covering of curved surfaces — Fold and saturate, then blot excess water with towel —

Silk fillet applied wet —

Circular fuselages may be covered in sections between formers ①, or in lengthwise strips ② —

When colored tissue or bamboo paper is used, exposed edges should be touched up with colored dope —

"Water dope" all covering applied dry by spraying with atomizer —

Planked parts can be covered in sections with jap tissue —

Pin parts to board before doping —

Fig. 7-2. Methods of Covering

86

closed, however, you can then apply the dope in smooth, heavy coats, if you want to.

Some builders avoid the "sinking-through" problem by doping with the wing or other surface held upside down. In this way the excess dope applied will collect by gravity on the *outer* surface and may then be brushed smooth. This works well, but is pretty hard on the arms.

An unusual method to prevent sinking through, which is quick, easy and very satisfactory, is to moisten the silk surface just before applying the dope. A piece of cotton dipped in water and with the excess squeezed out is rubbed over the surface (on large areas it is best to do this a few sections at a time). The point is to get a smooth coat of moisture on the silk which will close all the pores, but excess drops are not desired. Surprisingly, when thin dope is brushed lightly over this moistened silk surface, it will tend to stay on *top* of the threads, with little sinking through. It has been found that the dope may either be applied with a very soft brush or be sprayed. This method need only be used in areas, as on wings, where th   is unsupported cloth (that is, no wood sheet is under it), for these are the areas affected by sinking through. Often a second wet coat must be applied to seal up a few areas where the pores are still open. If nitrate dope is used for this "wet-doping" method, the dope will be smooth and clear when it dries. Butyrate dope will very likely blush severely; however, a couple of further coats of clear butyrate applied in the usual dry manner will generally cause the blush to disappear.

Of course, silk or nylon should be used only on planes that have a rugged framework to withstand their tautness. Small, lightweight

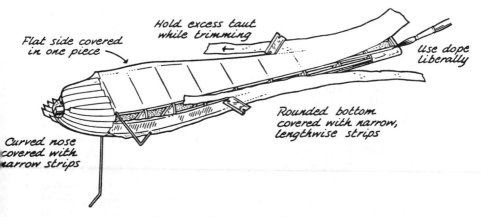

Fig. 7-3.   Covering the Fuselage

planes covered with paper may also warp. This action, which occurs mainly on wings and tails, can be minimized by a process known as plasticizing. This means that several drops of castor oil are well stirred into each ounce of dope. The slight amount of castor oil will prevent further pulling and will add a certain flexibility to the paper (without making it loose) so that it will not so easily tear or puncture. If a total of three coats is used, use plasticized dope only for the final one. If you use four coats, apply two plain coats, then two plasticized, and so on.

Many radio-plane builders prefer to use nitrate dope for most of the finishing, then put on the last several coats with butyrate to fuel-proof the surface. Generally, nitrate is cheaper; also, many feel it is easier to work with. It is getting scarcer in the hobby shops now, though, and some carry only butyrate. Nitrate can still be had from most large aviation suppliers, however. There is one thing to watch here: certain dopes are compatible; others are not. Even if of the same base (nitrate or butyrate), dopes made by different manufacturers may not be compatible; used together, they may cause wrinkling, peeling, or other unwanted effects—which means you will have to do the job over again. So it's best to make a test of materials if you wish to use different kinds together. The use of colored dope reduces the necessary number of coats. If, for example, eight coats of clear dope are needed for a certain silk-covered framework, perhaps four coats of clear plus two of color will give the same finish. Colored dope is heavier than clear, of course, which is why it is not used for *all* coats.

There are a few simple tricks in covering wings (see fig. 7–4). First, most wings will have dihedral, dividing the wing into two or more panels or straight sections, depending on the form of dihedral used. V-dihedral has two panels; tip dihedral, three; polyhedral, four. The top surface of a wing is covered with as many separate pieces of tissue as there are dihedral panels. The bottom of the wing should be treated similarly; separate pieces are preferable for each dihedral section, if there is undercamber.

The wing covering is attached to the four outside edges of the panel to be covered; that is, to the two end ribs and the leading and trailing edges. Run the grain spanwise. The material is pulled tight with the fingers until the adhesive holds the covering tight. The entire surface is then doped. Most builders prefer to attach the material to the end ribs first, and only after that to the leading and trailing edges. The covering is pulled fairly tight spanwise (but just tight enough to eliminate wrinkles) from front to rear. Otherwise there will be excessive sag between ribs,

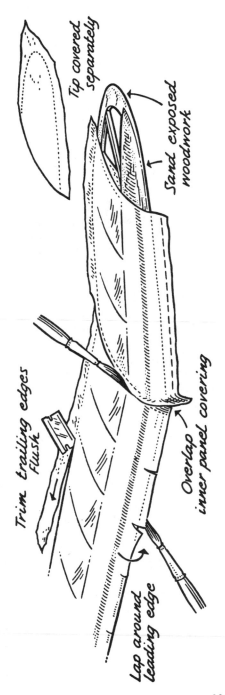

Tip covered separately

Sand exposed woodwork

Trim trailing edges
Flush

Overlap inner panel covering

Lap around leading edge

Fig. 7-4.   Covering the Wings

89

which distorts the airfoil shape. Wings with undercamber must have the covering stuck to each rib. One way to do this is to coat the underside of each rib with model cement before applying the covering; when the covering is doped to these surfaces it will stick better (run your finger along each rib to press the covering into the cement).

Cover wing tips with a separate piece of material, precut to the required pattern. Sand all cemented joints so that one piece of wood fits flush with its neighbor. See that dried cement does not jut out to snag the covering. Sand down every joint.

Sometimes silk or nylon may not pull up tightly when it is first doped. Exposing the work to the sun will often do the trick. If wrinkles are seen on a fabric-covered surface, before over-all dope is applied it is often possible to loosen the covering at the edges adjacent to the wrinkles by brushing on more dope; the wrinkles may then be pulled out and the edge redoped.

Always use a brand-new razor blade for trimming off excess paper or fabric. It will leave a rather frayed edge, even so, but this may be smoothed down with a bit of dope, rubbed out with a finger tip.

Tails are covered in the same manner as wings. The usual flat tail, either stabilizer or rudder, is covered with two pieces of material, one for the top and one for the bottom, or one for each side, as the case may be. When tail surfaces are water-sprayed, they should be pinned to the bench until the covering has dried and stretched. Great care should be taken to prevent warpage, which is quite likely with many tail surfaces, since some are flat-surfaced, and others are built with a lighter and less warp-resistant structure than are wings.

Regardless of the material used, all sturdy dry-covered wings should have their covering sprayed with water to pull the covering to drumlike tautness. If you have tried this and had your wing warp, you did not do it properly. Only one panel of a wing should be sprayed at a time, and this panel should be pinned tightly to the bench until dry. It will not stick to the bench when pinned down.

For spraying purposes, any household sprayer can be used. However, a paint sprayer is desirable because of the fine vapor it creates. Most paint sprayers have an adjustable nozzle for controlling the fineness of the particles in the vapor. An ordinary perfume atomizer makes a handy sprayer. Avoid actual *drops* of water when spraying your covering, as small tears may appear when the paper pulls tight. Don't stand too close to the part being sprayed, to avoid blowing the paper hard enough to damage it, and don't point the spray directly downward. Stand the wing, tail, or fuselage on which you are working against

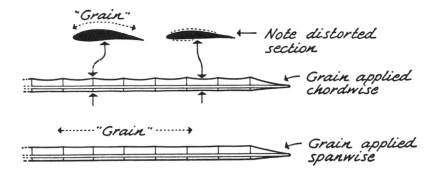

Fig. 7-5. "Grain" of Paper Covering

a nearby wall. Don't worry about water-wet covering sticking to the bench. If possible, avoid doping on a humid day; the dope may "blush," leaving large white splotches. Another coat of dope or even a coat of dope thinner will usually remove the blush.

While most indoor duration models are covered with microfilm, there is a beginner's category which specifies paper covering; a special very thin material called "condenser paper" is used; no dope or other tightening or sealing processes are needed, or possible, as the framework is too light to stand them. Microfilm itself cannot be purchased in sheets, as is other covering material; you must make it as you need it. A special liquid, somewhat akin to thin dope or lacquer, is carefully poured on a large surface of water (a bathtub is often used), where it immediately spreads out and sets. The skin is then lifted off on a wire frame (a coat hanger bent oval) and applied to the wing or other part. This microfilm solution may be purchased from some hobby specialists.

While silk, paper, and dope have been the standard covering and finishing materials for a long time, and nylon is also well tried, some new ideas have come along recently that show great promise. One is an epoxy finish that takes the place of (or under some conditions, may be used with) ordinary dope. Called Hobby-Poxy, it is a two-part material that must be mixed shortly before using. The "pot life" is fairly long and can be extended as required. Some very special techniques are required to get the best out of this material; we won't go into them deeply here, as the maker supplies detailed instructions. Briefly, since the surface does not dry almost immediately as with dope, great care must be taken to keep off dust. A real advantage is that with this epoxy finish only a few coats are necessary; with care, quite a good finish may be had with just a single coat. The material, like all epoxy, is extremely tough and is absolutely fuel-resistant (even the so-called "fuel-proof" dopes will sooner or later succumb to raw fuel on the surface). When properly applied, an exceptionally glossy, smooth finish can result.

Taking its place with paper, silk, and nylon is a new covering sheet called MonoKote. A thin, specially treated Mylar, it come in many brilliant colors, but here its likeness to other coverings ends. For Mono-Kote is self-adhesive and self-tightening and has the final surface finish built in. It is completely fuel-proof, of course. Most unusual point of all: you apply it with an electric iron! The sheet is laid on the framework and the iron (set to a medium heat) is run over the areas where it must adhere to the wood. It sticks strongly. When all rough edges have been ironed down, the iron is then run over open areas and over any wrinkles that may have been left in covering. They disappear like magic, and the entire surface tightens to glassy smoothness. That's all there is to the job. For repairs, a patch of the material may be ironed over the damaged area, and the edges are just about unnoticeable. Since no finish which must dry after application is needed, an entire model may be covered in one evening and be ready for flight the next day.

Decorations on model planes may be applied with colored dope as depicted in figure 7–6. A neat and very light method of decorating is to cut the required figures or pattern from colored tissue and dope it in place. A few coats of clear dope over the tissue will protect it and make it adhere permanently. Strips of MonoKote have been used for decoration, even on doped finishes, and you can buy in hobby shops a wide variety of self-adhesive strips in many widths and colors, plus a fine selection of decals. The latter are generally not fuel-proof and must be doped; this is a problem, as most decals wrinkle badly when dope is applied to their surface. This problem has now been solved, however, with the fuel-resistant decals that may be spray-doped for surface protection.

Before we leave this subject of covering and finishing, a few words on those most important tools: your brushes. It is very poor economy to buy cheap brushes, since invariably they will shed hairs and spoil your finish. Buy the very best you can afford; with proper care they will last many years. Figure 7–1 shows a brush kept in a closed jar with the handle projecting and with some dope thinner in the jar: It is best to keep a brush this way only while you are working on a model. When finished, remove it from the jar, clean it *thoroughly,* and store it dry.

When cleaning brushes that have been in dope, you can use dope thinner; however, this is often more costly than a universal solvent such as acetone. The latter will clean nitrate and butyrate dope and also many lacquers off brushes. Whatever you use, clean the brush by

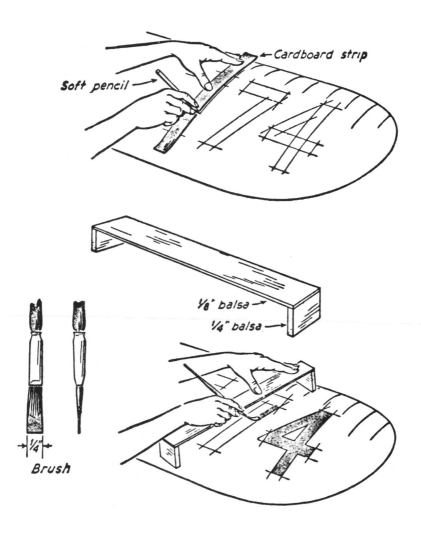

Fig. 7-6. Lettering of Wing Covering

"pumping" it up and down while flexing the bristles close to the metal ferrule. This gets the dope out of the "heel" of the brush, where it tends to build up and harden. In addition, the bristles may be brushed out on a newspaper with a stiff toothbrush (nylon is best). With this sort of care, your high-grade brushes will do a fine job for you year after year. They deserve as much care as your most expensive metal tools!

8

MINIATURE INTERNAL-COMBUSTION ENGINES

Before we get into engine specifics, it should be explained that most planes flown today with tiny internal-combustion (usually shortened to IC) power plants are termed "gassies." This is simply a holdover from early model days when free-flight planes were flown with either rubber bands or a "gas" engine (so called because it used gasoline fuel). The latter planes were then termed "gassies," and they are still widely referred to in this manner, even though few model-plane engines today utilize gasoline fuels.

Internal-combustion engines are divided into two large classes: the two-stroke-cycle and the four-stroke-cycle. Again, these terms have been shortened by popular usage to "two cycle" and "four cycle." Because our model planes require high power, simplicity, and light engine weight, the two-cycle engine dominates the field. The four-cycle engine, almost universal in automobiles, requires four piston movements for each power stroke, two up and two down. On the first stroke, the piston travels downward, creating a partial vacuum in the top of the cylinder, thus drawing in through the open intake valve the charge of vaporized gas. On the second stroke, the piston travels upward, compressing the gas mixture in the top of the cylinder, intake and exhaust valves now being closed. The timer now causes the spark plug to fire, igniting the gas-air mixture. This is the power stroke, the pressure driving the piston down, transmitting the force through the crankshaft to the propeller (or flywheel). The piston now travels up again, forcing the burned gases through the open exhaust valve. Then as the piston goes down again, a fresh charge of fuel is sucked in through the open intake valve, and the cycle repeats. Because of its mechanically operated valves, four-cycle gas engines are seldom used as model airplane power plants. They are complicated, relatively heavy, and costly; although they are considerably more efficient in their use of fuel than our two-cycle engines, this is a rather minor matter in model aviation.

The two-cycle engine provides a power impulse for every two piston movements: one up and one down. In this engine the fuel-air mixture is admitted initially into the crankcase, rather than into the cylinder. The crankcase is hermetically sealed. On the first stroke, the piston travels upward, compressing the gas vapor in the cylinder and causing a partial vacuum in the crankcase. As the piston moves upward, an intake port is opened so that the partial vacuum in the crankcase causes a fresh charge of fuel to be sucked from the carburetor into the crankcase. When the plug ignites the fuel mixture in the cylinder, the piston is driven downward for its second stroke. When the piston reaches its lowest point, it simultaneously uncovers both the exhaust port in the cylinder wall and, on the opposite side of the cylinder, the by-pass from the crankcase to the cylinder, permitting the fuel vapor in the crankcase to rush up into the cylinder. The pressure of the fuel in the cylinder helps push the exhaust gases out the open exhaust port. A baffle or raised ridge on the piston top prevents the fresh vaporized fuel mixture from racing directly across the cylinder and out the exhaust port on the opposite side. The baffle deflects the mixture upward.

The two-cycle sequence is seen in figure 8–1. Because it is easier to understand, we have used what is called a "side intake" engine here; the intake port is on the cylinder wall below the exhaust port and is opened and closed by the piston. Actually, this style of engine is seldom seen today; it has been found that rotary intake valves are much more efficient, for they allow a greater charge of fuel to be drawn into the crankcase. The majority of engines have the rotary built into the crankshaft; the air intake and "carburetor" project upward from the shaft bearing housing, just in front of the cylinder. Some engines are made with a rear rotary valve; here the intake is on the rear cover of the crankcase and admits fuel into the case via a disk valve which is ro-

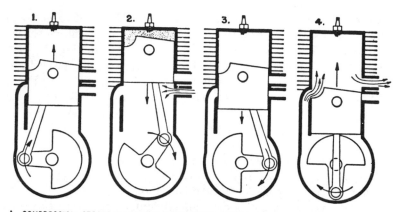

1. COMPRESSION STROKE — TURNING CRANKSHAFT FORCES PISTON UPWARD, COMPRESSING VAPORIZED GASOLINE IN CYLINDER. A PARTIAL VACUUM IS SIMULTANEOUSLY CREATED IN THE CRANKCASE.

2. POWER STROKE — INTAKE PORT IS OPENED, ALLOWING GAS VAPORS TO ENTER CRANKCASE. SPARK PLUG IGNITES GAS VAPORS IN CYLINDER, FORCING PISTON DOWNWARD.

3. EXHAUST STROKE — BURNING GASES FORCE PISTON DOWNWARD UNTIL THE EXHAUST PORT IS OPENED, LETTING BURNT GASES OUT.

4. INTAKE STROKE — GAS VAPORS IN CRANKCASE HAVE BEEN COMPRESSED DURING EXHAUST STROKE, AND WHEN PISTON UNCOVERS TRANSFER PORT, GASES RUSH IN, HELPING FORCE OUT THE EXHAUST GASES.

Fig. 8-1.   Two-Cycle Engine

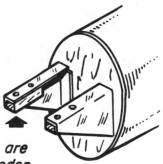

Metal engine mounts are bolted to firewall; wooden blocks absorb vibration.

Fig. 8-2.   Engine Mount

tated by the crankpin. Most engine men feel this is the most efficient setup of all, but it's more costly to make and more complex. Rear-rotary engines generally command a premium price.

In an engine with spark ignition, the charge (in either two- or four-cycle engines) is ignited by an electric spark at the plug, just as in your auto engine. A timer on the crankshaft controls the electric circuit, con-

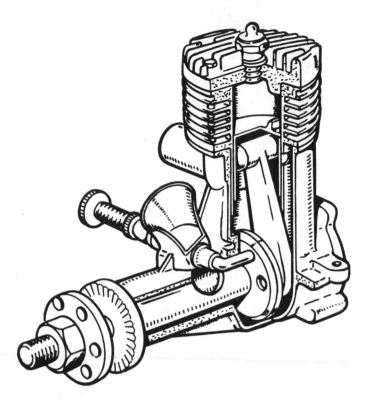

Fig. 8-3.   Shaft Rotary Valve Glow Engine

sisting of a spark coil, condenser, and battery. Early modelers found most of their engine troubles were produced by the spark-ignition system, and shortly after World War II glow ignition developed rapidly. A few spark-ignition engines are used today, but mostly in "old timer" free-flight events, where the object is to fly prewar planes with prewar engines. Spark ignition is also used in some model-boat engines where the weight of the ignition apparatus is not so important.

The glow-engine operating sequence is exactly the same as the spark sequence, whether two-cycle or four-cycle, but, due to use of special fuel, the compressed charge in the cylinder is ignited at the proper instant by a glowing coil of wire, part of the "glow plug." This plug has a center terminal to which one end of the wire coil is welded, the other end being fastened to the plug body. To start glow engines, it is necessary to attach a "starting battery" to the plug. The current required to heat the plug is rather high (most take several amperes), and fairly heavy batteries are needed. Heavy dry cells are popular, and smaller special starting batteries are offered by some manufacturers; they have a special internal composition suited to this task. Small nickel-cadmium

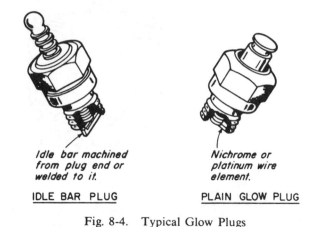

Idle bar machined
from plug end or
welded to it.

IDLE BAR PLUG

Nichrome or
platinum wire
element.

PLAIN GLOW PLUG

Fig. 8-4.   Typical Glow Plugs

cells are very popular and very compact; a cell of the size equivalent to a flashlight D cell (about $1\frac{11}{32} \times 2\frac{13}{32}$ inches) will give many engine starts when fully charged and may be recharged dozens of times. After the engine starts to run, the starting battery may be disconnected and the engine will continue to run. The heat of combustion (and the alcohol fuel, which reacts with the glow-plug wire) cause the plug to remain hot, producing ignition without all the heavy components required in spark systems. The fuel composition, style of glow plug, and other factors determine the exact instant of ignition of each charge. Weather is also a factor. Glow ignition is very practical and reliable, however.

Even after glow engines were well developed, some modelers preferred the spark-ignition style, since by shifting the timer position these engines could be slowed down for test flights and so forth. But glow-engine techniques have now been developed to the point where these light and potent power plants can be idled down almost to a "tick-over" if needed. Good idling is one of the prime requirements of radio-control engines (in the larger sizes especially), and today we have it in profusion, along with the light weight and simplicity of glow ignition.

As noted earlier, spark-ignition engines normally ran on a fuel mixture of gasoline to which was added heavy mineral oil. But glow fuel is based on an alcohol fuel mixture, and the lubricant is generally castor oil (either natural or artificial). Special additives are included in most fuels to promote better mixing of the alcohol and castor oil, to give more power, to promote easier starting, and so on. Fuel mixing is quite a complex business today, though most glow engines will run well on a plain mixture of methanol (a form of alcohol) and castor oil; in fact, the rules of some international IC engines model-plane events specify such a mixture, which is provided by the sponsors.

Glow plugs come in two main sizes (short and long) and in many makes and "heat ranges." The proper ignition point for a given engine and fuel is assured by picking the proper plug (and also by taking into account local atmospheric conditions). Engine makers specify what is best for each of their engines, of course, and most supply a suitable plug. Modelers who wish to get the absolute maximum power from an engine often mix their own fuels to suit the immediate conditions (including changes of temperature or humidity on a particular day—or even at a particular *time* of the day!). The average glow engine, however, is surprisingly tolerant of weather and fuel, and most will generally give good operation under all weather conditions with a mild fuel, of which many are on the market.

A few of the smaller engines utilize "glow heads"; here the hot wire coil is built right into the cylinder head, which unscrews easily for replacement. On larger engines, the glow plug itself is replaced, of course. Glow plugs gradually wear out in use, and when the wire coil is "open" —that is, no current will pass through to heat it—the plug must be replaced. Actually, glow plugs are often replaced before they open, as they get gummed up with burned oil, the glow gets weaker and weaker, and the engine may become hard to start, lose power, or idle poorly.

We must mention briefly here still another type of model IC engine, very popular in Europe, though not widely used in the United States. This is the so-called "diesel." A more exact term is "compression ignition" engine. In the spark-ignition engine, the fuel charge is fired by a precisely timed electric spark. In the glow engine, the fuel ignites at the proper instant (timing influenced mainly by fuel composition and glow-plug design) by contact with the glowing wire coil in the cylinder head. The compression-ignition engine needs no "fire" in the cylinder, as the specially volatile fuel ignites when the fuel-air charge has been compressed sufficiently to raise its temperature to the firing point. This requires far greater compression than that used in either spark or glow engines. The true diesel engine fires in the same manner, but such engines used in cars, trucks, and so on inject the fuel directly into the cylinder when the charge of plain air has been raised to the ignition point. Model diesels, however, draw the fuel-air mixture in and compress it just as do model glow and spark engines.

Because of the high pressures, model diesels must generally be more ruggedly built and are therefore heavier. They are amply powerful, easy to handle (when you are accustomed to them), and, of course, dispense with all expendable components such as batteries and glow or spark ignition plugs. Diesels generally give more mileage for a given weight of

H

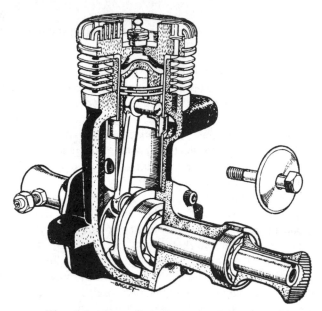

Fig. 8-5.   Rear Rotary Valve Glow Engine

fuel than do glow engines; thus they are often used in model-plane categories where fuel economy is paramount; Team Racing, for example.

Most diesel engines have a screw lever on the cylinder head, by means of which the cylinder compression may be varied, which changes the timing of the ignition. Thus the engine can be adjusted to run well on different fuels and under varying weather conditions. Diesel fuel usually contains kerosene, oil, and ether (the latter is the "firing" agent for the fuel mixture), but many other materials are added or substituted.

You will hear of "ringed" and "lapped" engines. The latter are by far the most numerous, and the term means that the piston is fitted extremely closely to the cylinder by a machine process called "lapping." Such engines take fairly careful breaking in, but have a good life if they are handled properly. In the larger sizes (.45 to .60 cubic inch) it has been found preferable in some uses, such as radio control, to allow a little looser piston fit and to equip the piston with one or two rings (auto-engine pistons generally have three rings) to effect the seal. One big reason for this construction is that a ringed piston may be made of aluminum alloy, which is much lighter than the iron alloy used in lapped engines and thus causes less vibration. The piston ring or rings may be replaced to restore pep to such an engine after it has had long use.

Fuel must be mixed with air and admitted to any engine as a vapor. Everyone knows the tremendous explosive qualities of gasoline vapor;

100

other fuel vapors are similarly powerful. Also, the amount of fuel, once it is vaporized, must be controlled to suit the speed at which the engine is being run.

Both vaporization and amount of fuel are controlled by a needle valve. This is nothing but a long, pointed, rodlike piece of metal that screws into a long tube. Imagine a piece of metal tubing. To one end the fuel line is connected and in the other goes the needle valve. In the middle is a tiny hole. When the needle is screwed all the way into the tube, it covers this small hole. No fuel can pass. As the needle is unscrewed, fuel flows from the fuel line out the hole. The needle can be delicately adjusted to close more or less of the hole as necessary.

How does the fuel become vapor? When you flip the propeller to start the engine, fuel is sucked through the hole in the needle valve and, once the engine begins to run, the fuel becomes mixed with air that rushes through the venturi, or air-intake passage. The relationship of the small hole in the needle-valve body and the venturi is very important.

As we have already seen, the upward movement of the piston inside the cylinder causes a partial vacuum in the crankcase. Thus, when the intake port opens, the rush of air through the venturi causes the liquid fuel to be blended with air—to be vaporized. The action is similar to that of a perfume atomizer. Only when the mixture is fairly close to the ideal will the engine start and run well. The needle valve enables the user to accomplish this adjustment to suit all conditions.

We hear the intake and needle valve of model engines referred to as the "carburetor"; actually, this term refers to a much more complex fuel-mixing unit, such as that found on automobiles. The proper term for the venturi and needle valve on the average engine is "mixing valve." However, multispeed engines nowadays are becoming more and more complex; some have as many as four or five variable adjustments to allow reliable operation over a speed range from idling to top power. Such units can probably be considered carburetors, and they are getting more complicated all the time.

The needle valve allows the user of the simplest engine to slow it down a great extent; this is done by allowing more fuel to go in for a rich mixture. The engine runs somewhat roughly and has much less power, but speed can be cut only a moderate amount by this means. If the fuel is too rich, the engine simply quits. The simplest throttle setup cuts down the fuel and air mixture together; this will allow considerable speed reduction. If this is carried too far, however, again the engine stops. The simple intake throttle does cut down the fuel volume, but it cannot keep the ratio of fuel to air correct as it is closed. The fuel mixture is invariably too rich with the throttle closed. Not only is this a poor mixture for good running, but it tends to quench the glow plug. (All the extra fuel simply cools the plug so much it cannot fire the mixture.) Two means to overcome this are common. An adjustment called an "idle bleed" is found on many engine intakes; it serves to lean the mixture at closed throttle settings (that is, to reduce the amount of fuel in the fuel-air mixture), but has no effect when the throttle is wide open. To keep the glow plug hot at low speed, an "exhaust damper" is fitted to the engine and coupled to the intake throttle. The damper helps to slow the engine by itself (a fairly wide speed range can be had with just the damper alone), because it restricts the exhaust port and tends to hold some of the burned fuel of each charge in the cylinder. Because it thus retains some of the hot gases, the glow plug is kept up to ignition temperature at low engine speeds. Practically all modern engines which operate over a wide speed range have coupled intake and exhaust throttles. With the other adjustments on the intake throttle mentioned above, a modern variable-speed glow engine of the type popular for larger radio-control planes may have a reliable speed range from as low as 2,000 rpm (amply low for the purpose) to 10,000 rpm or considerably more. It will also operate smoothly and reliably between these extremes. We have the needs of the competition radio fliers to thank for this development. Reliable high and low speeds are of interest to the Navy carrier control-line fliers as well.

As we mentioned, the starter-battery leads must be attached to the glow plug, then removed as soon as the engine is running smoothly. A common way to attach these leads is by means of alligator clips which, as the name suggests, have serrated jaws for grasping wires or terminals. If you use such clips, be sure you get small ones for model work from your hobby shop. Large ones grip too tightly and may loosen the center portion of the glow plug. Slip-on connections are better. There are many types, depending on the kind of glow plug being used. Ask your dealer for the proper connection for your particular brand of plug. The connection slides over the plug, automatically making all necessary electrical connections without risk of short circuits. Once the engine starts, the clip-on is easily pulled off.

A prop wrench is essential because props frequently come loose in starting or may break on contact with the ground when landing or taking off, requiring replacement. The use of pliers on a prop nut will quickly round the corners, making it difficult to tighten or loosen the nut. Many makes of engines are shipped with such a wrench in the box.

I-1/2 V

HEAVY-DUTY STARTER

Bend to adapt to
different engines

HANG-ON STARTER

Fig. 8-6.   Starting Batteries

It will be found that this wrench is cleverly designed to perform many special purposes, frequently fitting, in one way or another, every removable part on the engine, including the back crankcase cover plate.

For bench testing and break-in, engines should be firmly mounted and may be supplied by the fuel tank that comes with them, if any. Some of the smaller engines do have such tanks, but the majority of all sizes today do not, so you must mount the tank and link it to the needle valve with fuel-proof tubing. (Actually, we know of *no* such tubing supplied today that is truly fuel-proof; most will either harden or soften with continued use and must eventually be replaced; some fuel tubing does have a fairly long life, however.)

How do you know when the engine is broken in? Turn or screw in the needle valve while the engine is running (to lean out the mixture) until the engine reaches it obvious maximum number of rpm. The smoky exhaust will disappear, and the radical change in sound will be easily detected. Now, if the engine continues to run steadily, holding a constant rpm until the fuel is exhausted, it is ready for flying. If, on the other hand, the engine seems to run up and down hill, alternately slowing and speeding, it requires more breaking in. It is good practice not to run the engine for more than 30 seconds the first time you try it. If your engine is new, it may require breaking in before full-throttle operation for an extended run is possible. Therefore, it is recommended procedure to let the engine run off a few tanks of fuel at reduced throttle. This is done by screwing out the needle valve, after starting, until the engine runs with a rich mixture, indicated by a smoky exhaust and slower running. Well-made engines, particularly the bigger ones, may consume a couple of cans of fuel in this process. New engines should be operated at first on sport, not racing, fuel. Sport fuel does not permit the high rpm of more potent mixtures so that the engine does not heat up as much. If you have only a powerful fuel at hand, add 5 to 10 per cent of its volume in castor oil. For the duration of the break-in period use a prop slightly smaller than the recommended size

103

for the particular engine. The experts tell us it is much better to run a new engine for short periods—say, five minutes—and let it cool off considerably before restarting. This is said to do the best job of mating the metal parts. As with an auto engine, careful breaking in pays dividends in longer engine life and more reliable running. Don't rush the process, but take the maker's advice on break-in.

Here is a suggested method for starting glow engines:

1. After selecting the desired propeller, position it on the crankshaft. If you face the engine from the front and turn the shaft counterclockwise with your fingers, you will feel the piston come up against compression inside the cylinder. The prop then should be on the shaft diagonally in such a manner that the tip to your right is slanted upward in the two o'clock position. This position minimizes breakage when the plane lands. It also makes for easy and natural flipping and minimizes the number of times the prop will kick free.

2. After the tank is filled with fuel, some raw fuel must be fed up to and into the engine. Some fliers prefer the choke method. This means that a finger is placed over the open end of the venturi while the prop is turned until fuel is observed to flow through the fuel line up to the needle valve. A couple of extra flips at this point induces enough fuel vapor into the cylinder to give a pop and perhaps a start. Others prefer to prime. This means that a jet of fuel is squirted into the exhaust port. The prime should be small, consisting of just a few drops; anything more should be run off by tipping the engine and blowing away the excess. When priming, it is still necessary to choke slightly in order to fill the fuel line; otherwise the engine will start, run off the prime, and then strike an air space in the fuel line before the raw fuel reaches the needle valve.

Squirt the prime against the piston through the port; the piston prevents an excess of fuel getting into the cylinder. Flip the prop a few times before attaching the booster leads. Should an engine become flooded, remove the glow plug (with the proper wrench, never with pliers) and invert the engine, at the same time holding the venturi in the lowest position. The excess fuel will drain out the various openings. Spin the prop with the finger to make sure that the excess fuel is ejected through the glow-plug hole. Lower the piston by turning the shaft and blow through the exhaust ports. Blow excess fuel off the glow-plug filament.

3. Once the engine is primed and fuel has been drawn into the line ready to run, attach the starter clip-on connections and flip the propeller smartly in a counterclockwise direction. If the prop stops with a loud bang or smack, you have overprimed. Remove the starter leads, check the prop for looseness and change in position, then flip it over several more times, attach the leads once more, and attempt to start. If the prop does not stop short again with a bang, continue to flip up to a dozen times or until the engine begins to run. If there is no action, prime again lightly and flip again.

Sometimes you will hear a very mild pop, perhaps the instant you flip the prop, then maybe another pop. This means that the engine is on the verge of starting, so continue flipping until it runs. There is a slight excess of fuel in the engine, but not enough to cause flooding.

4. When the engine starts abruptly and runs for only a second or two at very high rpm—just a brief scream—the fuel mixture is too lean. The engine merely ran off the prime. Open the needle valve another quarter turn, and so on until the engine runs satisfactorily.

If the engine runs, but at a very low and faltering number of rpm, with a smoky exhaust, the needle valve is open too far and must be shut down one-quarter turn at a time. If the engine continues to run but slows down—but without the telltale smoky exhaust that indicates a rich mixture—the mixture is just a trifle lean. Open the needle valve a tiny bit at a time till it will sustain top speed. If the mixture is too rich, the engine may run at quite good speed, but a bit irregularly. You may hear it go into four-cycle operation, which means the mixture is firing only every second revolution. You can detect the change in exhaust note, and the engine will slow down considerably, of course. Also, you will notice the telltale smoky exhaust. To correct this, turn in the valve a little at a time.

Rich running in flight will do no harm to the engine; it just wastes fuel, and you don't get maximum power. Lean running can definitely be harmful, however; when running lean an engine gets much hotter than normally, and if allowed to continue doing so, it may seize up and quit abruptly. Expansion of overheated parts raises friction until the engine has to stop. An engine can often be heard running just on the verge of being too lean by an exhaust sound often termed "cackling";

this is a sharp cracking sound that can be heard over the normal exhaust note. If your engine runs this way, the mixture should definitely be enriched a little.

An engine that is properly adjusted should run out an entire tank of fuel without becoming too rich or lean, of course. If it does not, if it refuses to keep running in flight or even on the test stand, it could mean the tank is not at the right height in relation to the needle valve, or it may be too far from the valve. Generally, the tank top should be level with the needle valve in a free-flight plane, though it could be somewhat higher. For a control-line plane the fuel line at point of exit from the tank should be on a level with the needle-valve body. For radio control, it is usual to position the tank so its center (vertically) is on a level with the needle valve. In any case, tanks should be kept as close to the engine as possible, to minimize the distance the engine must draw fuel. An engine with poor crankcase compression may not be able to pull fuel more than a few inches; if in good shape, the same engine could likely raise fuel six inches or more.

Should an engine refuse to start—assuming it is not old and worn out, with a leaky crankshaft bearing that lowers crankcase compression —check the voltage of your starting battery. This should be done with the starting leads on a good glow plug; checking voltage without this load on the battery can tell you very little. A dry cell should show no less than about $1\frac{1}{4}$ volts at the battery terminals. Check right at the plug and you will note the voltage is lower, due to resistance in the leads and connections. Make sure the leads are in good shape, all soldered joints secure, and the terminals on the battery screwed down tight. Remove the glow plug from the engine, and check to be sure it is not defective. You should see a bright red glow from the coil. This may be hard to see in bright sunlight, so shield the plug and check again.

When an engine which is known for its easy starting and good running suddenly develops trouble without explanation, try these hints:

1. Is the fuel line clogged? Sometimes flecks of dirt may be seen through the transparent fuel line at the point of attachment of the needle-valve body. This probably means that there is dirt in the valve as well, perhaps even closing off the tiny hole in the needle valve.

Remove the flexible line from the needle-valve body and squirt fuel through it. Most tanks have three openings: one for the fuel line, one for filling, and one a vent which allows air to escape when you fill the tank. Hold your finger over this vent, attach the squirt gun to the filler tube, and squirt fuel through the tank and out the opening to which the fuel line attaches. Swish the fuel around the tank and blow through the filler opening while holding the vent closed. The pressure will jet a stream of fuel out the fuel-line tube.

Remove the needle-valve body and, if the hole is clogged, work out the dirt with the point of a pin. Attach the filler tube to one end of the body and squirt fuel through it. Then close the far end with the finger so that the force of the fuel under pressure is directed out the tiny hole. Replace the valve body, being sure that the small hole is in its original position, which usually is downward out of sight, facing the shaft, or inward facing the crankcase in rear-valve engines.

2. As directed above, make sure the hole in the needle valve is properly placed. If the engine has been disassembled, the needle-valve body may have been improperly replaced, or it may have been turned accidentally.

3. The glow plug may be weak. If this is the case, the engine will run with starter battery connected, but will stop immediately when the lead is disconnected; or the engine may always stop within a few seconds after the leads have been disconnected. Replace the plug. A further check is to see if the engine will keep running with the battery connected.

4. If the engine has been run extensively and has given lots of service, it may have developed a loose-fitting bearing, permitting crankcase compression to be lost. This can be detected by a wobbling crankshaft. Ordinarily, the crankshaft will not wobble, but if, on picking up the engine and pushing a prop tip in a fore-and-aft direction, you can feel play in the bearing, then it probably needs replacement.

5. Glow plugs may be loose or damaged, permitting cylinder compression to be lost. Such compression may leak around the base of the plug or up through the center piece where the insulated material separates the contact from the outside of the plug. If the plug is loose, tighten it, but if the core piece is loose, replace the plug.

6. If the engine gradually slows down after minutes in the air, and it is known to be thoroughly broken in but is still fairly new, a less powerful, cooler-running fuel may be required, or some oil may be added to the hot fuel mixture. Be sure, also, that your needle valve is not set a hair too lean. On long engine runs there

is a tendency for the engine to lean out toward the end of the run; this is due to the fact that, as fuel is consumed, there is less weight of fuel to create pressure at the needle valve; or the level of fuel may have dropped to the point where pressure has disappeared and the engine must depend entirely on suction to make the fuel flow. So open the needle valve a little and note the results on subsequent test flights.

While they may start and run at top speed, radio-control engines may refuse to idle at low speeds. There may be a variety of reasons for this, depending on the engine and type of throttle, but a basic requirement for good idling is an "idle bar" glow plug. Oddly enough, some engines do not come with such a plug (some imported engines have no plug at all when you buy them). The idle bar is either machined from the plug body metal or welded to the body, just below the wire coil. It tends to keep big blobs of fuel from striking the hot coil of wire (many engines, especially if the mixture is not properly adjusted for idling, will run quite rich at low speed, which means the fuel is not completely vaporized and larger droplets are coming into the cylinder) and cooling it so much that the engine stops. For good idling, as well as good top speed and power, special additives are required in glow fuel. Many fuel manufacturers sell several mixtures, one of which is intended for radio-control engines; this usually costs more than common "sport fuel" (which might work fine in an engine where a wide speed range is not required), but is well worth the difference.

In many areas of the country it is becoming increasingly difficult to find flying sites for engine-powered model planes, especially if there are houses within a mile or so. The main objection of the average citizen to model-plane flying is *noise!* The song of a model engine at top speed may be music to the ear of a modeler, but it means only irritation to others. There has been growing interest in silencers or mufflers for model engines; quite a few European countries forbid *any* model-engine operation without a muffler. Because of this, muffler development, at the present time, is much farther ahead there than in the United States, and most mufflers have to be imported; practically none are made in this country. Fortunately, the overseas makers can supply units to fit many of the engines that are popular here. The term "silencer" is a misnomer, since we are not trying to take away *all* the exhaust noise (if this could be done, it would be found that the propeller itself makes a great deal of racket). The term "muffler" is probably a better one. What it does is to remove the harsh high-pitch sounds of exhaust

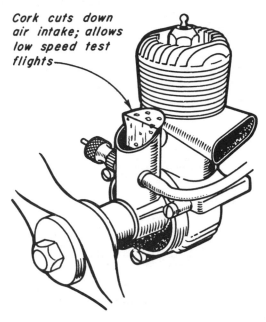

Cork cuts down air intake; allows low speed test flights

Fig. 8-7. Venturi Restriction

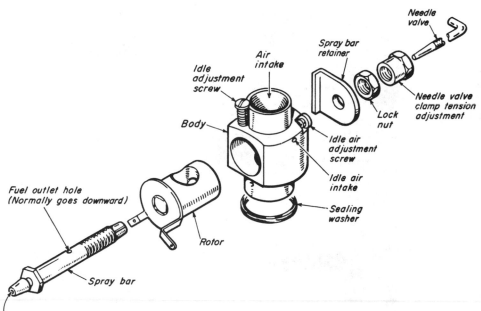

Needle valve

Idle adjustment screw

Air intake

Spray bar retainer

Body

Needle valve clamp tension adjustment

Lock nut

Idle air adjustment screw

Idle air intake

Fuel outlet hole (Normally goes downward)

Rotor

Sealing washer

Spray bar

Fuel intake

Fig. 8-8. Variable-Speed Intake Throttle

which are by far the most irritating. Many radio fliers who operate with clubs which have muffler rules say they hate to fly in other areas where unmuffled engines are common, for they find the noise very distracting.

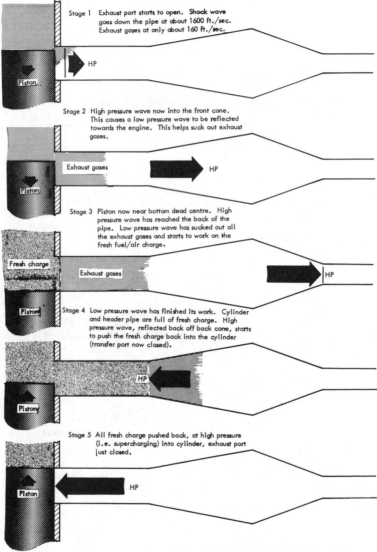

Fig. 8-9.   Principles of Tuned Pipes

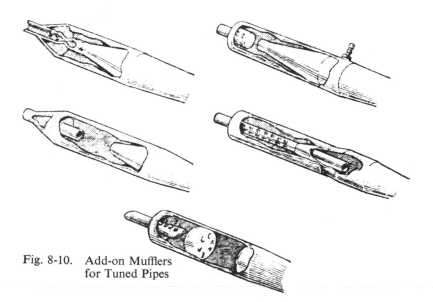

Fig. 8-10. Add-on Mufflers
for Tuned Pipes

It is no great job to build a muffler that will quiet the exhaust satisfactorily, but to do this and not lose a large portion of the engine power is another matter. It seems probable that the best compromise between reasonable noise reduction and retention of top power and rpm would come where an engine manufacturer developed both the engine *and* the muffler as a matched pair. Unfortunately, at this time we have very few examples of this; most mufflers are simply add-on units.

On the average, mufflers probably take some 5 to 15 per cent of power, there being many variables in the matter, of course. They do tend to afford longer engine runs from a given amount of fuel. Also, it is usually possible, and even preferable, to remove the exhaust throttle when a muffler is fitted to an engine. The back pressure from the muffler itself (which is what robs engine power) is usually sufficient to keep the plug glowing at low engine speeds.

Model-engine muffler research has just scratched the surface so far, but already we have types that not only quiet the engine to a remarkable extent but also *increase* engine power. These are the "tuned exhaust" units, utilized so far mainly on control-line speed engines. They are bulky and are good over only a rather narrow speed range; but they show what can be done with enough research.

9

TANKS

Let's first discuss the fuel-feed and tank problems posed by the typical high-powered contest free-flight airplane. Even though the engine may have to run but 12 seconds, it is difficult to avoid having the motor lean out after a few seconds, cutting down power or causing failure. Leaning out means that the proportion of air in the fuel mixture is increased; running rich means the opposite. It is important to maintain as constant a fuel pressure as possible throughout the engine run. Since the consumption of fuel necessarily reduces the fuel level, it follows that pressure must vary, depth of fuel in the tank being one of the factors. There are several ways the builder can minimize these fuel-pressure changes and then adjust his needle valve to handle whatever change remains.

The two principal factors that bear on fuel pressure in the free-flight machine are the distance of the tank from the engine's needle valve and the vertical location of the tank in relation to the needle valve. The farther the tank is mounted from the engine, the greater the draw or distance that the engine must suck the fuel. The ability to draw fuel varies widely from engine to engine, depending on crankcase compression and other factors. Even if the engine can run with a long draw, it may be difficult to start and to keep running. Obviously, the tank should be located as near as possible to the engine.

The relation of the tank to the needle valve, meaning whether the tank is located high or low within the plane, must be precise for reliable operation. If the tank is placed high above the engine, the fuel flows downhill of its own accord and floods the engine. On the other hand, if the tank is positioned much below the needle valve, the engine will have to pull fuel against gravity. The tendency will be to run lean. Therefore, it is customary to place the top of the standard free-flight tank at the needle-valve level. The free-flight tank may be a cube or a cylinder, but its three main dimensions are roughly similar. A long tank is bad for a free-flying model due to the surge of fuel to the back of the tank upon launching. For the small Half-A free-flight planes, the glass portion of an eyedropper has been found very useful. The glass dropper is held to the side of the plane close to the engine with a metal strap and tiny screws, or simply clasped by a strip of tape cemented (then fuel-proofed) over the glass and to the plane. A piece of fuel line runs from the lower extremity of the glass tube up to the needle valve. The reasons for using such a tank include the ease of estimating the amount of fuel for a flight (the tube may be marked with small lines to show the various amounts of fuel that result in certain-length motor runs) and also simplicity, economy, and lightness. The proper vertical position for the eyedropper tank is from one-third to one-half its length above the needle valve. Make tests and move the tank up or down accordingly.

A very simple tank for small free-flight planes consists simply of a coil of fuel tubing (lower right in fig. 9–1). Running time is checked to find out how long the tubing must be before it is coiled. Be sure the tubing is not kinked shut at any point during the coiling; the end must be open, of course.

In the control-line field, an ingenious experimenter developed the wedge tank. The point of the wedge was placed toward the side of the plane that would be on the outside of the flying circle. Centrifugal force would push the fuel into the point of the wedge. The fuel-line tube was carried to the rear outer corner of the tank, or rear tip of the wedge. Since fuel tended to be pushed back by acceleration and outward by centrifugal force, this fuel line literally was good to the last drop. Nor did the inventor's cleverness stop there. The normal air-vent tube at the top of the tank was extended to reach but not touch the inner bottom surface. Another vent tube was attached to the bottom surface, extending up through the tank almost to the top inside surface. When the plane flipped over on its back, the bottom vent became the top vent, and the former top vent now admitted air. In other words, this tank operated equally well whether right side up or upside down. But the wedge tank was not suited for speed models. Here, centrifugal force is extremely severe; the wider a tank, the more fuel presses against the side of the

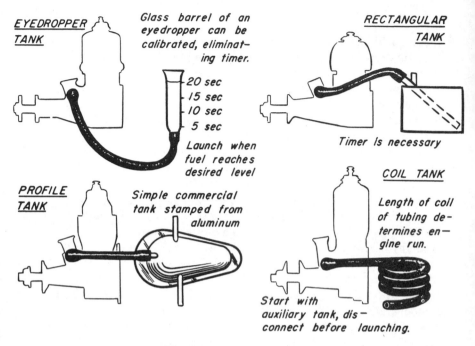

EYEDROPPER TANK

Glass barrel of an eyedropper can be calibrated, eliminating timer.

20 sec
15 sec
10 sec
5 sec

Launch when fuel reaches desired level

RECTANGULAR TANK

Timer is necessary

PROFILE TANK

Simple commercial tank stamped from aluminum

COIL TANK

Length of coil of tubing de-termines en-gine run.

Start with auxiliary tank, dis-connect before launching.

Fig. 9-1.   Free-Flight Tanks

tank on the outside of the circle, and the wedge tank is a wide tank. The answer for speed flying proved to be a long, high, narrow tank. Because of cramped quarters in the speed model and the interference of various parts with the tank location, all sorts of weird tank contours are resorted to. Speed builders invariably construct their own tanks.

With the development of stunt flying and the wedge tank that made it possible, it was first thought that only a wedge could be used. Some builders now claim that a square tank can be used with equal success. As a matter of fact, today we have tanks of many shapes: square, round, wedge, high rectangle, diamond, and even a combination of square and wedge.

In control-line planes, tank position is even more critical than in free-flight jobs. In addition to affecting any normal tendency to lean out or richen up, the position of the tank may determine whether or not a stunt job will run as steadily on its back as when upright. The feed line must be exactly on a level with the needle-valve body on stunt machines.

Many tanks, especially the larger sizes, have an internal baffle to stop surge. Surging of fuel results from sudden acceleration and deceleration and is particularly noticeable in long tanks.

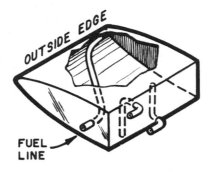

Fig. 9-2.   Stunt Tank

You may hear fliers refer to clank tanks and to clunk tanks. There is a real difference. The first clank tanks were developed for control-line stunters; they were brass rectangular units. The fuel pick-up tube that connects to the needle valve terminated in a short straight end placed about midway on one side. A slightly larger tube bent in L-shape pivoted on this end; it was weighted at the open end, so it would always tend to swing wherever the fuel might be, despite violent maneuvering. When an empty tank was shaken, you could hear the swivel clanking against the sides. The clank tank has been quite popular in radio control, having evolved to a long circular shape. The swivel is free to turn a full 360 degrees on its tubing-pivot support. The larger sizes have a baffle, which not only prevents surging but supports the long feed tube which runs fore and aft.

Clunk tanks are entirely different, though the object is the same: to assure steady fuel feed regardless of plane maneuvers. These tanks are invariably made of fuel-proof plastic and usually have a screw-on cap through which pass all the necessary tubes. The feed pipe ends a short distance inside this cap, and onto it is forced a length of synthetic rubber tubing (this tube must be able to stand immersion in fuel without becoming stiff or rotting, and surgical rubber has been found useful here). A small weight is forced into the flexible tube at its far end, and a hole through the weight allows fuel pickup. The weight naturally flops around in the tank, under the urge of gravity and centrifugal force; since the fuel does the same, fuel feed is assured at all times. When these tanks are shaken, a dull clunk results; hence the odd name!

Clunk and clank tanks are widely used for radio-control stunt planes, but are really not required for sport planes which might do just a loop or two occasionally. The clank and clunk tanks allow lengthy inverted flight, of course; the weight in clunk tanks even will fall to the forward end of the tank (along with fuel) in a lengthy nose-down maneuver.

115

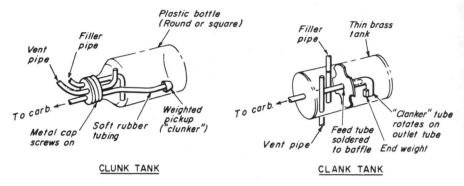

Fig. 9-3. Clunk and Clank Tanks

Some modelers find it necessary to build their own tanks to fit special fuselage shapes or odd operating conditions. The material used is shim brass or tin. Tin may be obtained from old fuel cans, and, though thicker and heavier than shim brass, is quite all right for normal flying where absolutely top performance is not demanded. First, from experience with standard tanks and the length of motor run you desire, sketch out your design to suit whatever particular purpose you have in mind. Next, prepare accurate patterns on thin, stiff cardboard and use them to scribe on the tin or brass the outlines of the parts you will cut out with tin snips. Allow appropriate overlapping edges for soldering and bending. Mark and drill the holes for the vents and fuel line before beginning to cut the metal. The cut, flat pieces of metal may be bent over a sharp-cornered hardwood block with a small hammer. Small flaps or flanges may be bent with needle-nosed pliers. Soldering should be done with a hot, clean iron and resin-core solder. In assembling the feed tube and vents, be sure that the inner ends are in the desired positions, at the rear of the tank or some corner, as the case may be. The metal surfaces to be soldered should be absolutely clean. Better soldering results will be had if a *very mild* flux is used; a good formula is 20 per cent zinc chloride, 20 per cent glycerine, 60 per cent ethyl alcohol. A druggist will make up several ounces of this mixture for 50 cents or so. It is most useful on metalwork where resin-core solder will not/do a good job (it is fine for soldering music wire, for example). After soldering and testing for leaks, the tank should be cleaned out well with plain alcohol, or, in a pinch, fuel can be used, due to its alcohol base.

A common error made by the beginning tank builder on free-flight tanks is not to run the feed line to the back of the tank. If the feed tube does not reach the rear of the tank, the fuel will surge away from it when the plane is launched. Another mistake is to forget to clean out the tank or not to be sure that it is leakproof! To pressure-test the tank for leaks,

116

put a long piece of fuel tubing over one of the vents or the fuel-line connection; then close off the other two openings and submerge the tank in a bowl of water. Blow through the tubing and watch for bubbles.

So-called balloon tanks are used in several forms. In one type, a small, round toy balloon has a piece of fuel tubing inserted at the open end and firmly bound; this is the fuel-feed tube to the needle valve and is the only opening from the tank. The tubing extends close to the far wall of the balloon and has a V-notch cut in the end, so it won't be closed off if it comes against the inner wall while the engine is pulling out fuel. Fuel is forced into the balloon with a rubber squeeze bulb; then the fuel-tubing inner end is held uppermost, the squeeze bulb disconnected, and all air forced out of the balloon. The latter should not be filled enough to cause the rubber to distend (when the filler tube has been removed). The balloon is mounted in the model in a compartment where it can "flop around" so that the fuel tube is always pulling fuel, regardless of gravity or centrifugal force. No vent is required, as atmospheric pressure tends to squeeze the balloon flatter as fuel is withdrawn. Such tanks are used in control-line stunters.

Another form of balloon tank is popular in control-line speed planes. This one consists of a fountain-pen bladder, with a feed tube bound into the open end. Often a small rubber balloon is placed over the pen bladder and held with the same binding. This style of tank is filled till it definitely distends and is used that way; the pressure feeds fuel to the engine at quite a steady rate until the tank is empty.

Pressure feed in still another form is utilized in both control-line and radio planes. Here the tank is of metal, and pressure is fed to it from a tap into the engine crankcase. Needless to say, after it is filled, such a tank must be completely sealed, as must be all the tubing and fittings in the system.

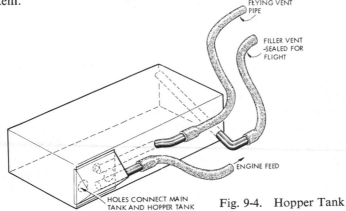

Fig. 9-4. Hopper Tank

10

RUBBER MODELS

Quite a few years ago, just about every model-plane enthusiast got his first taste of flying by building a "Baby ROG," a cute and lively little plane with 9- to 12-inch span, with just a simple stick to hold the parts and act as a fuselage. These little jobs could give hours of fun indoors, or outdoors in very calm weather. They had just a skeleton wing outline, covered with thin tissue, and a prop made of thin balsa steamed to correct shape. They were an ideal starter to instruct youngsters in the facts of powered flight. There were kits for them at very low cost, and you can get similar kits today. One manufacturer's range which is particularly suitable is that known as the "EeZee Bilt" series by Keil Kraft. They vary from 16 to 22 inches wingspan. Take a half-dozen kits to some group such as a Boy Scout meeting, and you can soon be staging rubber duration contests. Molded plastic props replace the fragile balsa of the old time ROG's, give better performance, and are virtually unbreakable.

It is just a step from such models to those that will give much longer flights and resemble more nearly the rubber duration planes being flown in national and international competition today. Since its purpose is to attain a model of reasonable performance and minimum complication, the small-fuselage plane is of simple construction. The fuselage almost always is a box, and the wing is squared off with parallel leading and trailing edges with blunted tips of sheet balsa or block. When the wing span is less than 15 or 16 inches, sheet-balsa construction is advisable throughout. The fuselage sides are easily cut out and put together by means of a few key formers. The wing can be flat sheet balsa up to ap-

118

proximately 12 inches of span, cambered for greater strength and lift. Camber may be imparted by putting several strips of dope crosswise (that is, chordwise) to the wood on one side, or the wood may be dampened and held in position on the bench over a few sheet-balsa ribs. It will hold the desired shape when dry. With more than 18 inches of span, it is better to build up the wing with spars, edges, and ribs. Sheet balsa may be used on wings up to 24 inches in span, or even larger, when special attention is given to structural design, but in these larger sizes it tends to be much heavier than tissue-covered wings. Sheet can be used, however, for a fuselage of any size.

The most popular size for sport rubber craft is 20 to 24 inches, with about 30 inches the practical limit. Hard $\frac{3}{32}$-inch square longerons or medium-hard $\frac{1}{8}$-inch square longerons make fuselages that will stand any amount of banging around. A one-spar wing is adequate, although the builder may also use two spars or multispars.

Because the weight of the rubber motor is distributed over most of the length of the fuselage, this type of model must always have a very long nose in order to balance that weight at the correct CG. Roughly speaking, there is almost as much rubber length in front of the wing as there is behind it. On the model with wing span of 2 to 2½ feet, the trailing edge of the wing will rest about ½ to 1 inch behind the point where the plane balances without the wing in place. From chapter 2 it will be recalled that the distance between the mid-chord point of the wing and the same point on the stabilizer is called the "tail moment arm." Also, that rubber models run to higher aspect ratios than gas models. In the sizes we are now discussing, an 8:1 aspect-ratio wing (a higher ratio would reduce the chord to an inefficient dimension) would result in a chord of 3 to 3¾ inches. A moment arm of 50 per cent of the span would provide a fairly long fuselage. For example, 50 per cent of 25 inches would provide a 12½-inch distance between the two mid-chord points. In figuring up the total fuselage length, this would leave one-half the wing chord to be added, also one-half the stabilizer chord, plus whatever the nose length happened to be. Half the wing chord would be 1½ inches, half the stabilizer chord possibly 1 inch, thus giving 2½ additional inches, or 12 plus 2½ inches, or 14½ inches, plus the nose length. The nose, not counting the actual nose block and propeller, should be at least half the tail moment arm for an average sport-type rubber model. This would make another 6 inches, or a new total of 20½ inches over-all fuselage length. From this it may be seen that an approximation of minimum length may be made as 75 per cent of the wing span.

What features should you include in a rubber-powered plane? First,

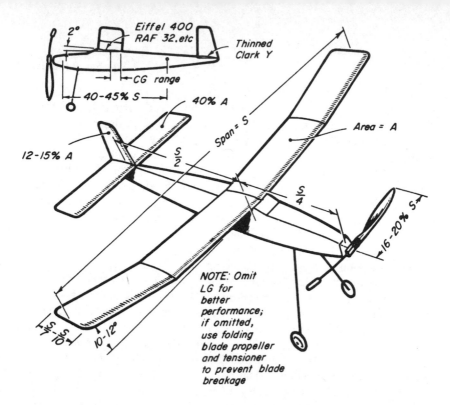

Fig. 10-1. Sport Rubber Model Proportions

a knock-off wing which may be held to the fuselage with a couple of loops of ⅛-inch-wide rubber (or equivalent rubber bands). It is advisable to allow a flat area atop the fuselage where the wing will sit of at least 1½ chord lengths; this will allow you to shift the wing back and forth for perfect balance. The landing gear should be bent from ¹⁄₁₆-inch-diameter music wire—ample size for this model.

As explained in chapter 6, the key to rubber-model performance is the propeller. You can start with a normal two-blader, later trying folding blades or a single-blade style for comparison.

On very small planes of 1-foot span or so, the freewheeling prop will not make much difference, and the folding prop is rather difficult to make due to the smallness of the hinges and fittings. As spans grow to 20, 24, 30 inches and beyond, it becomes desirable to use at least the simple freewheeler because of the improved performance and greater durations possible.

On small- and medium-size designs with long landing gears to protect the prop, the freewheeler will give good service. On contest types, landing gears are omitted for maximum efficiency and reduced weight. With either a freewheeler or folding prop, some sort of tensioning device must

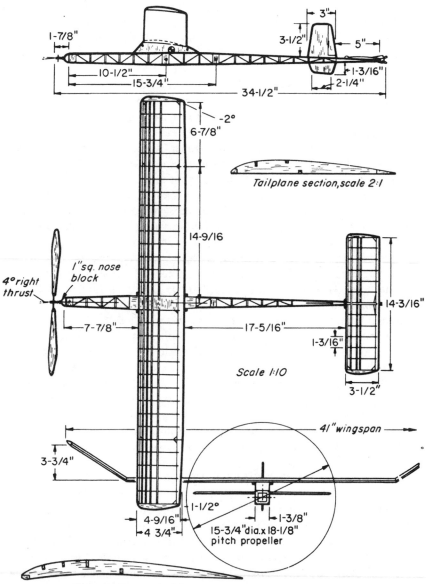

1-7/8"

3"

3-1/2"

5"

10-1/2"

15-3/4"

34-1/2"

1-3/16"

2-1/4"

-2°

6-7/8"

Tailplane section, scale 2:1

14-9/16

1" sq. nose block

4° right thrust

7-7/8"

17-5/16"

14-3/16"

1-3/16"

Scale 1:10

3-1/2"

41" wingspan

3-3/4"

1-1/2°

1-3/8"

4-9/16"

4 3/4"

15-3/4" dia. x 18-1/8" pitch propeller

Wing section, scale 1:2

Fig. 10-2. Modern Competition Rubber Model

be utilized to keep the rubber tight enough, when it is almost run down, so it won't shift position in the fuselage and change over-all balance.

Rubber length has a direct effect on flight duration. Small craft like baby ROG's and little fuselage or cabin machines which do not have tensioning devices can be given only slight slack in the rubber. Slack is the surplus length of the rubber, as measured between the shaft hook and the rear rubber support. When tensioning devices are employed, it is common to use rubber mo ors that are roughly double the required length. The tensioning prevents the motor from unwinding completely, so it remains taut between hooks at all times. The extra length allows many more motor turns. When the rubber is stretched out and wound with a winder, at least triple the normal number of turns may be put in without breakage. The baby ROG or stick types can have their rubber detached from the rear hook for stretch-winding. Make a small S-hook which passes through the rubber loops and engages the tail hook which is built into the plane. In the cabin-type fuselage, a hardwood dowel is inserted through the rear of the fuselage. This dowel can be pulled out when it is necessary to replace rubber motors. When a freewheeling or a folding prop is used, the shaft is bent to form a winding loop in front of the prop. To wind the plane, one person serves as anchor while the other pulls out the prop and nose block assembly from the front. The winding hook goes through the loop on the prop hub.

The experienced modeler knows that the thrust line must not change from flight to flight; otherwise the flight pattern will vary, perhaps disastrously. He keys, or marks, the nose block so it will always be inserted the same way. On small models the block is simply made a snug fit in the fuselage nose, so it will not fall loose as the rubber unwinds. On larger planes it may be preferable to use stronger fastening for the same reason. However, if the propeller shaft has a tensioner arrangement, the unwound motor will always stay tight enough to prevent the block from dropping loose.

The shaft bearing should be of metal to prevent wear, though on small models a tiny plate of thin plywood may do well enough. Nose blocks of large rubber planes are often built up of many crossed plies of hard balsa, shaped to the desired over-all contours.

Too many builders take care of the front end properly and pay scant attention to the rear rubber anchor. The accepted method is to insert a piece of birch dowel crosswise through the fuselage. Sheet balsa of the same thickness as the longerons is cemented between the crosspieces on the sides of the fuselage, between which the dowel will extend. On small planes of less than 24-inch span, ⅛-inch dowel is suitable. Use 3/16-inch for up to 36-inch span and ¼-inch dowel for larger machines. Two large but light fiber or aluminum washers are cemented to the inside of this sheet-balsa fill-in—the holes are the same size as the diameter of the dowel—to help anchor the dowel and to prevent it from crushing the fill-in. Grain of the fill-in is fore and aft, not up and down. The dowel should fit snugly enough not to slide out, but loosely enough for it to be removed without much pressure. To assist the helper holding the plane for stretch-winding, the dowel is allowed to extent out from either side of the plane at least ½ inch on a big model. On larger contest planes, dural metal tubing is sometimes used. When it comes time to wind the plane, the helper simply slips a stiff metal rod through the tubing and then is able to retain a firm hold.

As rubber begins to wear, it will stretch and become longer. To prevent rubber loops from sliding off hooks for this cause, the loops may be slipped over a rod held in a vice or any other handy projection. Grasp the rubber close to this rod or peg and stretch it out a few inches. Have someone wrap a thin piece of rubber around the rubber motor at this point and tie it tightly. A small loop will result in the end of the motor when you let it snap back to normal length. Such a loop makes it easy to slide the rear rubber dowel in and out of the motor.

As explained in chapter 6, a rubber-tensioning arrangement is a necessity in large rubber models, due to the relatively heavy motors used. Be sure your tensioner works smoothly and reliably. There are quite a few other ways to link the shaft to the propeller; that depicted in figure 6–3 is just one that has worked well. The main thing is to be certain the shaft moves forward under spring pressure when the motor is nearly unwound, so the projecting end of the shaft at the forward edge of the rubber hook will properly engage its stop pin, or screw, as shown in the sketch.

Some fliers feel the rubber itself must be "tensioned" before it is installed. Others claim this uses up valuable turns that could be turning the propeller and therefore is not worth while. Probably the best way to prove or disprove this is to try it on your own model. One method is to loop the end of the rubber motor over a doorknob, then stretch the motor out for 8 or 10 feet. The strands are then divided into three portions. If you have twelve strands, for instance, there will be four in each group. Approximately 35 winder turns are wound into each group of strands separately. As the winder is passed from one group to the next, a wood peg or perhaps a clothespin is inserted through the winder end of each group. A helper then holds that finished group at the same stretched-out point. After all groups are partially wound in this manner, they are braided together into one motor. This is done by means of the pegs or clothespins, which give a convenient grip. A helper can use his fingers to slide the braids along evenly as they are made. After the entire motor is braided, it is allowed to return to its original length. When installed in the plane, it will take a few more turns for sufficient tensioning.

Though we've saved it till last, probably the most important factor in rubber model-plane flying of any size is care of the rubber itself. Proper handling and storing are most important. Competition rubber fliers expend more care on their motors than do most owners of glow engines. It should be understood that model-plane rubber is far from uniform, even with the advanced manufacturing knowledge of today. One reason may be that the rubber we use is such an infinitesimal portion of total rubber usage that not much time is expended in perfecting it; instead we modelers seem to get the dregs.

First, rubber should *always* be lubricated before use. This will allow more turns to be packed in and will help prevent the strands from chafing and eventually breaking. The simplest lubricant is plain castor oil. This is used by some competition fliers, while others prefer various combinations of soft soap and glycerine thinned with water. Equal parts of soap and glycerine, thinned with about twice the weight of water, will do as a start. In either case, the lube must be well rubbed into the rubber strands; that is, you must make sure each individual strand is coated. All excess must be wiped off, or it will foul the inside of the fuselage as the motor unwinds. The castor oil will last quite a while, but the soap-glycerine mixture tends to dry out as the water evaporates.

Many competition fliers wash their rubber motors after each flying session. This takes off the lube, of course, but it also removes any tiny pieces of grit that can cause nicks in the rubber. After washing and drying, the rubber is well dusted with talcum powder and stored in a cool, dry spot. The experts often will store each motor individually in a jar with a tight screw top. The motors must be relubricated when they are again to be used, of course. Most sport fliers won't care to go to all this trouble; but at least they should use castor-oil lube and keep the rubber out of the sun and dirt.

Rubber must always be stretched when it is wound, for this will allow safe storage of many more turns. For sport planes, stretch two or three times the original length; start decreasing the length as you reach about two-thirds maximum turns, and continue to decrease until the rubber is of normal length for the plane when winding is complete. Stretch-winding can allow many more safe turns to be packed into the rubber motor of *any* rubber-drive model, be it the little Baby ROG or the big contest Wakefield plane. How many extra turns depends on many factors—the kind of rubber, how old it is, the sort of lube, and so on—but 25 per cent increase is probably a good figure, and this allows a very worth-while increase in flight duration.

It is difficult to specify just how many turns may be put into a rubber motor. Again, conditions vary widely; among other factors are those noted above and, of course, the number of strands, rubber cross section, length, and so on. Brand-new rubber usually won't take as many turns without breaking as will that which is "worked in"; again, the experts carefully precondition their motors before competition use. An experienced modeler can tell pretty well when winding how near he can come to maximum winds without breakage. This is something you must learn from long experience. To aid the less expert rubber flier, we include two tables of safe turns you can apply to various motors, both with brown rubber (which is not often found nowadays and originates from the U.S.A.) and with the black Pirelli rubber. The latter is used almost exclusively by the experts, who feel it gives better results in competition flying. It is available from only a few sources in the country, generally those catering to the free-flight rubber experts. However, since it is considered "the best" by those who really know, we feel it worth while to include the information here. (Almost every contest flyer uses Pirelli rubber. It is bought in bulk, about a kilogram at a time, and strips are selected for use.)

You can determine directly from the first table how many turns you can put into any brown-rubber motor of reasonable length and number of turns and of the three most popular rubber sizes. Note that the turns specified are for rubber that is stretched and lubricated. The chart for Pirelli black rubber is for one size only: 6 mm by 1 mm. This imported Italian rubber is roughly ¼-inch wide. The motor length in this table is the length when the rubber is new; Pirelli stretches about 10 per cent after it has been wound a considerable number of times. The number of turns specified is quite conservative, since some of the top rubber fliers use 7 to 8 per cent more turns for a given motor than we show. However, this table is a good guide for the average sport flier. Needless to say, the table assumes the proper lubrication of the rubber (in this case by castor oil) and the proper stretch-winding.

As we have pointed out, rubber varies quite widely from batch to batch, even from the same factory. Therefore, flying experts make tests to check each batch they buy to get an idea of how it compares with earlier lots. A good batch is just as important to these fliers as is the occasional "hot" glow engine which is considerably better than countless others of exactly the same type and make.

Rubber Models

MAXIMUM SAFE TURNS—$\frac{1}{8}'' \times \frac{1}{30}''$ BROWN RUBBER

STR	TURNS/IN.	20″	22″	24″	26″	28″	30″	32″	34″	36″
2	115	2300	2530	2760	2990	3220	3450	3680	3910	4140
4	80	1600	1760	1920	2080	2240	2400	2560	2720	2880
6	64	1280	1408	1536	1664	1792	1920	2048	2176	2304
8	55	1100	1210	1320	1430	1540	1650	1760	1870	1980
10	50	1000	1100	1200	1300	1400	1500	1600	1700	1800
12	44	880	968	1056	1144	1232	1320	1408	1496	1584
14	40	800	880	960	1040	1120	1200	1280	1360	1440
16	36	720	792	764	836	908	980	1052	1124	1196
18	34	680	748	816	884	952	1020	1088	1156	1224
20	32	640	704	768	832	896	960	1024	1088	1152
22	30	600	660	720	780	840	900	960	1020	1080
24	27	540	594	648	702	756	810	864	918	972

MAXIMUM SAFE TURNS—$\frac{1}{4}'' \times \frac{1}{30}''$ BROWN RUBBER

STR	TURNS/IN.	20″	22″	24″	26″	28″	30″	32″	34″	36″
2	80	1600	1760	1920	2080	2240	2400	2560	2720	2880
4	56	1120	1232	1344	1456	1568	1680	1792	1904	2016
6	44	880	968	1056	1144	1232	1320	1408	1496	1584
8	37	740	814	888	962	1036	1110	1184	1258	1332
10	33	660	726	792	858	924	990	1056	1122	1188
12	29	580	638	696	754	812	870	928	986	1044
14	27	540	594	648	702	756	810	864	918	972
16	25	500	550	600	650	700	750	800	850	900
18	23	460	506	552	598	644	690	738	782	828
20	21	420	462	504	546	588	630	672	714	756

MAXIMUM SAFE TURNS—$\frac{3}{16}'' \times \frac{1}{30}''$ BROWN RUBBER

STR	TURNS/IN.	20″	22″	24″	26″	28″	30″	32″	34″	36″
2	94	1880	2068	2256	2444	2632	2820	3008	3196	3384
4	60	1200	1320	1440	1560	1680	1800	1920	2040	2160
6	54	1080	1188	1296	1404	1512	1620	1728	1836	1944
8	46	920	1012	1104	1196	1288	1380	1472	1564	1656
10	42	840	924	1008	1092	1176	1260	1344	1428	1512

STR	TURNS/IN.	20″	22″	24″	26″	28″	30″	32″	34″	36″
12	38	760	836	912	988	1064	1140	1216	1232	1308
14	35	700	770	840	910	980	1050	1120	1190	1260
16	32	640	704	768	832	896	960	1024	1088	1152
18	28	560	616	672	728	784	840	896	952	1008
20	25	500	550	600	650	700	750	800	850	900

To determine maximum turns of any motor, carry horizontal line to right from number of strands until it intersects a vertical line representing the motor length; e.g., 12 strands of $\frac{1}{4}''$ flat, 30″ long, have 870 turns maximum under ideal conditions. On very hot or cold days, turns will be cut down appreciably.

The maximum safe turns given are for motors that are stretched while winding. For hand-wound motors, deduct 20 to 30%.

Turns Table for Pirelli Black Rubber (6 mm)

Length (inches)	Number of Strands							
	4	6	8	10	12	14	16	18
12	458	377	326	291	267	246	230	218
13	497	408	353	314	289	266	249	236
14	535	439	380	338	312	287	268	254
15	573	471	408	363	334	307	288	273
16	611	502	435	387	356	328	307	291
17	649	533	462	411	379	348	326	309
18	687	565	489	435	401	369	345	327
19	725	596	516	459	423	389	364	345
20	764	628	544	484	446	410	384	364
21	802	659	571	508	468	430	402	382
22	840	690	598	532	496	451	422	400
23	878	722	625	556	512	471	441	418
24	916	753	652	580	535	492	460	436
25	955	785	680	605	557	512	480	455
26	993	816	707	629	579	533	499	473
27	1031	847	734	652	602	553	518	491
28	1069	879	761	677	624	574	537	509
29	1107	910	788	701	646	594	556	527
30	1146	942	816	726	669	615	576	546
Turns per Inch	38.2	31.4	27.2	24.2	22.3	20.5	19.2	18.2

Data from Frank Zaic and Charles Sotich.

11

CONTROL-LINE MODELS

The term "control-line model" means a plane attached by means of steel wires to a small handle, usually U-shaped, which is held in the flier's hand. Small planes may use fish-line or dacron control cords, rather than the heavier steel wires. Many of the plastic ready-to-fly planes are so equipped. The model is captive in that it is limited to flying a circle around the pilot. Movements of the control handle are transmitted through a bellcrank arrangement inside the plane to its elevators. When the handle is tilted back, the elevators move up; when tilted forward, the elevators move down. In this way, the plane can be caused to take off, fly inverted, perform loops and other intricate maneuvers, and then land. Probably the simplest method for flying a captive airplane is to attach a single line to it which is connected to a pylon or pole on the ground. When the plane is released, it flies a steady circular path. The drawback to this arrangement is that the pilot can exercise no control over the plane. The idea applies best to very small Half-A powered models which, in this case, frequently are of all-balsa construction with a profile-type fuselage and sheet-balsa wings and tail. For them, light fish line or .008 or .010 wire is suitable. It is essential that this type of round-the-pylon model be balanced or trimmed very much nose-heavy, even if the CG falls well in front of the wing. An eye-

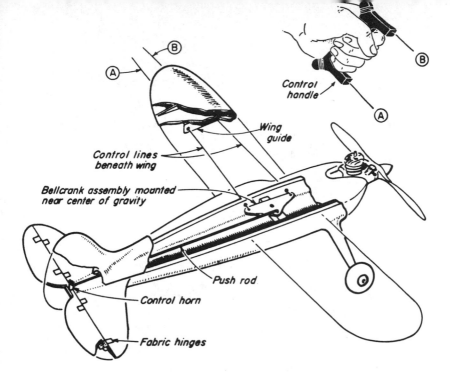

Control
handle

Wing
guide

Control lines
beneath wing

Bellcrank assembly mounted
near center of gravity

Push rod

Control horn

Fabric hinges

Fig. 11-1. Control-Line Model

let is screwed into the side of the fuselage at the CG position, and the line is fastened to the eyelet. A piece of wood, wire, or any other material that will serve as a guide, just forward from the leading edge of the wing (on the side of the plane to which the line is attached), holds the control line in its proper position. The line may also be attached to the end of a fish pole held by the flier; in this case, by moving the tip of the pole up and down considerable variation of flight path may be achieved. Real stunt flying does not come, however, until you use a movable elevator, and with the proper plane this will allow advanced stunting.

Control-line planes come in many types and sizes. For the beginner there is the primary trainer, usually an all-balsa profile creation of extreme stability, strength, and simplicity. As a rule, the trainer is able to perform nothing more violent than a wingover or simple loop. Profile means that the fuselage is a very thick sheet of balsa on edge. Most of the plastic ready-to-fly planes are copied after real plane configurations. Such models are packaged with engine in place and include control handle, control cords, and so forth.

After the trainer comes the stunt model. Here, more wing area is included and construction is much lighter. In many cases, the entire airplane, excepting the tail surfaces, is of built-up construction. Greater

129

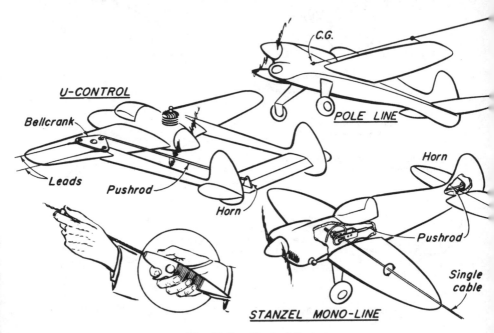

Fig. 11-2. Control Systems

power, lighter weight, more area, and more violent control-surface movement insure top maneuverability. In many cases, profile-fuselage construction is combined with a built-up wing covered with paper, silk, or nylon. Many advanced stunt airplanes have wing flaps, which are hinged surfaces attached to the trailing edge of the wing. These flaps are connected to the control-moving linkage in such manner that the flaps tilt up when the elevators tilt down, and vice versa. When the flaps tilt down, they tend to increase the lift of the wing, helpful when the plane performs an abrupt change in direction. It matters little whether the stunt model is upright or inverted in flight. The wing has a symmetrical section; in other words, the curvature is exactly the same on the top as on the bottom. In order to lift, such a wing must fly at a slight positive angle of attack, but since both sides are the same, the plane will fly inverted just as well as upright. While the trainer generally has a rather long fuselage to insure steady flight, the stunter is shorter, so that it will maneuver abruptly. Such planes are thus sensitive on the control; they react very rapidly and positively.

Combat planes are highly maneuverable, very fast stunt ships, refined to the ultimate in simple, speedy construction and light weight. The combat model must turn on a dime and must be considered expendable because of the frequent collisions during heat of competition. Briefly, two, sometimes more, planes are flown simultaneously against

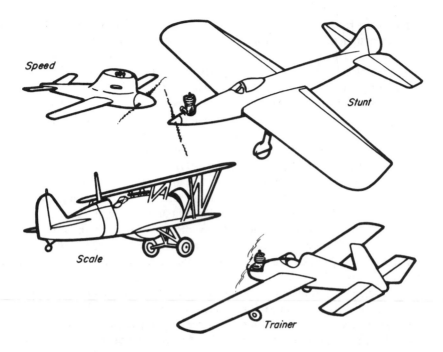

Fig. 11-3. Relative Sizes of Various Control-Line Types

each other. Each trails a crepe-paper streamer. The object is to cut or remove the enemy's streamer while protecting one's own streamer. Points are given for the number of attacking passes, the amount of streamer removed, and so on. Loss of the streamer amounts to a "kill." Most combat planes have little or no fuselage, with lightly built, paper-covered wings. To save weight, landing gears are usually dispensed with. The models have to be launched by hand.

The most exquisite miniature scale planes imaginable can be built and flown by the U-control method. Some of these planes take many months to build and duplicate an infinite amount of detail found on the real craft, such as rockets, lights, retractable landing gears, working wing flaps, instrument panels, seats, seat belts, make-believe controls, and accurately scaled engines and paint schemes. In most cases, the scale plane has very limited performance, being capable of straight and level flight, wingovers, and at most a mild loop. However, skillful fliers with large, lightly built, powerful scale planes have been able to put these fine craft through all the maneuvers called for in the stunt-flight pattern.

The team racer was developed in California and was intended to be flown in actual races with two, three, four, or more fliers in the center of the circle. Such planes were required to have cockpits, minimum wing area of 125 square inches, engines from .140 to .300 cubic inch, and a fuel tank of only one fluid ounce capacity. Races had enough laps for at least one refueling stop to be required, and possibly more. A very experienced "pit man" was needed to refuel the plane, restart the engine, and launch the plane in the absolute minimum of time. For a while this event was quite popular at larger meets, but it has lost favor in recent years. However, team racing is a popular international event, and is regularly flown at S.M.A.E. contests. So too is the team race class for smaller motors of 2.5 cubic centimetres known as Class ½A. Although contests have tended to be dominated by a few especially proficient teams there still remains a very fair chance for the careful newcomer. One essential is a need for a good engine and much patience in determining its most efficient operation.

Rat racing is a somewhat simplified form of team racing, featuring several planes flying at once for a large number of laps. No scalelike features are required, nor is there any beauty judging, so rat racers are generally rather austere and are easier for the nonexpert modeler to construct. The races are run in various heats, with 35 laps, 70 laps (one refueling stop), and 140 laps (two refueling stops). Engines range up to .40 cubic inch. As in team racing, rats must ROG, but they are not limited in fuel-tank size. Rules and restrictions in general are kept to a minimum so that modelers who have felt the very sophisticated team-race rules and planes are beyond them will be encouraged to try rat racing instead.

An interesting variation of the scale model is the carrier job. These planes are created for participation in the Navy carrier event in which a scaled-down carrier flight deck (curved, of course) is placed in the circle. The model must take off from the deck, then perform both fast and slow-speed runs, and attempt a deck landing. Sandbags and stop cords are stretched across the deck as on a real carrier. The plane has a tail hook which is retractable. Since it is important to be able to vary power in flight in order to make slow- and high-speed runs, carrier planes are equipped with two-speed engines. Control of engine speed is attained by equipping the engines with throttles similar to those widely used in radio control. The throttles are operated by means of a third control line (see figure 11–12). In some planes, electrical signals are sent over the normal two control lines (which in this case are insulated), and a light servo in the plane moves the throttle.

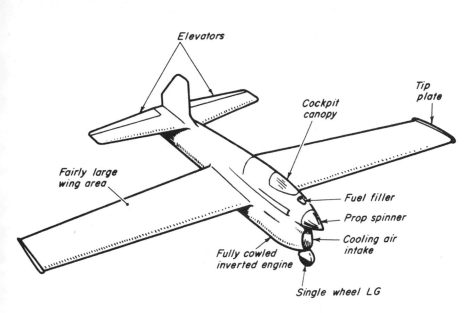

Fig. 11-4. Representative Team Racer

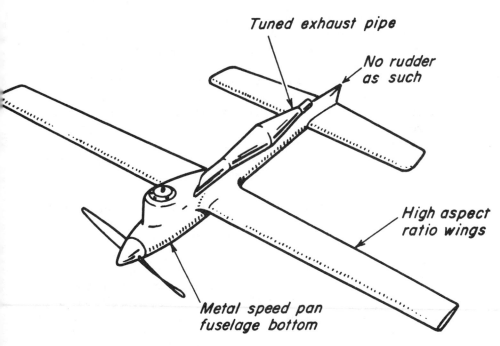

Fig. 11-5. Speed Model Proportions

Probably the most advanced of all U-control types is the speed model. Competition is divided into four classes: Class Half-A, up to .05-cubic-inch displacement; Class A, .051 to .1525; Class B, .1526 to .300; Class C, .301 to .650. These hornets are extremely small in all classes. They are very heavily built in order to stand the engine vibration and the wear and tear of skid landings on concrete runways. No landing gears are employed. Take-off is from a dolly, usually a wire cradle having three or four wheels. (Classes Half-A and A usually are hand-launched due to small size.) When the plane picks up sufficient speed to fly, it lifts from the dolly and is on its own. A speed model is timed over a certain number of laps, which are averaged to show the maximum speed attained. This may be faster than 190 mph (actual) in Class C. High-speed engines are used, as are special hot fuels and small high-pitch props.

Construction includes hardwood (sometimes metal is used), balsa, and plywood. The fuselage consists of two shells, an upper and a lower. The engine, tank, and usually the control system are mounted inside the bottom shell. The top shell lifts off for easy access to the interior. The bottom shell may be of hardwood or metal, the top shell hardwood or balsa. Cast-magnesium bottoms are on the market. These afford better engine mounting and cooling, hence higher rpm and greater speeds. They also stand up better under the battering of high-speed landings. Wings are either shaped from solid wood, like pine, or made up of a single sturdy spar wrapped with thin aluminum sheeting to form a top and a bottom surface. This metal sheeting is flush-riveted along the trailing edge. Tail surfaces are usually plywood, although metal can be used. Speed engines usually are started by means of an electric motor starter operated from an old car battery.

We can't say just who was the "inventor" of control-line flying, but certainly the late Jim Walker of Portland, Oregon, did the most to publicize this form of flying by putting on exhibitions in every part of the country. Walker had developed a method of controlling the elevator of a model plane by means of two wires fastened to a small U-shaped handle which the operator held in his hand. His experiments culminated in a patent on this control system.

The heart of the Walker invention control system is the bellcrank which is securely mounted inside the fuselage or on the wing close to the fuselage. The bellcrank is pivoted at the center; small holes at the ends of the two long arms provide for the attachment of the leadouts, which are music-wire pieces running through the wing, over it, or under it, depending on the configuration of the plane. The other end of each

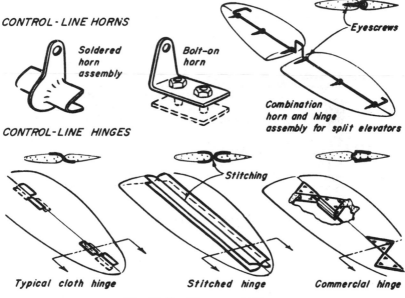

Fig. 11-6.   Bellcrank and Linkage

CONTROL SYSTEM PROPORTIONS		
	Size	For more rapid response
A	2-1/2"	decrease
B	1/4"	increase
C	1/2"	decrease

CONTROL - LINE HORNS

Soldered horn assembly

Bolt-on horn

Eyescrews

Combination horn and hinge assembly for split elevators

CONTROL-LINE HINGES

Stitching

Typical cloth hinge   Stitched hinge   Commercial hinge

Fig. 11-7.   Horns and Hinges

leadout terminates in a loop to which the actual control lines are attached. A heavy music-wire pushrod extends back from the bellcrank to the control horn affixed to the elevator or elevator spar.

Extremely simple in principle, the control system must be properly installed for safe, reliable flying. The first requirement is to suit the strength of the system and the size of its components to the size, weight, and speed of the aircraft. A Half-A sport-flying plane may be flown on dacron lines or other sturdy lines like lightweight fish line or thin music wire. Wire should be .008 to .010 in diameter. Flexible wire is advisable for these small craft. The line may attach directly to the bellcrank (only in small models) or to music-wire leadouts running from the bellcrank to a point outside the guide plate near the wing tip. These leadouts can be of some such diameter as .022, .024, and so on. The pushrod can be of $\frac{3}{64}$ or even $\frac{1}{16}$ music wire. The bellcrank may be made of thin plywood or aluminum or may be bought finished from a hobby shop. The horn may be purchased or made from thin music wire with a loop, through which the bent-over end of the pushrod is inserted.

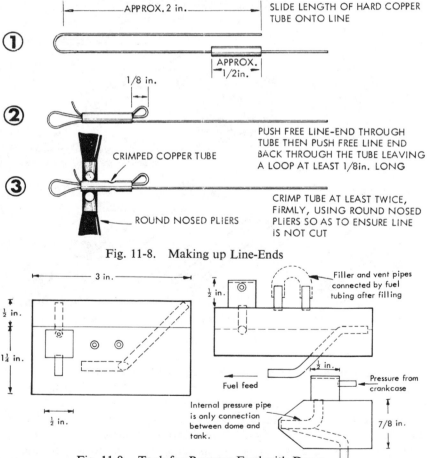

Fig. 11-8.   Making up Line-Ends

Fig. 11-9.   Tank for Pressure Feed with Dome

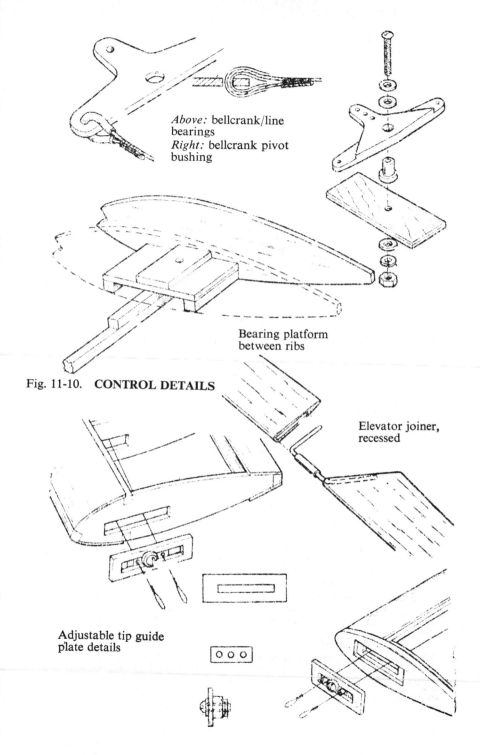

Above: bellcrank/line bearings
Right: bellcrank pivot bushing

Bearing platform between ribs

Fig. 11-10. **CONTROL DETAILS**

Elevator joiner, recessed

Adjustable tip guide plate details

Control-Line Models

In larger models, it is imperative to use sturdy control components firmly installed in the plane. The lines have to be thick enough to transmit torque and to withstand tension. Planes entered in actual competition must be submitted to pull tests before they are allowed to fly. The pull test is performed by having one man hold or anchor the model while the other holds the handle and pulls heavily on the end of the lines. A scale is attached between the lines and the handle. A certain number of pounds of pull is specified as the minimum that guarantees safety for each size of plane. These tests insure that the control system is strongly installed within the structure and cannot break loose and that no wires or joints will fail under stress of high-speed flight. The test for the larger-size control liner calls for as much as 32 times the weight of the model, which indicates how strong you should make your airplane. Line diameters and line lengths are shown in the accompanying table.

Speed Model Specifications F.A.I. INTERNATIONAL

(a) Maximum cylinder capacity of motor 2.5 c.c. (.1526 cu. in.)
(b) Total minimum area 2 sq. dm. per c.c. (508 sq. in. per cu. in.)
(c) Maximum wing loading per unit of area 100 gr. per sq. dm. (32.8 oz. per sq. ft.)
(d) Minimum control line diameter two line system only 0.4 mm.
(e) A control handle with rotating lugs, radius not exceeding 4 cm. will be used.
(g) A standard fuel of either 20/80 or 25/75 oil/alcohol to be used without additions.
(h) Line length 15.92 metres (52 ft. 2¾ in.).
(i) Course is 1 km. (10 laps).
(j) Pull test to be equal to 15 kg.

S.M.A.E.

Class I	up to 0.9 c.c.
Class II	0.91 to 1.50 c.c.
Class III	1.51 to 2.50 c.c.
Class IV	up to 2.50 c.c. (F.A.I. Class)
Class V	2.51 to 5.00 c.c.
Class VI	5.01 to 7.00 c.c.
Class VII	7.01 to 10.00 c.c.
Class VIIN	Novice class using 0.40 cu. in.

Distance to be flown. The distance to be flown must be a minimum of 1 km., the minimum radius of each circle being: Class I: 13.25 m, 12 laps per 1 km.; Class II: 47 ft. 5¾ in., 11 laps per 1 km.; Class III: 52 ft. 2¾ in., 10 laps; Class IV: as F.A.I. International; Class V: 58 ft. ½ in., 9 laps; and VI: 19.90 metres (65.29 ft.), 8 laps per 1 km; Class VII: 19.90 m. (65.29 ft.), 8 laps per 1 km.

Team Racer Specifications

N.B. All S.M.A.E. classes must have model weight marked on inboard wing tip in 20-mm numerals and letters in grams. Class B and Goodyear must have effective fuel stop devices. S.M.A.E. CLASS ½A

(a) Maximum engine capacity 1.5 c.c.
(b) Minimum projected wing area 6 cm.² (93 sq. in.)
(c) Maximum fuel capacity 6 c.c.
(d) Minimum width of fuselage at cockpit shall be 40 mm.

(*e*) Minimum depth of fuselage from top of cabin to bottom of fuselage or in the case of an open cockpit model, from the top of the pilot's head to the bottom of the fuselage, shall be 75 mm. Engine cowling immediately adjacent to the engine shall not be included in fuselage depth.

(*f*) Minimum landing wheel diameter shall be 25 mm.

(*g*) Distance between centre of control handle and centre line of model in flight shall be 14 m. (45 ft. 11¼ ins.), minimum wire diameter 0.25 mm (0.010 in.).

(*h*) Pull test is 20 × model weight.

S.M.A.E. CLASS B

(*a*) Engine capacity 2.51 c.c. to 5 c.c.

(*b*) Minimum projected wing area 9 dm.^{2} (140 sq. in.).

(*c*) Maximum fuel capacity 30 c.c.

(*d*) Minimum width of fuselage at cockpit shall be 50 mm.

(*e*) Minimum depth of fuselage from top of cabin to bottom of fuselage or in the case of an open cockpit, from the top of the pilot's head to bottom of fuselage, shall be 100 mm.
Engine cowling immediately adjacent to the engine shall not be included in fuselage depth.

(*f*) Minimum landing wheel diameter shall be 25 mm.

(*g*) Distance between centre of control handle and centre line of model shall be 17.69 m (90 laps. equal 10 km.) (180-lap final). Minimum wire diameter 0.4 mm.

(*h*) Engines must be silenced to a level not exceeding 82 db at a distance of 7 m.

(*i*) Pull test is 30 × model weight.

F.A.I. INTERNATIONAL CLASS

(*a*) Maximum engine capacity 2.5 c.c. (.1526 cu. in.).

(*b*) Minimum projected surface area (wings and tail) 12 dm.^{2} (186 sq. in.).

(*c*) Maximum fuel capacity 7 c.c. Only one tank permitted.

(*d*) Minimum width of fuselage at cockpit shall be 50 mm.

(*e*) Minimum height of fuselage at cockpit shall be 100 mm.

(*f*) Distance between centre of control handle and centre line of model shall be 15.92 m. (10 laps equals 1 km.).

(*g*) Maximum weight of model 700 gm.

(*h*) Minimum cross-section of fuselage 39 sq. cm.

(*i*) Line thickness shall be not less than 0.3 mm. Mono line is not permitted. (100 laps for heats, 200 laps for finals.)

(*j*) Minimum pilot head dimensions: height 20 mm.; length 14 mm.; width 14 mm.

(*k*) Minimum wheel diameter: 25 mm.

Other S.M.A.E. Racing Classes

GOODYEAR CLASS

(*a*) Maximum engine capacity: 2.5 c.c. (diesel only).

(*b*) Models shall be models of Goodyear racing planes that have flown in Goodyear or Continental Trophy races or other N.P.R.P.A. formula 1 races.

(*c*) Model profiles shall be within 5% of scale linear dimensions. The scale being ⅛ except where noted below. (Note: to help scaling up plans—all full-size aircraft are required to have a minimum wing area of 66 sq. ft. Therefore all models must have a minimum wing area of 9.6 sq. decimetres (148.5 sq. ins).

(*d*) Tail area may be increased by 25% over scale area to permit safe handling, either by increasing the mean chord and span equally, or, provided that the appearance of the model is not drastically altered, by increasing the span alone.

(e) Models shall be painted in a scale-like fashion, ie. in a colour scheme that might have been used on the full-size aircraft.

(f) The racing number of the full-size aircraft shall be displayed in similar positions on the model.

(g) The entrant's S.M.A.E. number shall be displayed in a similar position to the licence number on the full-size aircraft.

(h) Models shall have profile fuselages with a maximum width of 26 mm, excluding cheek cowls, and motors shall be uncowled. Fuselage side cheeks shall be permitted in so much as they do not cowl the motor. All motors must be side-mounted.

(i) Mono wheel undercarriages are permitted. The undercarriage need not be affixed to the model in the same place as the full-size aircraft. The undercarriage leg(s) shall emerge from the fuselage profile at approximately the same position as the full-size aircraft.

(j) The entrant, if so requested, shall produce a three-view drawing to substantiate the scale outline of his model. The drawings shall be from a source acceptable to the contest director.

(k) Distance between the centre of the control handle grip and the centre line of the model shall be 15.92 metres (52 ft. 3 ins).

(l) Minimum line diameter: 0.3 mm (0.0118 ins). Monoline is not permitted.

(m) Pull test is 20 × model weight.

(n) Restraining strap connecting engine to bellcrank pivot of at least 7 strands mandatory.

RAT RACE CLASS

(a) Maximum engine capacity: 3.5 c.c. (0.21 cu. ins).

(b) Line length from the grip of the control handle to the centre of the model shall be 17.69 metres.

(c) Minimum line diameter: 0.4 mm (0.0148 ins), or cable of equivalent cross sectional area. Monoline is not permitted.

(d) No restrictions are placed on the wing area, fuselage cross-section or fuel tank capacity.

(e) Models must fly in an anti-clockwise direction.

(f) Models shall pass a general safety inspection prior to each race or heat.

(g) A team shall consist of a pilot and a maximum of two mechanics.

From the wire sizes above, the sport flier can easily figure out what sizes he should use, taking into account model speed, line length, and plane weight. Better to err a bit on the safe side; your model might not fly quite so fast, but it will fly safely!

On the bigger, more powerful machines, the builders usually insert bushings through the holes in bellcranks where wires will attach and through the looped ends of the leadouts, in order to minimize cutting effects of the part on the wire during long service.

The length of line used depends on the size of the plane and size of the flying site. Too long lines on too small or underpowered a plane will result in inadequate control and the model's coming in on the lines, especially in a wind. Too short a set of lines on too fast and powerful a plane will make it hard to fly and almost impossible to stunt, for it will circle the flier too quickly. For sport flying, therefore, common sense dictates the line length. As a rule, Half-A models are flown on

35-foot lines if they are light and fast; otherwise, shorter lines must be tried until the plane seems to perform satisfactorily. For general flying of planes equipped with .19's to .29's, but where performance is not on the hot side, 50- to 60-foot lines are about right. Stunting is done on 50- or 60- or even 70-foot lines, the latter if the ship is fast and powerful. As a rule, lines come in lengths of 26, 35, 52, 60, and 70 feet.

Anchor a bellcrank firmly. The pivot bolt should pass through thick plywood or a wood block faced with ply, and the whole unit should be mounted between ribs in the wing center section (for example) so that the entire assembly cannot pull sideways. Support the pushrod at one or more points along its length—more on big models—so that it cannot bend or buckle under load. Very often the pushrod will bow when the flier applies down elevator, which puts the rod under compression instead of tension. Secure the control horn well on the elevator, covering over the cement joint with a piece of nylon tape or cloth cemented in place. On larger planes, control horns should have holes through which small bolts can be inserted to hold the horn rigidly in place.

On all control-line craft larger than Half-A it is advisable to provide some method of preventing control pushrods from pulling out of control horns or from wing-flap horns. A washer should be soldered over the end of the wire after it has passed through the hole in question.

If you design and build your own, consider these requirements (this applies to the kits as well). You will not want abrupt or erratic control responses. Starting with the handle, the lines should not be attached at the widest spacing (many handles have two or more sets of holes to vary the line spacing), as this gives maximum elevator movement. On the bellcrank, the pushrod should be attached at the hole nearest to the pivot. Later, when you become more adept, the pushrod may be inserted through the hole farthest from the pivot.

The end of the control pushrod that attaches to the elevator control horn should be inserted through the hole nearest the outer end of the horn. The nearer to the elevator the pushrod drives the horn, the greater will be the elevator travel and hence its reaction. Elevator area on the trainer generally is somewhat less than 50 per cent of the horizontal tail area. Control area on the speed plane is about one-quarter the total horizontal area. On stunt, it may run as high as two-thirds, with 50 per cent the average.

Reels and handles vary widely in price and quality. An adjustable handle is a nice thing to have. Very often when you attach your lines to the plane for the first time, you will find that the elevator is either slightly up or down when you hold the handle in neutral position. If

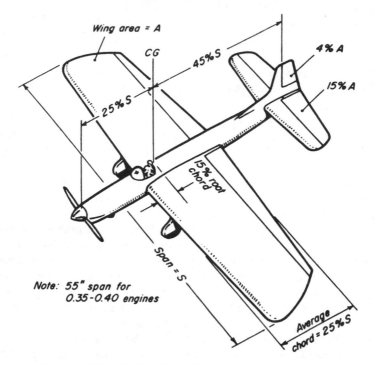

Fig. 11-11. Stunt Model Proportions

you tilt the handle to put the elevators in neutral, the handle must always be held in that position between maneuvers. Adjustable handles
have a clamp screw which can be loosened while an adjustment is made,
then tightened again. Some reels are designed to serve as handles.

As far as the control system is concerned, this leaves the bellcrank,
leadouts, pushrod, control horn, and elevator hinges. Bellcranks come
in a variety of forms. The simplest is a triangular piece of fairly thick
dural metal with holes bored for attachment of the lines and pushrod
and for the pivot. The more expensive ones have pivot bearings. Some
even have the leadouts in place. For small planes, a 2-inch bellcrank
is suitable; for larger sizes, 2½ or 3 inches. Elevator hinges take many
forms. The most popular consists of thin strips of linen or pinking tape
which cement to both stabilizer and elevator. For instance, a cloth
hinge may measure ½ × 1 inch for a large stunt model. Half the
length of this hinge should be thoroughly cemented to the top surface
of the stabilizer, then tucked down between stabilizer and elevator so
that the second half of the strip may be cemented to the bottom surface of the elevator. Another hinge would be placed immediately adjacent to the first hinge, but would be cemented to the top side of the
elevator and the bottom side of the stabilizer. One pair of these hinges
should be attached close to the tip of the stabilizer and elevator and

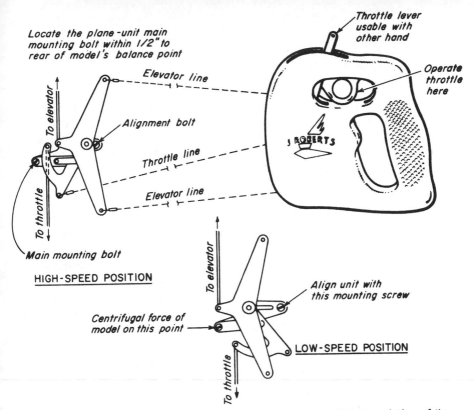

Locate the plane-unit main
mounting bolt within 1/2" to
rear of model's balance point

*Throttle lever
usable with
other hand*

Elevator line

*Operate
throttle
here*

To elevator

Alignment bolt

J ROBERTS

Throttle line

Elevator line

To throttle

Main mounting bolt

HIGH-SPEED POSITION

To elevator

*Align unit with
this mounting screw*

*Centrifugal force of
model on this point*

LOW-SPEED POSITION

To throttle

NOTE: The three-wire flight control system allows any desired variation of the
engine throttle by movement of the trigger in the control handle, but such variation
has no effect on elevator action. Conversely, elevator movement will not shift engine
speed. All three wires always have the same tension; so they may be smaller in diameter
than the two elevator wires normally required.

Fig. 11-12.   Three-Wire Control System

the other closer to the fuselage in the same manner. Two more sets of
hinges should be installed on the other side of the plane. For speed
models and high-powered stunt planes, it is advisable to use some sort
of sturdy metal hinge which is fixed in place with small screws or nuts
and bolts.

To adapt the dimensions given in figure 11–11 to various-size stunters suitable for different classes of engines, use the span of the large
plane in the illustration as the denominator in a fraction and the span
of other sizes as the numerator. If you divide the numerator by the
denominator, this factor will be reduced to a convenient decimal which
can then be multiplied by all the dimensions of the drawing. The plane
in the figure is for engines of .45- to .60-cubic-inch displacement and
has a 52-inch wing span. For .19 to .35, make the span 42 inches; for
.075 and .09, 34 inches; .049 to .065, 24 inches; .035 to .045, 20
inches.

Very few speed-model kits exist. Some concerns do market the metal bottoms or speed pans in sizes to suit different classes. The individual speed builder plans his design around the proper-size pan. Some enthusiasts arrange to have their own pans cast. Any foundry that pours aluminum and magnesium will do the job reasonably, provided you supply the pattern. It should be carved from mahogany or pine, hollowed to have a wall thickness of about $\frac{3}{32}$ inch.

As with every other model-plane field today, there is a bewildering array of accessories on the market; such things as control horns, bellcranks, surface hinges, ready-to-use lines, and so on are available in great variety. Aside from speed planes, you can also get a variety of models in kit form for most engine sizes and most classes.

The accompanying table will enable the reader to adapt a standard-speed tank design (fig. 11–13) to whatever size model he has in mind. Note that the dimensions are given in letter form in both the illustration and the table.

Speed Tank Table

Engine	A	B	C	D	E
.19	2	½	1	½	⅜
.29	3	½	1⅛	¾	⅜
.49	3½	⅝	1¼	1	½
.60	4½	⅝	1¼	1¼	½

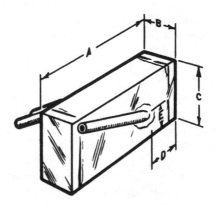

Fig. 11-13. Speed Tank

Some fatal accidents have occurred in the United States and in other countries to modelers who flew their control-line planes too near high-tension wires. A fatality may occur even if neither the model nor its wires touches the high-tension line: the high voltage can jump a considerable distance to the control wires, which are grounded through your body. *Since you have no way of telling how high a voltage may be in wires even on wooden poles, it is best to be suspicious of all such wires.* DO NOT FLY NEAR POWER LINES!

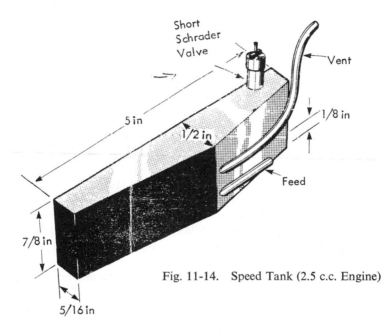

Fig. 11-14.   Speed Tank (2.5 c.c. Engine)

12

CO₂ AND
DUCTED FANS

Increasingly popular among enthusiasts for small models due to its economics and silent operation is the CO_2 engine. The CO_2 to drive the subminiature gas engine is stored in a little aluminium flight capsule, which may be recharged several times from a standard steel Sparklet soda-syphon bulb, which is bought from your chemist in boxes of ten.

The process of charging is very similar to that adopted for refilling a gas cigarette lighter (although of course the gas itself is quite different!). It is interesting to study the behaviour of a liquefied gas in certain clear plastic lighter refill cartridges, since it will make the reasons for many of the following phenomena more easily understood.

With this understanding, a good method of control can be exercised over the number of recharges obtained from each Sparklet bulb and over the duration of the resulting engine runs.

If the flight capsule is charged from a Sparklet bulb held nozzle down, liquid CO_2 flows into the small flight capsule; this we will call a liquid charge. If, on the other hand, the Sparklet bulb is held nozzle up during charging, the flight capsule will receive little or no liquid—only gas, and a much shorter engine run subsequently results. In the following pages we will refer to this as a gas charge. (Fig. 12-1).

Gas connections between flight capsule and engine should be arranged so that no liquid CO$_2$ reaches the engine. The flight capsule connection must therefore be arranged from the highest point, although the engine may be mounted in any position relative to the capsule.

If the flight capsule connection is too low, liquid CO$_2$ will reach the cylinder head valve and this results in the engine slowing right down and little bits of ice being ejected from the exhaust ports! The length of run is also greatly reduced.

Very different results are obtained from the alternative charging methods. In comparing gas and liquid charging patterns it is interesting to observe that whereas in the former the first charge always results in the longest run, in the latter the first one is always considerably shorter than the second run.

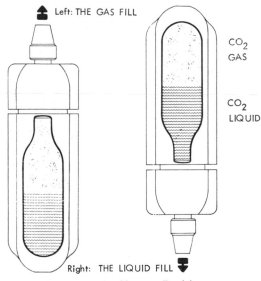

Fig. 12-1.   CO$_2$ Charger Positions

Only three good runs are obtained from a single Sparklet bulb with liquid charges. The fourth run is really too short for anything except test flying, and yet it seems a pity to throw away the bulb when there is still quite a lot of gas in it. The answer is to employ a second bulb, and after charging the flight capsule as though for a fourth flight, top it up from bulb 2. In this way you use less gas from the second bulb, because there is already quite a lot of gas in the flight capsule from bulb 1.

Repeat the procedure for flights 5, 6, 7 and 8, but on 8 replace bulb 1 (now well and truly drained) with a new one and pump in a charge from this one as well. Then carry on with bulbs 2 and 3.

In this way four fairly consistent runs can be achieved from each Sparklet bulb—an efficiency increase of 25 per cent. Careful marking of the bulb is, of course, essential, because the lowest numbered bulb must always be used first to avoid reverse gas flow from the flight capsule to the charging bulb!

Exposed coils of copper gas pipe between engine and capsule assist efficient gas expansion and heat generators which, when used in this section of pipe, enable the engines to be used efficiently in cold weather when the ambient air temperature is too low (below 50°F) to allow adequate gas expansion.

Airframes for these comparatively expensive little engines are so cheap and quick to build that it is essential to have the power plant easily transferable between models.

There are nevertheless occasions when the flight capsule can only be built into the framework in an inaccessible position, and if the gas pipe is then permanently attached to the engine, it becomes impossible to change the engine unless you have some spare cylinder-heads which you can leave attached to the permanently installed gas pipe.

To overcome this problem Doug McHard devised a simple means of attaching and detaching the gas pipe from the cylinder-head requiring no machining, and the details are shown in figures 12-2, 12-3.

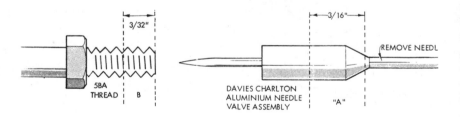

Fig. 12-2. Needle Valve Parts for CO$_2$ Head

If you have some modest workshop facilities an even neater job can be made using a section of brass 6 BA bolt drilled and then soldered over the cylinder-head tube and a 6 BA tapped length thick-wall brass tube with a 6 BA screwed insert in the top end in place of the aluminium needle valve sleeve.

Make sure that the soft PVC washer is a tight fit within the sleeve. It is also important to ensure that the washer faces are cut parallel and

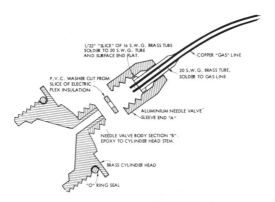

1/32" "SLICE" OF 16 S.W.G. BRASS TUBE
SOLDER TO 20 S.W.G. TUBE
AND SURFACE END FLAT.

COPPER "GAS" LINE

P.V.C. WASHER CUT FROM
SLICE OF ELECTRIC
FLEX INSULATION

20 S.W.G. BRASS TUBE,
SOLDER TO GAS LINE

ALUMINIUM NEEDLE VALVE'
SLEEVE END "A"

NEEDLE VALVE BODY SECTION "B".
EPOXY TO CYLINDER HEAD STEM.

BRASS CYLINDER HEAD

"O" RING SEAL

Fig. 12-3. Detachable Head

flat—use a sharp razor blade. If you can countersink the two faces butting against the washer a more efficient gas seal will result. An incidental but significant advantage of this attachment is that it enables the cylinder to be more easily rotated to adjust the engine revolutions.

One of the most practical propellers for the average flier is the 5½-in. Williams Bros. nylon prop. Wooden props are more efficient, but it must be admitted that their rigidity is likely to bend or even break the thin prop attachment bolt following a turn-over landing.

A scale model DH2 was built by Doug McHard as an example of the type of aeroplane made possible by the CO$_2$ engine, which with rubber power would be impractical and for free flight power would require dead ballast weight to achieve the correct CG. No ballast weight is used in the DH2, which weighed just a fraction over one ounce in flying trim. First time never-miss starting in that cage of booms and wires is also a valuable "plus" and the total absence of fuel mess means that you can really build like a rubber model. The absence of engine scream produces a wonderfully realistic effect in flight.

Doug's Heinkel He 46 (19 in. span) has a flying weight of 22 grammes (about ¾ oz.). The engine is adjusted to turn at about 3,250 revs (upon starting) and this produces a gentle climbing flight which, on a single flight capsule with a liquid charge, gives durations of around 1½ minutes.

This He 46 is an adaptation of the rubber-powered original (plans for which appeared in *Aeromodeller*, April 1970), and one reason why it was originally chosen for rubber power was its relatively long nose, which distributes the rubber weight more efficiently about the CG. No such design limitations exist with a CO$_2$ engine and, in fact, a short nose layout has certain advantages, for it removes the temptation to move the flight capsule to and fro along the fuselage to achieve the correct CG. If the flight capsule, because of a long nose, ends up too far to the rear of the CG, the weight of a liquid charge can seriously upset the power trim. It is always better to locate the flight capsule as near as possible to the centre of gravity. (Figure 12-4 for a typical sport model conversion.)

It would be difficult to find a shorter-nosed subject than the Fokker Dr. 1 Triplane, which is another subject in which Doug installed the Brown Junior CO$_2$ unit. This was originally a rather unsuccessful rubber model which has been made completely practical by the use of CO$_2$ power. Scale is 1/24, which makes the wingspan approximately 11$\frac{1}{2}$ in.

The choice of model for this new engine is wide to the point of being virtually limitless. Types which leap to mind as tempting projects, previously difficult or impossible for rubber power, are the whole range of interesting short fuselage types, the Westland Pterodactyls and a host of flying wing prototypes such as the Waterman Arrowbile, as well as all those early flying machines with lots of frame and very little fabric like the Bleriot Monoplane model, which always looked wrong with a rubber motor showing through the rear fuselage. Mounting is simplicity itself. (Fig. 12-5.)

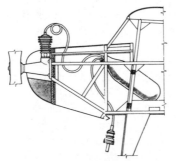

Fig. 12-4. Sport Model CO$_2$ Conversion

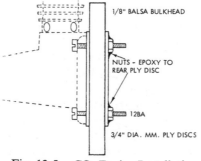

Fig. 12-5. CO$_2$ Engine Installation

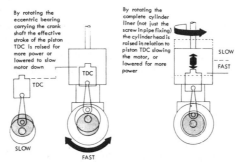

Fig. 12-6. Cylinder/Piston Adjustment Methods

How about the all-twin and multi-engine types which are immediately ideal with a central flight capsule linked to both engines (all four if you are a millionaire)? The CO_2 engine will run quite happily in either direction, so all torque problems can be overcome by counter-rotating props! Alternatively, differential throttle settings will enable torque effects to be fully countered and all engines from a common capsule must stop at the same time. See Figure 12-6 for an explanation of how the two difficult systems of cylinder compression adjustment work, and Figure 12-7 for sections of the units.

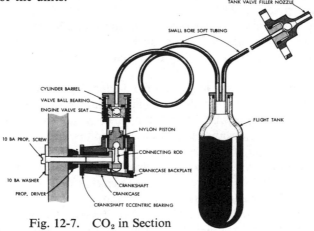

Fig. 12-7. CO_2 in Section

Although there is a marked power surge upon starting the engine, it is nowhere near as acute as with a rubber motor, and the gradual reduction of power as the pressure falls produces a most realistic transition between power flight and glide.

It is worthwhile to experiment with various propeller/throttle combinations for each model. Sometimes it is better to use a large propeller and high throttle setting to achieve a given engine run and in other cases a smaller propeller at medium revs will produce almost exactly similar flight patterns. With a small propeller (down to 3 in.) something like 7,000 r.p.m. can be achieved, but duration of run at these revs is, of course, very short.

Practical Ducted Fans

With the advent of the jet engine and subsequent practical use to which it was put as a power plant for aeroplanes, the piston-engine prop-driven aircraft has become obsolete for fast transport and new shapes and forms fill the ever-decreasing air space of the world.

Thus when we come to model jet engines and jet aeroplanes, the comparative evolution of model aeroplanes with their real counterparts comes to a grinding halt. There have, of course, been such power plants typified by the Dynajet reaction jet, fired with white spirit and producing immense thrust for a short time. They are used on control line models, but by and large they are both over-noisy and over-hot for model use by the average aeromodeller. Jetex solid pellet fuelled rocket motors are ideal for small free-flight models, but certainly not practical for a radio-controlled model.

There is, of course, the possibility of building a miniature jet turbine engine but, again, a high degree of technical know-how would be necessary not only to make it but also to maintain it in operations on the flying fields.

This leaves us with the long-accepted ducted fan method of propulsion.

It is not clear who actually invented the ducted fan system, but there are records of the Coanda ducted fan powered aeroplane built in 1910 and the famous Caproni-Campini CC2 aeroplane in 1941 driven by this method of propulsion. The engine (piston) was amidships, driving a turbine compressor in a duct. The machine flew well at speeds of above 200 mph. Jumbo jets fly with an extreme development of fan-jets and the fabulous Hawker Harrier uses a "cold" fan too.

In the field of model aviation a number of names spring to mind when ducted fan designs are mentioned: Phil Smith, designer of Veron, who produced such well-known kits as the Lavochkin and the Fairey Delta II; another experimenter was Mr Newbold who produced a ducted fan "Vampire" for control-line flying which was successful; in America, Mr Schnitz produced a number of articles on the subject; John Coatsworth, who experimented with amazingly good results on the Centrifugal type of impeller; and last but by no means least, perhaps the most successful of all pioneers, the late P. E. Norman.

P. E. Norman and Phil Smith favoured the axial-mounted fan, which for all practical purposes seems to be the most efficient and most effectively simplest to build and put into operation; and it has been widely adopted throughout the modelling world, entering production in the U.S.A. as the "Scozzi" and "Kress" designs and in Sweden as the "Boss".

It is probably true to say that "P.E." was one of the first aeromodellers to fly a successful DF model, his first machine being a model of the then new Soviet fighter, the Mig 15, the year being 1950 and the place, the Downs near Ashford, Kent.

Then, in the late 1960s and early 1970s, "P.E.'s" son Marcus entered the ducted fan scene using radio control of the latest type and established immediate success. Marcus Norman's achievements with home-constructed DF units were described by him in the *Aeromodeller Annual*. Here are his observations, which over the years have proved to be very practical.

Basic function of the DF unit is to suck in at one end of the duct, increase the velocity at which it is travelling by means of a fan, and then expel the speeded up mass of air through the rear end of the said duct, thus producing an opposing force upon the duct and therefore propelling it forward by means of the "jet stream".

Therefore a DF unit must consist of:

(a) A duct (or pipe) intake.
(b) A fan (or impeller).
(c) A motor of some form to drive the fan.
(d) A duct efflux (rear end hole).

The ducted fan unit relies on the volume of air passing through the duct; rather than compression of that air before expulsion through the efflux. (In a jet engine, compression of air is essential before ignition with the kerosene and subsequent expulsion thrust.) From this it can be at once appreciated that the "ducted fan" is not a jet engine in the sense of the word as we know it.

Marcus's father "P.E." discovered that if the efflux area was decreased too much, the resulting effect was to cause the fan blades to stall and therefore the amount of thrust being delivered was cut quite dramatically. (This is quite effectively illustrated when one puts one's hand over the efflux of a duct, the revs immediately drop.)

Likewise, if the efflux area is large (i.e. the same size as the fan circle area), then the same result is observed, although to a lesser degree. In consequence to these results, therefore, it is obvious that there is some ideal "in-between". "P.E." found that an efflux area of between 75%

and 80% of the fan circle area produces the best results. Slight reduction or enlargement of these sizes is possible nowadays; this is probably due to the greater power that is now available from the newer glow plug engines, but 68-70% would be a minimum, and maximum 88-90% of the fan circle area to maintain the degree of efficiency that is needed for a unit. (Fig. 12-8.)

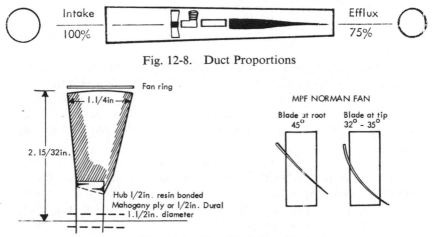

Fig. 12-8.   Duct Proportions

Fig. 12-9.   Fan Blade Detail

The "intake" area should ideally be 88-100% of the fan circle area, and the two most efficient types would appear to be either "Elephant Ear" intakes, as on the Supermarine "Scimitar", "Swift" or "Harrier", and they must still add up to the 88-100% required, or "open" type intakes as on many Russian types, i.e. Mig 15, etc.

The "fan" should be very carefully made and is the most important factor in the DF unit. Size is determined by power plant to be used, and with an ideal number of five blades. (Fig. 12-9.)

The engine used should be of the best power-weight ratio that is obtainable. Ideally .40 cu. ins. capacity.

The efflux area should ideally be 75-80% of the fan circle area. Once again it can take the form of "Elephant Ear" type—this is where the tail block is inserted in the centre of the efflux to take the fin and rudder, etc.—or of the straight through "open" hole type. In the case of the "Elephant Ear" type, the two outlets must add up to the 75-80% of the fan circle area required.

A cone behind the engine and tank in the rear duct probably increases efficiency slightly and helps to straighten out the flow of air passing through it.

The most effective position of the fan is at approximately one-third of the length from the intake end as can be seen in figure 12-12. However, a variation on this can be made with no apparent detrimental effect: the nearer the fan is to the intake the more effective the "sucking" motion; but the length of the rear duct is then greater and so there is possibly added friction between the airstream and the duct walls, and likewise if the fan position is too far back, the "sucking" motion of the fan is reduced and hence less air drawn in until the model is actually moving. It is interesting to note that when in a high-speed dive, the engine of a DF unit does not appear (or rather sound) as if it is over-revving itself, as does a prop-driven aeroplane, even though air is being forced into the intakes at quite high velocity. However, there are other factors to be taken into consideration, the main one (and probably the most important) being the CG position of the finished model.

The CG position will depend on the shape of the wings. With a straight wing the best position for the CG (depending on the camber) is generally considered to be approximately 33% of the chord from the leading edge of the wing, and this still holds good with the DF type of model.

With a delta wing, CG positions vary according to the sweep of the leading edge of the wing.

An average position of the CG on a delta planform would be 58% without reflex on the trailing edge, or 55% with reflex on the trailing edge (reflex = washout).

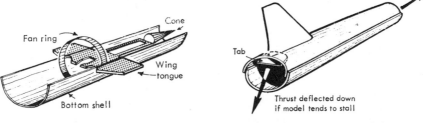

Fig. 12-10. Engine Mounting   Fig. 12-11. Downthrust Tab

An average position for the CG on a swept wing without washout would be 56%, and 54% for a swept wing with washout on the trailing edge. The variation between swept and delta wings is partly due to the "bite" out of the trailing edge of a delta shape thus forming a swept shape. It will be noted that the 60°, 70° and 80° swept wings have CGs in approximately the same positions as their delta counterparts.

The best method of mounting the engine and tank in the duct is to

CO_2 and Ducted Fans

incorporate one engine-cum-wing tongue mount through the duct at right angles and on a horizontal plane and on the Centre Line of the duct (figure 12-10).

The fan itself runs inside a pre-made ring with a clearance of approximately $\frac{1}{32}$" all round. The ring is fixed to the engine mount-cum-wing tongue, and it is upon this structure that the duct "shells" are fixed. Marcus Norman makes his tongue-engine mount from $\frac{1}{4}$" resin bonded ply, and it has always proved a good sturdy method of construction.

An unusual and important trim tab that will be required is the downthrust vane (figure 12-11.)

If too much downthrust is incorporated, the effect of the vane on the model will either dive under power or need a lot of up elevator to make it climb. If, on the other hand, the model has not got enough downthrust it will stall. With this type of model it is a kind of "rushing" stall, and one can tell soon after take-off whether this is due to insufficient downthrust, as it will quite suddenly put the nose up and wallow down in a stalled attitude. One can make an adjustable downthrust vane if so required. With RC models one does have the use of the elevator, but if for instance a lot of "down" is required to fly the model level, then when the engine cuts and it is in glide, a lot of alteration of trim will be necessary so a fixed vane is useful.

Type	Fan dia.	Depth duct	Width duct	Total length	Span	Scale wing area	Weight	Max. wing loading
"Scimitar"	4 15/16"	5"	7"	48 1/8"	32"	2.25 sq. ft.	4-4 1/2 lb.	2 lb./sq. ft.
"Gnat"	4 15/16"	5"	6"	56 1/4"	39 3/4"	1.5 sq. ft.	4-4 1/2 lb.	2.25 lb./sq. ft.
"Phantom" Dassault	4 15/16"	5"	7"	66 2/3"	43"	3.3 sq. ft.	4 1/2-5 lb.	1.8 lb./sq. ft.
"Etendard" Dassault	4 15/16"	5"	6 1/4"	48 3/4"	34"	2.5 sq. ft.	3 3/4-4 lb.	1.5 lb./sq. ft.
"Mystere"	4 15/16"	5"	5"	40 1/2"	39"	2.6 sq. ft.	3 3/4-4 lb.	1.5 lb./sq. ft.
Mig 15	4 15/16"	5"	5"	39 3/4"	37"	2 sq. ft.	3 3/4-4 lb.	1.8 lb./sq. ft.
Mig 17	4 15/16"	5"	5"	39 3/4"	36 1/2"	2 sq. ft.	3 3/4-4 lb.	1.8 lb./sq. ft.

This table gives a rough guide to some scale models that have been built. In most cases each type requires increase in wing area intake and efflux sizes. However, out of the types mentioned, the two French types "Etendard" and "Mystere" are nearest to the formulae required. One problem with the "Mystere" is that it has a low wing, but a small amount of cheating could put the wing (still using the tongue and box method) in a low mid-wing position.

The basic idea is not to be ambitious at first, and anyone wanting to build a DF model should not attempt to make a scale model his first project. Figure 12-12 illustrates a typical "straight-wing" design.

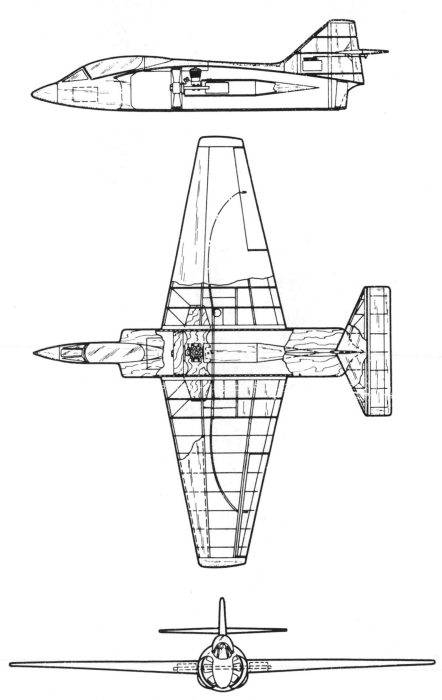

Fig. 12-12.   Straight-Wing Ducted Fan Design by Marcus Norman

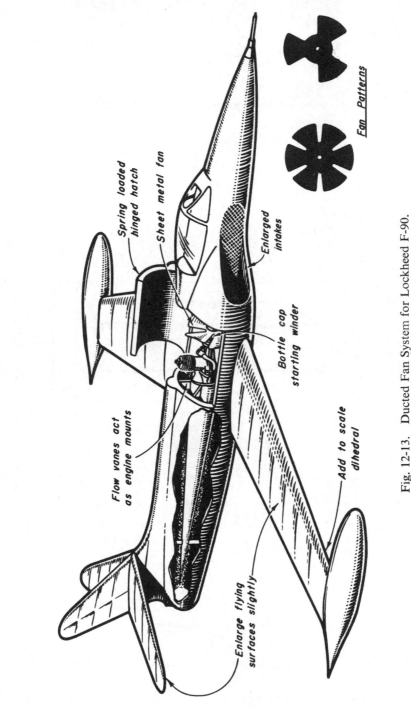

Fan Patterns

Spring loaded
hinged hatch

Sheet metal fan

Enlarged
intakes

Bottle cap
starting winder

Flow vanes act
as engine mounts

Add to scale
dihedral

Enlarge flying
surfaces slightly

Fig. 12-13.   Ducted Fan System for Lockheed F-90.

13

GLOW-ENGINED
FREE-FLIGHT
MODELS

Free-flight machines fall into three general classifications (see fig. 13–1). First, there is the contest-type free-flight, engineered for maximum climb and an efficient glide. Second, there is the sport variation, more realistic looking than its thermal-hooking (or thermal-riding) brother, somewhat heavier, and equipped with a smaller engine for more gentle flying. Third, there is the flying scale and semiscale craft, most always rather small in size and powered with one of the little, but potent, Half-A or under mills.

What makes a good contest free-flight machine? Let's begin with the rules. Through the years, they have changed many times, always seeking to limit performance. In the beginning, one could make any kind of design, equip it with any engine, and fly it with all the fuel he could cram in a tank. Since many planes were lost, fuel was soon limited to ¼ ounce per pound of plane weight. Planes still flew away, and the next limitation was a 30-second engine run. This did not work for very long, and it has been successively reduced until today hand-launched contest gassies (there are few ROG's any more) are allowed only a 12-second engine run—and planes are *still* being lost! Wing-loading specifications, weight rules, and other methods have been tried, but most were dropped because processing of planes at contests simply took too long; besides, these limitations still do not prevent flyaways. Practically all the larger contest models—glider, rubber, and gassie—are now equipped with dethermalizers. an arrangement which brings the plane gently to the ground shortly after the maximum flight time has elapsed. Figure 13–5 shows some popular schemes, but the pop-up tail is in most widespread use today.

Engines are so potent and glides so long that even dethermalizers don't always bring a plane down (rising currents are sometimes so strong that the plane goes on up, even after the dethermalizer has operated properly). A moderately strong wind will take a plane far downwind, and often out of sight, even before the dethermalizer goes off. Some free-flighters are experimenting with the use of simple radio-control steering in their models, to be utilized only to get a model back to the flying area *after* maximum flight time has passed. This has been found especially useful for test flying in small fields and congested areas, when radio steering is resorted to early in the glide. Such use of radio control has been termed "RAFF" (Radio Assisted Free Flight) by advocates, and while not included in present contest rules, it may become officially acceptable in time.

It is evident that the two main factors in peak performance are a fast, high climb and a lengthy glide. The design of such an airplane centers about the engine. To put it more accurately, the problem really is

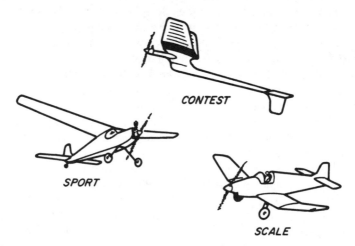

CONTEST

SPORT

SCALE

Fig. 13-1.　Free-Flight Glow Engine Model Types

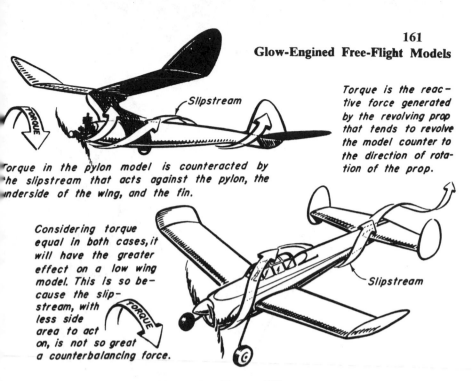

Torque in the pylon model is counteracted by the slipstream that acts against the pylon, the underside of the wing, and the fin.

Torque is the reactive force generated by the revolving prop that tends to revolve the model counter to the direction of rotation of the prop.

Considering torque equal in both cases, it will have the greater effect on a low wing model. This is so because the slipstream, with less side area to act on, is not so great a counterbalancing force.

Fig. 13-2.   Torque Effects

one of controlling the amount of power developed by the engine. Ever since 1938, when Carl Goldberg's pylon design appeared, this configuration has been favored for stability and reliability under power in a machine of reasonable size.

Modelers usually associate increased stability with a high wing location. In other words, the lower the CG in relation to the wing—this is termed "pendulum stability"—the more stable the design is expected to be (within reasonable limits, of course). However, the pylon configuration has some unique characteristics which have a more direct bearing on its fine performance. Three principal factors stand out. First is torque.

In the low wing, and even a moderate cabin-type layout, torque is a real problem, but on the pylon model the deadly torque force is not nearly so effective and actually may be canceled by another force. This factor is the slip stream, the twisting mass of air that blows back from the whirling propeller. This slip stream revolves in the same direction as the propeller so that it strikes against the upper left profile of the fuselage, pylon, and vertical tail (looking forward from the tail). Thus the slip stream tends to roll the model over to the right and into a right-hand turn. By controlling the height and area of the pylon and the vertical tail, the builder is able to overcome the torque and have a plane

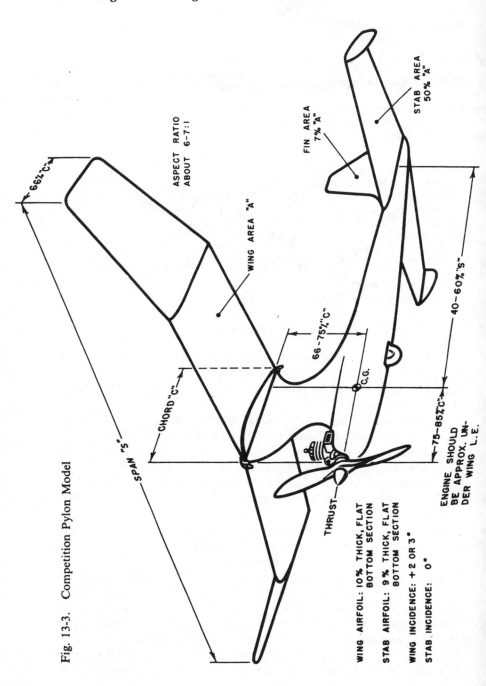

Fig. 13-3. Competition Pylon Model

SPAN "S"

66¾"C"

ASPECT RATIO
ABOUT 6-7:1

WING AREA "A"

FIN AREA
7% "A"

STAB AREA
50% "A"

40-60% "S"

CHORD "C"

66-75% "C"

C.G.

75-85%C"

THRUST

ENGINE SHOULD
BE APPROX. UN-
DER WING L.E.

WING AIRFOIL: 10% THICK, FLAT
BOTTOM SECTION

STAB AIRFOIL: 9% THICK, FLAT
BOTTOM SECTION

WING INCIDENCE: +2 OR 3°

STAB INCIDENCE: 0°

that turns slightly to the right. With high-powered pylons, the slip-stream effect generally exerts a much greater force than torque so that the danger to be avoided is a right-hand turn or spiral into the ground. It can also be shown, although this is more complex and rather theoretical, that the gyroscopic effect of a whirling propeller will produce a right-hand diving turn tendency when the nose of the model is displaced in an upward direction. From the practical standpoint, it will be found that if the slip stream is properly put to work, the airplane is controllable.

The third important factor results from the fact that the wing on the pylon model is high above the fuselage. Consider that the thrust line must obviously be considerably below the wing location and that the effect of the propeller thrust pulling forward, while the wing resists forward motion due to its drag, is to lift the nose skyward. The reader who is given to drawing diagrams will quickly see that the thrust is being exerted through a moment or leverage arm equal to the distance between the thrust line and the center of resistance of the plane. To combat this nose-up tendency, the free-flight designer resorts to a type of stabilizer which, having an airfoil section like the wing, generates lift. The faster the plane goes, the more lift the stabilizer develops to counteract the tendency of the plane to climb. At some point the lift of the wing and the nose-up tendency of the thrust will be balanced by the lift developed by the stabilizer. It would take an experimenter years to establish the precise relationship of these and other factors in the pylon, but inasmuch as the optimum values now are established, we can review them briefly.

The CG usually lies well back on the wing chord in airplanes using lifting-type stabilizers, being positioned anywhere from an extreme forward position of 50 per cent chord back to the trailing-edge position, and it averages about 75 to 85 per cent of chord.

The optimum stabilizer area appears to be about 45 per cent of the wing area. The stabilizer thickness ratio would work out to 8 or 9 per cent of the stabilizer chord.

A good, all-round aspect ratio for the wing that combines aerodynamic efficiency with structural strength is 6:1, perhaps as high as 7:1. Airfoil thickness varies between 9 and 13 per cent, averaging about 10 per cent. The 10 per cent thick airfoil is considered a thin wing and is desirable because it is also a fast wing, having less drag, with the probable result that the model gets higher during its 12-second engine run. Undercambered airfoils make construction more difficult and are harder to cover but may improve the glide, especially on more heavily loaded planes. Polyhedral is preferred to straight dihedral, but in either case the amount

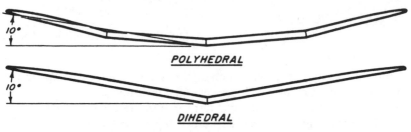

POLYHEDRAL

DIHEDRAL

Polyhedral is preferable to dihedral. In either case use approximately 10° tip elevation

Fig. 13-4.   Dihedral Measurement

of wing-tip elevation above a flat surface should be in the neighborhood of 10 degrees. The planform or outline shape of the wing varies, but there is no real need to use anything but parallel leading and trailing edges, at least out as far as the polyhedral break, with rounded or elliptical wing tips. The polyhedral break occurs about halfway out on the wing, or 50 per cent of the semispan, 25 per cent of the full span.

The wing should be set at a larger angle of incidence than the tail. The optimum angular difference is 2 or 3 degrees. The stabilizer is set flat at zero degrees of incidence so that the wing is made higher at its front edge, to place the wing at 2 to 3 degrees positive incidence.

In these high-performance pylon models, the wing is situated above the thrust line at a distance varying between two-thirds and three-quarters of the wing chord. It is advisable to use only as much pylon side area as is necessary for adequate strength; too much side area at this point may induce spiral dives under high power. Fuselage length is determined by the moment arm, customarily measured from the mid-chord point of the wing to the mid-chord point of the stabilizer. (Moment arms were discussed in chapter 2.)

To achieve the balance necessary for the success of the setup outlined above, the nose should not extend beyond the leading edge of the wing. The firewall or engine support should be at this point: the engine may project beyond. Still shorter noses, as well as longer ones, are used, but longer noses usually affect the power-turn characteristics adversely.

An overlarge fin area will cause the plane to head into the wind. This prevents the tight gliding circles essential for riding thermal currents and is therefore undesirable. Too small a fin area may cause the plane to rock to and fro as it climbs steeply, and when the plane is rolling from side to side, it may suddenly make a half roll until the nose is pointed down, when a fatal dive may result. A good average fin area is about 6 or 7 per cent of the wing area.

Every high-performance free-flight model should be equipped with a dethermalizer. Wise fliers know that no such machine should even be

164

given its first short test hop unless the dethermalizer is set and ready for action. Contest rules do not recognize duration beyond 5 minutes (a five-minute flight is termed a "max"), except on flyoffs when longer flight times may be specified. Therefore, even with no wind, when the plane might come down almost at the spot where it took off, the flier takes no chances and sets his dethermalizer for the time limit.

Although numerous devices have been tried, only two types have proved both effective and practical. By far the most popular is the pop-up tail. This is nothing but a stabilizer that is hinged in some manner at its leading edge and spring-loaded by means of a rubber band so that it will tip up at the rear. When the stabilizer assumes a large negative angle, it abruptly raises the nose until the model stalls. The plane descends in a nose-high attitude at a steep angle and a fairly high rate of speed. However, it will generally not be damaged upon reaching the ground. The trick is to get the angle of tilt so adjusted that the airplane will remain in a constant nose-high attitude and not just rock back and forth between alternate dips and stalls; this angle is approximately 45 degrees. Another essential condition is to have the stabilizer so keyed that it will not slide or twist when tilted, which would cause the rudder to be turned and so spin the airplane. A piece of thread may be run from the rear edge of the stabilizer (about halfway toward the tips) down to the rear tip of the fuselage. This tether prevents the tail from tilting beyond the desired angle and also keeps the rear of the tail from sliding to one side or the other. The leading edge usually is hinged or keyed in some manner—say, by a plywood tongue fitting into a slot cut in the stabilizer mounting platform—so that the tail remains accurately centered.

Two methods are used to operate this type of dethermalizer. One is a standard clockwork timer available in many hobby shops, and the other is a fuse. If the timer is employed, it is located well forward in the fuselage and has either a long, thin music-wire pull rod or a cord extending back to the tail release. The timer is wound just prior to launching. The fuse is simply a piece of string that has been soaked in strong saltpeter solution. The release for the tail consists of two short projections of music wire; one sticks out to the rear from the center of the stabilizer, and the other, just below the first wire, is attached to the fuselage itself. A small rubber band is looped lightly around both wires; it should be just strong enough to hold down the back of the tail. The fuse is inserted through the rubber band. When the burning fuse contacts the band, the latter will break, whereupon the tension of another rubber band tilts up the stabilizer.

The second dethermalizer idea is the drag chute, a small parachute which is folded and stored in a small compartment in the bottom of the

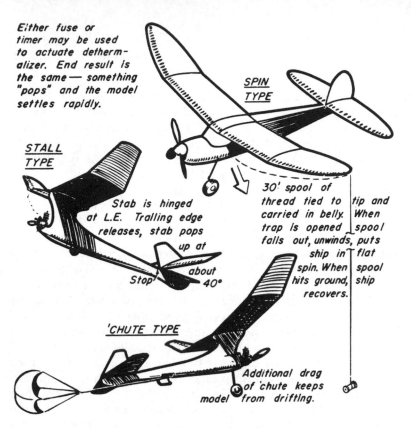

Either fuse or timer may be used to actuate dethermalizer. End result is the same — something "pops" and the model settles rapidly.

SPIN TYPE

STALL TYPE

Stab is hinged at L.E. Trailing edge releases, stab pops up at about 40° Stop

30' spool of thread tied to tip and carried in belly. When trap is opened spool falls out, unwinds, puts ship in flat spin. When spool hits ground, ship recovers.

'CHUTE TYPE

Additional drag of chute keeps model from drifting.

Fig. 13-5.   Dethermalizer Systems

fuselage, just beneath the wing. The compartment door is held shut by a rubber band through which a fuse is inserted. A small piece of asbestos attached to the underbody near the fuse will prevent igniting the model. When the door springs open, the chute falls out and opens, then drags out behind the airplane, slowing its glide so it descends quickly to earth.

In some areas and under dry weather conditions, a fuse could be a fire hazard, and a mechanical timer is mandatory. Many modelers now equip their planes with fuse "snuffer tubes"; a snuffer is simply a light metal tube only slightly larger in inside diameter than the fuse (which must be a snug fit) and attached firmly to the tail of the plane. It acts to snuff out the fuse fire when the fuse has burned to the rearmost edge of the tube. Needless to say, enough fuse is allowed to project to give the desired dethermalizer time interval, plus a little extra for leeway. In some areas, snuffers are mandatory on all free-flight models.

How big a free-flight model should be depends on the power plant, and where the contest or high-performance type is concerned, this depends on the event or class in which the design is flown. Rules define these classes of engines in free flight: Class Half-A, up to .050-cubic-inch piston displacement; Class A, .051 to .200 cubic inch; Class B, .201 to .300 cubic inch; Class C, .301 to .650 cubic inch. Total model weight is limited to 7¼ pounds, but there are no other restrictions. Wing areas vary widely for each engine category, reflecting real individuality in design concepts. The Half-A planes run from perhaps 200 to 400 square inches in wing area; many fliers utilize the same plane for both Half-A and A, with a .049 engine for the former and the practically identical .051 for Class A. This sort of dual use is also practiced with larger contest models. At the upper end of Class A, the wing areas run around 400 to 600 square inches with .09 engines. For engines of .29 to .35 size, the range seems to be from perhaps 650 up to 850 square inches, and the big Class C models have even larger dimensions. Great flexibility in design is possible under the present rules, where only engine size is specified, but we still have the old problem of lost planes due to flyaway! Where do we go next . . . ?

Large numbers of sport planes are flown free-flight with engines from .02 to .049, and within this range are also found many free-flight scale models. The rules specify a maximum engine size of .20 cubic inch for free-flight flying scale, but the majority of planes are rather small and utilize much smaller engines than this. Many .02-powered scale planes are seen in competition. These little ones can fly well, but are seriously handicapped if there is any wind blowing—and there almost *always* is at scale contests, or so it seems.

14

RADIO CONTROL

Prior to 1949 practically all radio-control work was accomplished on amateur radio band frequencies (mostly on the 6-meter band at 50 to 54 megacycles), but in that year the Federal Communications Commission authorized the use of 465 mc for model control, without the need for obtaining an amateur license. Meanwhile tests were being made of 27.255 mc also for radio control and under a simple license (such as was required for 465-mc operation) that did not require any knowledge of electronics or the radio telegraph code, unlike the amateur licenses which required considerable knowledge of both. The 27-mc spot looked very promising, and general use of it for radio control was authorized by the GPO in 1950. Very strict requirements had been set up for 465 mc, including actual test and approval of the equipment from each manufacturer; as a result, only two systems were ever approved. On 27.255 mc, however, requirements were much simpler, and soon there were a number of makes of equipment available and a number of kits for those who wished to save some money by constructing their own gear.

The radio control modeller is also subject to certain legal obligations. His equipment must only be operated within a certain wavelength band, or, as more usually specified, a specific frequency range which has been allocated by the GPO for radio control purposes in Britain. Regarding the permitted frequencies for model radio control operation, these cover the band 26.96 megacycles/second to 27.28 megacycles/second (11.12 to 11.1 metres wave length); 35.005 megacycles to 35.205 megacycles and 458.50 to 459.50 megacycles (VHF) have been approved from 1981 and avoid interference from CB transmissions.

Other frequency bands may be available for use in other countries and equipment designed to operate on them. Thus in America some equipment is designed to operate on the 50-54 or 72 megacycle bands; and in Germany on the 40-41 megacycle band. This again will not normally affect the average modeller, since, if imported, such equipment will be set for tuning on the British 27 megacycle band.

The accompanying table gives the color codes for antenna flags and ribbons designating the transmitter frequency. These are not mandatory unless you fly in an SMAE-organized contest. However, every RCer should fly a flag or ribbon to let other fliers know his exact frequency and to prevent two planes from being launched on the same frequency.

From 1981 one does not require a license for operation, nor is there any examination (as is mandatory for amateur licenses) required. Since it is generally felt that reliable model control, except for short-range operation such as with model cars or boats, rarely requires more

---

Standard Radio Control Transmission Frequency Spots

Modern radio control systems are tuned to transmit on any one of a number of exact 'spot' frequencies listed here. These 'Spots' are spread through the legal 26.96 MHz to 27.28 MHz waveband allocated by the GPO for operation of radio control model equipment. Each is identified by a colour code, and a pennant of the appropriate frequency colour should always be displayed on the aerial of your transmitter. In this way, other radio control enthusiasts can instantly identify the frequency on which you are operating, and will therefore avoid transmitting while your model is in the air. In this way, disastrous frequency clashes, resulting in damaged models, are avoided. The system is for your own safety as well as everyone else's.

Frequency	flag colour	
26.975 MHz	designated by flag colour	grey/brown
26.995 MHz	,, ,,	brown
27.025 MHz	,, ,,	brown/red
27.045 MHz	,, ,,	red
27.075 MHz	,, ,,	red/orange
27.095 MHz	,, ,,	orange
27.125 MHz	,, ,,	orange/yellow
27.145 MHz	,, ,,	yellow
27.175 MHz	,, ,,	yellow/green
27.195 MHz	,, ,,	green
27.225 MHz	,, ,,	green/blue
27.245 MHz	,, ,,	blue

Between 35.005 and 35.205 MHz there are a further 20 'spot' frequencies identified by a number system, *not* colours. Refer to dealers for information.

than .1 W power, practically all of our current transmitters *do not* have
to be licensed.

Now, with the regulations clear, what else is needed? First, of course,
you must have a transmitter and receiver, and they come in bewildering variety. For those who wish to delve more deeply into radio control, we strongly suggest buying some of the books mentioned in appendix II which go much more thoroughly into the matter than we can
possibly do here.

To understand how the radiated energy or transmitter "signal" is
electronically manipulated to achieve the desired response at the model's
control surface, we have to think of the receiver as a "sensor" which
detects the radio energy radiating from the transmitter.

In the earliest radio-control equipment the "control" was based upon
the simple reaction of the receiver to the transmitter signal. In effect,
when you turned on the transmitter, the receiver simply sensed the signal
and reacted in a constant way to the standard signal. These were the
simple "single channel" radio-control sets in which the receiver switched a
control "actuator" to achieve a single control function. Single channel
radio control is no longer manufactured.

Modern, multiple control function proportional equipment simply
builds on the basic signal and concept of the early RC systems. The term
"multiple control functions" implies the ability to control the movement,
both independently and simultaneously, of a number of separate model
controls. The expression "proportional" implies that the position
of the control surface is, for all practical purposes, infinitely variable
between neutral and full travel, the control surface faithfully following
movement of the transmitter control column.

In modern radio-control equipment, the transmitter signal is basically
the same but instead of being a continuous, unvarying emission, the
signal is electronically interrupted into a sequence of pulses so that these
interruptions form a coded message. The interruptions, or code, become
the "information" which tells the individual control surfaces where to sit,
in relation to the neutral.

In Figure 14-1 you will see that the signal radiating from the transmitter consists of deliberately grouped "information" pulses. Typically,
a number of variable length control pulses (one for each control function)
are followed by a long fixed-time synchronization pulse—a fixed reference
called a "sync. pause". It is longer in length than the sum of all the
control pulses, each of which is infinitely variable in length between
fixed extremes of time which represent the extremes of throw of a control
movement: for instance, 1.2 milliseconds (thousandths of a second)
would represent full "up" elevator, while 1.8 milliseconds would be full

"down" elevator position. In-between, a pulse length of 1.5 milliseconds represents the midpoint and would, in effect, be telling the control surface to sit at neutral.

Typically, the information code is repeated 40 times per second and the collective technical name of a single group of control pulses and accompanying synchronization pulse is a "frame".

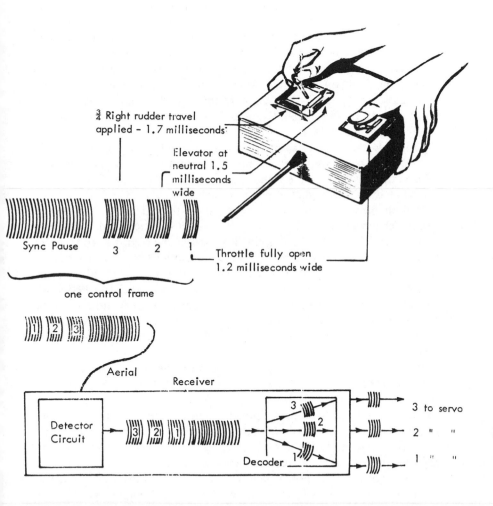

Fig. 14-1. Radio Control System

The required control positions are fed in at the transmitter via the control sticks, which are mechanically connected to variable resistances or "potentiometers". This is the point at which the pilot's commands, fed in by movement of the control sticks, are translated into the equivalent electronic impulses. It is the value of the resistance (or impedance) across the potentiometer which sets the length of the control pulse and thus the position of the control surfaces, faithfully following the positions of the control sticks.

The receiver is the sensor which detects and reacts to those transmitter signals. In a modern proportional RC system, however, the receiver consists of a detector circuit which is then linked to a further integral circuit, the function of which is to unscrabble that string of control information pulse codes and channel them to the appropriate control functions. In outline, what happens inside a receiver is shown in the lower half of figure 14-1.

Remember, we said that the code of control information, or "frame", is a sequence of pulses of signal. In other words, there is only one signal— broken up into pulses which run one after another in a continuous cycle punctuated by those synchronization pulses.

It is the decoder which turns what is, up to that point, still only a "single channel" signal like those old-fashioned systems, into independent control functions. In simplified non-technical terms, simply accept that the decoder is an electronic circuit with in-built criteria which allow it to understand that the long sync. pause is the start of an information "frame", after which control pulse No. 1 will always be channelled down the line of control output No. 1 and so on down the pulse train until the long sync. pause again "appears" and the sequence starts all over again, channelling the control pulse commands to the servos 40 times per second.

It is the servo which provides the motive power to move the control surface to the required position. The servo consists of a gear train and electric motor, mechanically and electronically interconnected with an electronic circuit called an "amplifier", and another variable resistance or potentiometer technically termed a feed-back potentiometer or "pot".

Servos have minds of their own, locked up in those "amplifiers", but at the same time they're real copy-cats too and in effect what they are trying to copy are the potentiometers back in the transmitter linked to the control sticks, which, in turn, are at the pilot's finger-tips. Do you begin to get the picture?

Without getting hyper-technical, when the RC system is energized by the battery, the servo amplifier generates its own "reference pulse", the length of which is governed by the position of and, therefore, the resistance (or impedance) across that little variable resistance.

Then, as soon as those incoming control command pulses from the transmitter are channelled in from the decoder in the receiver, the servo amplifier accepts them and compares the pulse lengths with those of its own internally generated reference pulses. See figure 14-2 for the basic idea. Any difference will cause the "comparator" section of the servo amplifier to energize its integral "drive" circuit, which will feed DC current into the electronic servo unit. The energized motor turns, driving the servo gear train, which in turn is mechanically connected to that variable resistance (or feed-back pot) which in turn is again, of course, electronically connected back to the servo amplifier, feeding back the value of its own resistance into the amplifier "comparator" circuit (now you get the meaning of that expression "feed-back pot"). As the variable resistance turns, driven by the electric motor via the servo gear train, it alters the length of its "comparator" pulse until it finally matches that of the incoming "command" pulse. At that point the DC current to the motor cuts off, and the servo stops, at exactly the point commanded by the position of the control stick back in the transmitter, the signal from which is set by the variable resistance to which it is connected. If you like—the servo has sought to follow the control position dictated by the position of that variable resistor in the transmitter—as we said, a real copy-cat!

And how does the servo move the control surface? Well, almost as a by-product really. The control output drive is on the shaft of the final or "output" stage of the gear train, which is also connected to the variable resistance, that the motor, via the gear train, is driving effectively to cancel to DC current. Figure 14.3 shows the internal mechanism of the servo and how motor, gear train and variable resistance are interconnected.

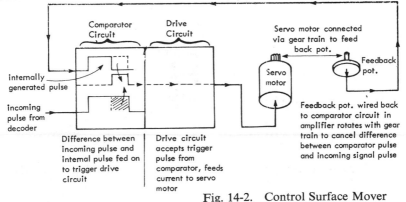

Fig. 14-2.   Control Surface Mover

Such then are the semi-technical basics of how modern proportional radio control works. Much of what goes on under those electronic circuits has been disregarded in order to give a simplified picture of how the control is achieved as in Figure 14-4.

Figure 14-5 shows a typical installation for the complete airborne pack of two servos (side by side), receiver and battery power pack. Note that the battery, the heaviest single item, is at the nose. In the next compartment is the receiver and behind that, under the wing, are the servos. This layout is a compromise of convenience and necessity. The battery pack is positioned nearest the nose to ensure that, in the event of a crash it does not tear through and damage the more vulnerable receiver and servos as would be the case if the battery were placed at the rear. Ideally, the receiver, being most vulnerable of all, should be placed behind the servos, but the practicalities of installation make such an arrangement inconvenient.

This general placement of equipment is helpful in achieving the correct balance of the model when complete, the final adjustment being made by shifting equipment components backwards and forwards in their installation compartments to achieve final balance.

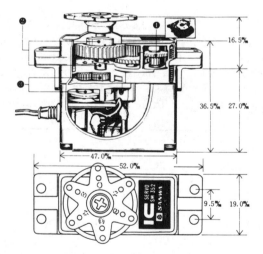

Fig. 14-3.   Servo Mechanism

1: Motor Drive   2: Output shaft bearings   3: Feed-back Pot Drive

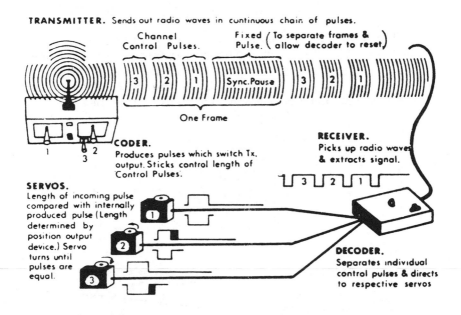

Fig. 14-4.   Complete RC System

Good installation begins before the airframe is constructed by laying the RC equipment over the plan to give a general idea of the installation requirements. Any installation aids, such as servo rails, switch mounts, push-rod guides etc., which may need to be built into the airframe as it goes together can be planned at this stage.

Early on in the construction stage you must decide which form of control linkage from servos to control surfaces is best suited to your model. Basically, you have a three-way choice: balsa push rods; flexible "snakes", or a closed loop cable. Balsa push rods are the oldest method of linking servo and control surface and in many ways still the best. Use hard $\frac{1}{4}''$ or $\frac{5}{16}''$ balsa dowel or $\frac{1}{4}''$ sq. strip. Take an adjustable control clevis with threaded wire rod, shape the wire to pass through a slot in the fuselage and bind to the control surface end of the push rod, sealing the thread with balsa cement. Ideally, the wire end should not be more than about 3" long to remain stiff under air-load. (Fig. 14-6.)

The servo end of the push rod also ends in a wire rod, preferably 16 swg. In the case of a rotary type servo output, a "Z" link is used to connect up. The rotary output of the servo disc must be removed from the servo to slip over the wire end, but when replaced, the wire is safely retained and cannot be removed, even by force. (Fig. 14-7.)

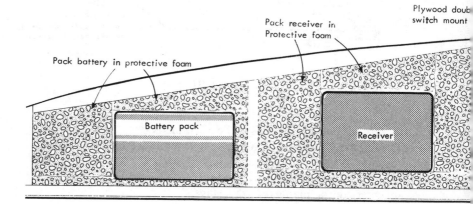

Pack receiver in
Protective foam

Plywood doub
switch mount

Pack battery in protective foam

Battery pack

Receiver

Fig. 14-5. RC Equipment Installation

Linear output servos require a slightly different connection arrangement. The output drive arm cannot usually be removed so that a simple snap-on/off keeper is required to hold the wire push-rod end in place.

"Snakes" are flexible push rods consisting of either a Bowden cable in a plastic tube, or two tubes (inner and outer), the latter usually of P.T.F.E. for minimum friction. (Fig. 14-8.)

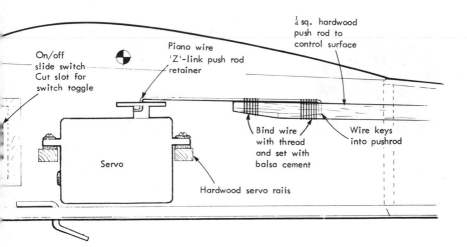

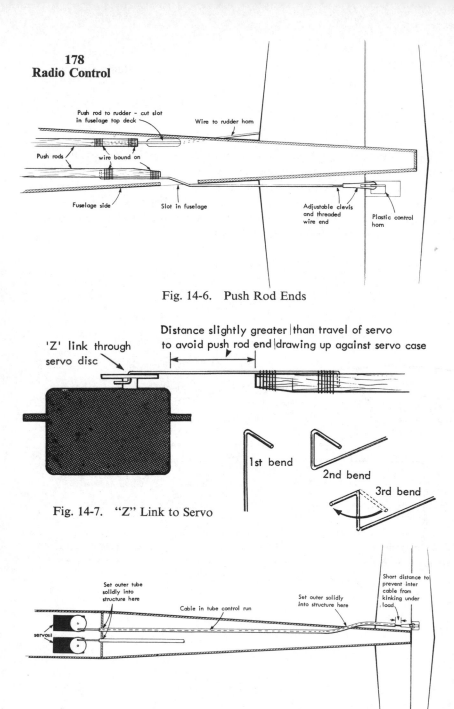

Push rod to rudder – cut slot
in fuselage top deck

Wire to rudder horn

Push rods

wire bound on

Fuselage side

Slot in fuselage

Adjustable clevis
and threaded
wire end

Plastic control
horn

Fig. 14-6.   Push Rod Ends

Distance slightly greater than travel of servo
to avoid push rod end drawing up against servo case

'Z' link through
servo disc

1st bend

2nd bend

3rd bend

Fig. 14-7.   "Z" Link to Servo

Set outer tube
solidly into
structure here

Cable in tube control run

Set outer solidly
into structure here

Short distance to
prevent inter
cable from
kinking under
load

servos

Fig. 14-8.   "Snake" Push Rods

The advantage is the ability to "snake" around internal parts of the airframe which, with a rigid push rod would otherwise need to be either removed or repositioned to permit free push-rod movement. Disadvantages are that in practice there is a limit to the amount of "snaking" that can be introduced without a build-up of friction which, in turn loads the servos, which draw excess current and reduces battery life. Particularly in the case of cable-in-tube, care must be taken to ensure the bare ends of the wire cable do not accidentally become kinked which will seriously impair the rigidity of the rod and may, under air-load, allow the control surface to "blow back" toward neutral, thereby reducing control effectiveness.

Linkage ends to both servo and control surface are similar to those of the push rod.

The Closed-Loop-Cable system, which consists of multi-strand control-line wire, is linked to a control horn on each side of the control surface. Properly set up, it achieves extremely precise control increments and has the advantage of minimizing weight at the rear end of the fuselage. In practice, it requires two adjustable clevises and is the most complicated of the three systems to set up to best advantage. (Fig. 14-9.)

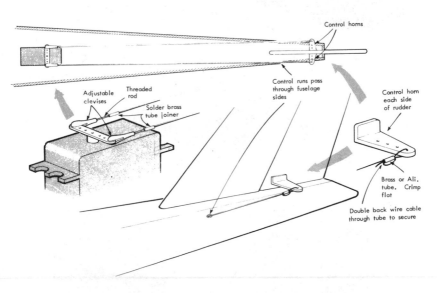

Fig. 14-9. Closed Loop Cable Controls

Whichever system is chosen, time and care must be taken to ensure unimpeded, friction-free linkage movement over the entire range of control surface travel. Any binding up, friction or fouling of the linkage will cause servo overload, leading to excessive battery drain. In really extreme cases, output transistors in the servo amplifier could be damaged and that will cost money!

Having roughly positioned the components of the RC system to achieve correct balance, commence by installing the servos, which can be either wood screwed to hardwood rails or direct to the internal faces of the fuselage sides using double-sided adhesive foam tape. (Fig. 14-10.)

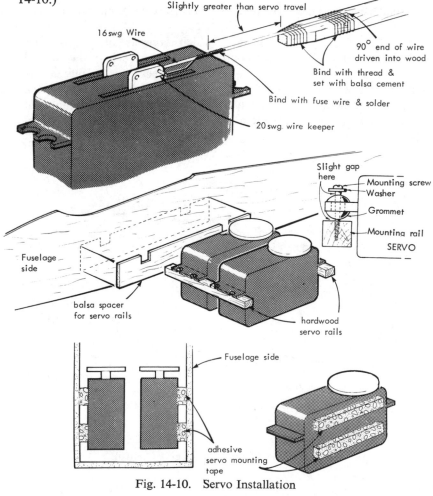

Fig. 14-10.   Servo Installation

Finally, receiver and power pack are installed into their respective compartments using foam packing so that each component is prevented from flopping around, but at the same time is not so rigidly packed that the cushioning effect of the foam is lost. Figure 14-5 shows the general arrangement.

Ensure that the leads from receiver to battery pack and servos are kept away from the receiver and be sure to run out the receiver aerial as far away from the servos as possible to avoid picking up any "noise" interference generated by the servo motors.

The technique for covering RC models is similar for nylon tissue or silk but is obviously different if plastic film is used. Whichever material is chosen, first decide the colour scheme. If necessary sketch out a three-view drawing with coloured crayons until a balanced design has been finalized.

Transfers are available in many designs and colours and can make a basic design look very attractive with little effort, but try to avoid covering every little area with some pattern. It is not always necessary to keep designs symmetrical, a simple large star on one wing doesn't necessarily mean the opposite wing also needs something.

If the model is to be covered in tissue, use heavyweight for the wing and lightweight for the remainder.

For nylon tissue or silk, prepare the airframe for covering first with two coats of sanding sealer, gently sanding after each coat with 300 grade or flour paper. This will seal the wood grain, prevent the surface grain "roughing up" when the covering is applied, and will also slightly soften, improving adhesion when dope is applied through the covering material. These covering materials should always be applied "wet". Cut the material about 1″ oversize all round. Crumple into a loose ball and hold under a running tap in lukewarm water. Gently squeeze out the excess water and carefully open out the ball. Clear dope should be used to stick the material around the edges only of the area being covered. Let the material dry thoroughly before doping over the whole area, especially over open frameworks. This will prevent the dope "blushing" when moisture is trapped beneath the surface, giving rise to a white streaky effect. If this occurs, allow to dry and apply further dope. This will reduce, though not always remove the effect. Use enough coats of dope to fill the material pores. Two coats should be sufficient for tissue but up to four may be necessary for nylon.

The wing should be covered in separate pieces starting with the under surface panels. The upper surface panels can then be wrapped around the leading and trailing edges and slightly overlapped on the bottom covering. The join lines will then be out of sight underneath the wing. The tailplane, fin and rudder should have the covering applied to the second side whilst the first side is still wet. Allow to dry and dope both sides in one go to prevent unequal shrinking stresses and warps developing.

All-sheet fuselages should be covered after completing the sanding sealer stage. Simply lay the dry tissue, lightweight this time, over the fuselage and paint the dope through. Start at the middle and work outwards, smoothing wrinkles as they occur.

If plastic film is to be used for the covering, the airframe should not be doped or sanding sealed. A light sanding overall is all that is needed for preparation. However, all loose dust must be removed as this will cause unsightly lumps in the covering. Use a small travelling iron or specialist film iron; the normal domestic iron is suitable on a low setting, but being very heavy arm ache quickly develops. Steam irons are less suitable as the underside is not smooth. The iron can be cleaned during operations if excess film adhesive builds up on the smooth iron face using steel wool or covering film solvent.

After covering the elevator and rudder can be permanently hinged with plastic film strip pegged in place with pins or pieces of cocktail stick.

Choose a calmish day for an initial test flight, preferably in the company of an experienced flier at the local club field. Check that the centre of gravity is as per the plan and add noseweight if necessary. See that the tailplane is set at the design angle and that all control surfaces neutralize. This should ensure a safe glide path. When satisfied, first flights can be attempted. Should the model appear nose-heavy, pack the tailplane with $\frac{1}{32}$" sheet under the rear. If the nose continues to drop, remove a little of the nose weight. Trim until satisfied that the model will penetrate into wind without loss of height. It may also be necessary to alter both the nose weight and tailplane trim if wind conditions vary, to give optimum performance. It is always safer to carry out a test flight with the model nose-heavy as control will be kept, whereas if the model is tail-heavy, stalling will occur with consequent loss of control at low airspeeds. When properly built and trimmed, loops and stall turns can be done as experience is gained.

15

FLYING
AND ADJUSTING

The control-line plane has several unusual features that tend to spoil its flight. One is the weight of the steel wires, tending to pull down the inside wing. Another is the air drag of the wires, tending to turn the nose in toward the center of the circle. Another is torque, which on an airplane that flies counterclockwise tends to roll down the left or inside wing tip. Added together, these forces create a pronounced tendency to roll the ship in toward the flier. On a windy day, the force of the wind against the plane as it flies upwind of the pilot on one side of the circle considerably magnifies this rolling tendency. Should the airplane move sideways toward the flier so that the control lines become slack, control is lost and the plane dives at full speed into the ground. Fortunately, these are simple difficulties to overcome. One expedient which quickly becomes second nature to the practiced flier is to step back whenever the lines become slack. Tension is restored and control preserved.

While taking up the slack is a necessary part of any U-control flier's technique, it is also essential to reduce any tendency of the plane to come in on the lines. These are the few simple adjustments. Torque is compensated for by slanting the thrust line 2 or 3 degrees toward the outside of the circle. Further insurance is provided by setting the rudder

183

toward the outside of the circle. On a large plane, the rear edge of the rudder should be displaced as much as ½ inch; on a small Half-A powered ship, ¼ inch should be sufficient. To overcome the weight of the lines, lead weight is placed in the outside wing tip. The proper weight may be determined by a simple test. Having put.a weight in place, hold the nose and the rear tip of the fuselage between fingers with unweighted side of the wing pointing at the ground. The counterweight should just roll the plane back to an upright position and continue rolling until the weighted tip is pointing at the ground.

The fore-and-aft sensitivity of the plane, which determines the response to elevator movements and the smoothness with which the plane flies when you try to hold level flight, is determined by many things. The CG position is most important, just as it is in free flight.

Not only does the location of the CG govern the sensitivity, if not the very flyability of the model, but the placement of the bellcrank pivot point and the amount of area and movement of the elevators all contribute to the flying characteristics of the plane. In fact, the bellcrank pivot point and the CG usually are considered as a combination. For example, if the plane is supported at both wing tips by the finger tips so that it teeters back and forth until the exact balancing point is located, the bellcrank pivot should then be so placed that the CG falls somewhere between the pivot and the front-line hole in the bellcrank. The nearer the CG is to the pivot, the more sensitive the model will be, other things being equal, and the farther forward the CG is, as on the front-line-hole position or even farther forward, the steadier-flying but less responsive the model becomes. Therefore, a very fast machine to be used for speed should balance on or about the front line, whereas the stunt plane which requires quick changes in position, rather than extreme steadiness in flight, should balance between the front hole and the pivot. Trainers balance forward; sport models, at an in-between position.

The speed plane does not have an offset rudder, usually does not have offset thrust, and never has a weight in the wing tip. This is true for several reasons, the important one being that the plane is not stunted and is not allowed to get high off the ground. Its timed run usually is made not higher than the flier's head. At its very great speeds, the heavy racing model develops centrifugal force which keeps the wires taut despite wind that would tend to slide the ordinary plane in on the lines toward the flier. Some racing planes even have thrust toward the inside of the circle to decrease pull on the lines for more efficient flying. Team racers fly level and do not require as much compensation as stunt planes.

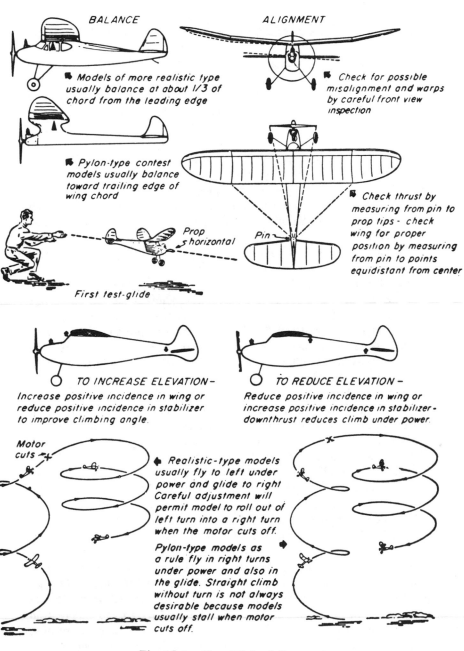

Fig. 15-1. Free-Flight Adjustments

Some stunt models utilize tricky features in design to eliminate the wing-tip weight.

The beginner should make a special effort to remember that the wind, however slight, should be allowed for in planning a flight. This is why: if the plane is permitted to take off into the wind, it is apt to climb high right after take-off and will be positioned at high altitude on the up-wind side of the circle before speed is built up to guarantee sufficient force to keep the lines taut. Most accidents happen at this point, as lines go slack and the plane dives into the ground. Take-offs should always be made downwind. For similar reasons, all possible stunts, such as loops and vertical 8's, should be made on the downwind side of the circle, where the wind tends to blow the craft away from the flier and to keep the lines taut. Stunting on the upwind side is always dangerous. It is easy to know where to begin a stunt because the wind can be felt on the back, and some quickly identifiable object, like a house or tree, may be picked up out of the corner of the eye.

Since free-flying models are not restricted in any direction, their adjustment is more demanding. The flier must know what the plane was doing on its last flight to make proper corrections for the next hop.

What makes the glider fly? When it is thrown into the air, the momentum from the launch provides the flying speed necessary for the wings to develop lift. Why, then, doesn't the glider tumble to earth as soon as this momentum is used up? The answer is that the glider noses down, and the force of gravity then becomes a substitute for a propeller, providing thrust to maintain forward speed and lift. The glider then coasts downhill. Assuming that the glider is properly proportioned and hence inherently stable, the modeler has only to balance it fore and aft, so that it does not dive or stall, and then turn the rudder slightly for any desired turn. This fore-and-aft balance is the factor on which all further adjustments are based. It is this simple: if the glider stalls, add weight to the nose; if it dives, remove weight from the nose.

Directions and plans for hand-launched gliders always show clay, lead pellets, or other weight attached to or inserted in the nose. Gliders require weight in the nose in order to have the CG properly located in relation to the chord of the wing. Select an open area, covered with tall grass if possible, and throw the glider lightly ahead. Do not point the nose skyward. Point it at a spot on the ground about 25 feet away. If the nose rises abruptly so that the model seems to falter, drop its nose, and dive to regain speed, it is stalling and requires more nose weight. On the other hand, if it dives to earth, remove some of the weight. Properly balanced, the machine will slide along smoothly and travel 6 to 10 times as far as the elevation above the ground from which it was launched. Once trimmed, the glider may be thrown harder, with the nose pointed up a little and the plane slanted off slightly into a right-hand turn (or left-hand, if you are left-handed). If the model is still tail-heavy, it will loop smartly. The trick is to bend the rudder slightly to the left and then throw the glider in a natural right-hand turn. After the momentum of launching is dissipated, the glider will gradually come out of the right turn and, putting down its nose to maintain speed, will enter a left turn in response to the rudder.

The soaring or towline glider may require an extra touch. In order to catch thermals or rising currents of air, a miniature plane must circle tightly. But since the towline glider must be towed aloft by means of a long cord attached to a hook beneath its fuselage (when overhead, a small piece of rag tied near the end of the cord causes it to slide off the hook, releasing the model), deflection of the rudder will cause the towliner to turn during the launch and possibly dive. If the flier doesn't immediately ease up on the cord, the plane will continue around and down into the ground. To make possible a straight launch, the hooks beneath the fuselage are mounted more to one side than the other. These hooks are placed on the same side as the desired turn. Thus, if the glider is to turn right, the hooks are mounted beneath the fuselage close to the right side. The off-center pull of the towline then equals the turning force of the rudder, and the climb is straight ahead until the model releases the line and the rudder takes over unopposed.

Some fliers prefer to achieve the desired straight tow but circling glide by a special rudder arrangement. This usually consists of a spring- or rubber-band-loaded tab on the rudder; tension of the towline holds the tab straight, allowing a straight-up tow; but when the line drops away, the tab is caused to shift to the desired turn position. To obtain a straight launch, the towline is caught over a movable hook, which in turn is attached by a fine wire or string to the side of the rudder opposite the string or rubber adjustment device. The result is that the pull on the towline during launching is transmitted to the rudder, holding it straight despite its trimming device. When the towline drops off the hook beneath the body, the trimming device is free to move the rudder.

Once you understand the simple tricks of balancing a glider, you can readily master the rubber-powered prop-driven planes.

The first thing to be sure of is a calm day. Early morning or late evening is usually the best testing time. Avoid wind because it will buffet the model and make it difficult to judge the effects of the adjustments you make. If the plane is a small, simple one, the kind of terrain doesn't

188
Flying and Adjusting

matter, but if the craft is at all fragile and of built-up construction, select a grassy area for maximum protection. The model is hand-glided
(with the motor unwound) from a standing position; aim the nose at
a spot on the ground about 25 to 35 feet away and give the plane a
light forward toss, not much more than a gentle shove. A severe throw
will cause the craft to zoom up steeply, where it will stall and then dive
into the ground. Too easy a launch will not provide enough flying speed,
and the plane may seem to fal. to the ground. Vary the strength of the
launch on several attempts in an effort to get the plane to glide smoothly
toward the imaginary spot. This will quickly indicate whether it is nose-
heavy or tail-heavy.

To correct a stalling tendency which will appear if the model is tail-
heavy, add pieces of solder to the nose, moving the CG forward. This
is satisfactory for sport flying, but contest fliers prefer not to add weight
because it may substract seconds from the flight duration. If the wing is
strapped on with rubber bands, you may slide the wing back a trifle,
moving the CG forward in relation to the wing. Or you can decrease
the amount of lift exerted by the wing by placing a thin sliver of hardwood under its trailing edge; or increase the lift of the tail, tending to
force the nose down, by adding such a shim under its leading edge. Use
any of these corrections or all in combination, making repeated test
glides until the plane appears to glide properly. If the plane is nose-
heavy, the exact opposite measures should be taken. (That is, less nose
weight, more wing incidence, less—or even negative—tail incidence.)
Now, at last, the power plant may be used.

One of the secrets of good adjusting is to iron out glide faults and
then pass on to final adjustments which affect the working propeller.
On the first short power test, put perhaps 50 turns in the rubber and
hand-launch the model just as if you were making a hand glide. Don't
throw the craft, and don't point its nose upward. If a stall or dive results, don't forget that the plane already is in gliding trim and that
previous adjustments must be left alone. Any bad power effects must
be controlled by altering the position of the thrust line. To stop the
stall, a sliver of hardwood is inserted behind the top of the nose block,
which angles the thrust line down at the front. This is called "downthrust." If the plane dives (this is unlikely), the opposite correction is
made. On the low-wing types, upthrust may possibly become necessary.
Rotation of the propeller will bring into play two forces not encountered
in the glider: torque and slip stream. Torque is compensated for by
adding right thrust. If slip stream takes effect, it will decrease the effects
of torque. The important thing to remember is to make all corrections

a little at a time, making short flight after short flight until the model performs smoothly. Only then begin to add power, either more turns on a rubber model, or a hotter engine run on a gas plane. Additional adjustments to the thrust line will be required from time to time as power is increased.

The rubber model performs most satisfactorily when it is caused to circle to the right, both under power and in the glide. You will note that until now nothing has been said about turn. It is all but impossible to set the rudder for the proper-sized turn when making hand glides because the plane is not airborne long enough to see a complete turn performed. But as those 50 motor turns are applied for the first power tests, the plane will be high enough when the prop stops for you to see how the plane glides, and then to set the rudder slightly to the right to cause a barely perceptible turn. If you can, make this rudder setting before arriving at the full amount of right thrust necessary to make the plane turn right under power, because the rudder will also affect the power portion of the flight. On most rubber-powered planes, it will be found that it is necessary to set the rudder to the right for the right-turning glide and to offset the thrust line to the right as well, to keep the plane from spiraling into the ground to the left under the effect of torque. As power is increased from flight to flight, the glide will stretch out, giving the flier a better opportunity for judging its quality. He may detect a slight stall or dive, which can be corrected by the methods used during the first hand-glide tests.

The expert may see his plane circling wide but stalling slightly, as its nose rises and dips. At this point, he will turn his rudder more severely to make the turn still tighter, and the stall disappears. If the turn was too tight to begin with and the plane was gliding too fast, he would apply less rudder, increasing the diameter of the turn and creating more lift to help support the craft.

Some bright modeler once noticed than an airplane could be made to turn tightly without banking steeply and that this appeared to boost the duration of the glide. He did this by tilting the stabilizer so that one tip was higher than the other. The model will always turn toward the higher stabilizer tip, or it will turn toward whichever wing tip is lower in relation to the stabilizer. Sight along the plane from the rear when tilting the stabilizer. Modern contest planes utilize the tilting stabilizer almost exclusively because by some odd quirk it has little or no effect on the plane's power in flight, but radically affects its glide. Therefore, thrust is controlled by tilting the thrust line, while the glide circle is determined by tilting the stabilizer. On high-powered machines, every

Straight flight   *Turning*

NOTE: This transition is quicker if model is adjusted for turns.

Fig. 15-2.   Turn Adjustment

slight bit of rudder offset has an acute effect on power, so that, in the case of such models, it is wise to leave the rudder tab alone or even to eliminate it entirely.

In the case of the rubber model, which turns right both under power and in the glide, it may help to warp the right or inside wing tip. An increase of $\frac{1}{16}$ inch in the incidence at the wing tip of a 6-inch-chord wing should be sufficient. The warp itself may be engineered by holding the wing tip over a steaming kettle until the paper softens slightly, then holding the wing with the tip at the desired angle until the covering becomes taut again.

Another condition that the practiced flier allows for is the wind. No model will fly the same in a wind as it does in a calm. It is necessary, therefore, for the modeler to learn as quickly as possible how much nose weight, or shimming of wing or tail, is necessary to balance his craft for windy-weather gliding. The power adjustments remain the same.

Adjusting and flying the free-flight gas model are much the same as for the rubber-powered one, although the builder has more of a choice as to how he wishes the plane to fly. It was noted that a rubber model should be adjusted to circle to the right, both under power and in the glide. This adjustment is referred to as right-right. In gas modeling, the plane may be made to circle either way, either under power or in the glide. For example, the most popular system is to circle right under power and left in the glide. This would be called right-left. Some builders even prefer to circle left under power and right in the glide, or left-right.

First power tests for a free-flight gassie can be ticklish. It is desirable to limit the amount of power. Most builders set the needle valve for a very rich, slow-running mixture or plug the intake, leaving only a small air hole.

A better system is to put the propeller on backward during early tests. The reversed prop seems to develop from one-half to two-thirds the normal thrust and, what is important, to have approximately the same amount of torque. If your new pylon persists in nosing up, it means that more lift must be had from the tail. If the area is correct, the stabilizer should be replaced with one that is slightly thicker. If this has been done and it is felt that the stabilizer airfoil section is at the practical limit of thickness, the best solution is to remove some of the incidence from the wing and to move the CG farther back on the chord.

A common difficulty on the cabin type of original design is a pronounced tendency to nose down, as if to start an outside loop, when extra flying speed develops. It is common in cabin models to have less nosing-up tendency under power, so that stabilizer areas may be somewhat smaller, down to as small as one-third the wing area, and not as thick in cross section as on the pylon model. When the cabin plane is trimmed to balance at one-third the chord, it won't require a lifting tail section, and a symmetrical one is substituted. Balanced farther back so that the tail carries part of the load, a slight lifting section may be required, such as a ratio of tail thickness to tail chord of 6 to 8 per cent. The diving tendency may be cured by adding wing incidence, using less tail incidence, or moving the CG back, provided the plane still is able to glide properly. Otherwise it is necessary to make a smaller and/or thinner stabilizer.

Low-wing model airplanes frequently prove bad fliers. The low-wing type has its thrust line positioned high in relationship to the center of drag of the machine, therefore creating a nosing-down tendency at high speed. This is exactly opposite to the normal tendency for the pylon type. However, the low-wing model may glide excellently, which makes the solution seemingly a mystery. The secret is to maintain an angular difference between the incidence setting of wing and stabilizer. The wing incidence will almost always be more positive.

16

SCALE MODELS

Over the years scale models have always been of absorbing interest, be they flying replicas or otherwise. Some years ago the making of wood "solid scale" models (as opposed to flying types) was the principal activity of many modelers. Today such modelers generally turn to plastic scale models, which we'll mention a bit later.

The beauty of the solid type of replica (see fig. 16–1) lies in its ability to duplicate any airplane in existence. One does not have to be concerned with whether or not the machine would make a good flier. The solid also is a pleasant project for those long winter evenings and bad days when one can't go out-of-doors.

It is customary to build solid scale aircraft to some convenient scale. Popular scales are ⅛ inch to the foot, ¼ inch, and 3/16 inch. Thus a plane that is 40 feet in span in real life would come out at 5 inches as a scale model in ⅛-inch scale, or 10 inches in ¼-inch scale. The scale used depends on the types of plane the builder wishes to make. Storage space, cost of materials, and the amount of labor are also factors in choosing a scale. So is the size of the airplane being copied. In ¼-inch scale, a B-36 bomber would have a wing span of almost 6 feet! Even in ⅛-inch scale this would be a walloping big 3-foot ornament. It would seem that 1/16-inch scale is the largest one practical for larger types of aircraft. The trouble is that one likes to make all one's models to a standard scale so that a fighter is in proper relation to a bomber companion. So, weigh all these pros and cons before picking your scale.

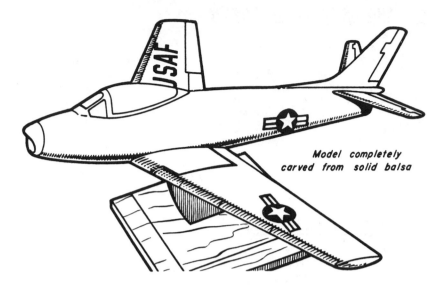

Model completely
carved from solid balsa

Fig. 16-1.   Solid Scale Model

Many home-built replicas are made of solid pieces of wood. Balsa is most used, but many builders interested in durability and ease of finishing favor a harder wood like pine. The building procedure is to draw the side view of the fuselage—its profile—on a clear-grained block of the proper length, width, and depth, allowing a slight margin for safety. The profile is then cut out, preferably with a power jigsaw, or with a coping saw. The cut is made sufficiently far ' outside the pencil marks to permit final sanding without reducing the accurate dimensions of the part. After cutting the side profile, the top profile is marked and the process repeated. The blanked-out fuselage is then shaped to the cross sections indicated on the plans. The wing and tail surfaces are made in the same manner. As a rule, external details, like an extended landing gear, are sacrificed, the model being placed on some kind of attractive stand.

The plastic scale industry has grown to huge proportions, not only in the United States but in other countries. These concerns just in the airplane field manufacture millions of kits, with the result that the prospective builder has a bewildering variety from which to chose. Models range from well before World War I right up to the present—and indeed into planes that will be seen in the future! Not only are these plastic replicas very accurate—in many cases the designers work from drawings of the original aircraft, or are able to take their measurements from the real thing—but quite a few of them have working parts. You can get bombers that actually drop bombs and planes with workable parts such as propeller, retractable landing gear, and cockpit canopy.

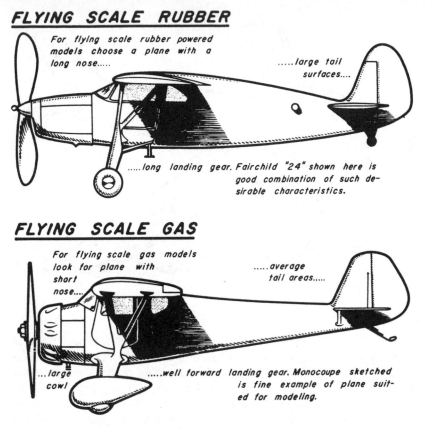

FLYING SCALE RUBBER

For flying scale rubber powered models choose a plane with a long nose.....

.....large tail surfaces....

.....long landing gear. Fairchild "24" shown here is good combination of such desirable characteristics.

FLYING SCALE GAS

For flying scale gas models look for plane with short nose....

.....average tail areas.....

...large cowl

.....well forward landing gear. Monocoupe sketched is fine example of plane suited for modeling.

Fig. 16-2.   Free-Flight Scale Model

There are plastic scale models in which you can actuate the controls from the cockpit. Going a little further in the airplane field from the planes themselves, there are some marvelous scale models of airplane engines; again, some of them have many moving parts.

Most of the kits have parts molded in a brownish material, which will take colored finishes (of a special variety) so that you end up with a very colorful and exact replica. Also, most kits include decal sheets for numerals, military insignia, and such features. Plastic kit makers have found how to metalize their parts where needed. Thus, if a kit is for a military fighter, the appropriate parts may come in a metallic finish to simulate aluminum. Not only that; different parts may have different metal textures, as is so often the case on the real planes.

To do a top-rate job, many of the plastic parts must be trimmed to remove "flash," thin edges left by the molding dies. A careful builder will work on these parts just as painstakingly as will the builder of a flying model plane, and the finished models are truly miniature gems. The

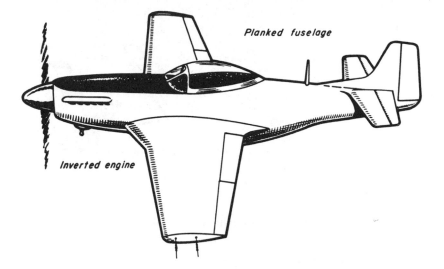

Planked fuselage

Inverted engine

Fig. 16-3.   Glow Engine Control-Line Scale Model

parts are held together by a special plastic cement, a very watery liquid
that actually melts adjacent surfaces and fuses them together.

While detailed plans, of the sort accompanying balsawood kits, are not
necessary, the drawings and instructions with plastic kits not only show
how the parts should be assembled, and the proper sequence, but give
explicit instructions on finishing and coloring. Indeed, the application
of proper color, markings, and finish is one of the most fascinating
parts of this work to many plastic builders.

The flying scale model is a more exciting challenge. Some planes have
excellent reputations for fliers in model form. Others are mysteries. Dare
you try one? Some, obviously, will lend themselves to free-flight gas
construction, such as the Monocoupe, with its squared fuselage, generous wing, and short nose for balancing the weight of the engine. Others,
like the long-nose Fairchild 24, will make good rubber-powered planes
because the weight of the rubber will be sufficiently far forward to prevent tail-heaviness (see fig. 16–2). Prop-driven planes of many types,
like Mustang fighters (fig. 16–3), will work wonderfully well when
flown on wires with a control handle or by radio control. Even the spectacular modern jet fighters can be made to fly by means of ducted-fan
power plants. All these methods are described in chapter 12.

You can even model Navy or Air Force types with side-by-side jets,
for a true two-engine flying model. The spans and weights depend on the
size and power of the engine you employ. Needless to say, the lighter
for a given size, the better your model will perform, especially in the
glide after the fuel has burned out. For the very advanced builder, large

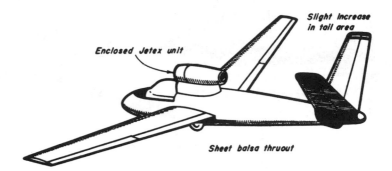

Fig. 16-4.   Free-Flight Jetex Sailplane Model

control-line scale models of jet fighters may be built with Dynajet power. A simple variation of the scale jet flier is a semiscale approach where a sheet-balsa fuselage is substituted for a built-up fuselage. In other words, the plane has a profile like the real thing, but its top view reveals no width to the body. Such a model is extremely simple to construct, especially when the wings and tail are made from sheet balsa.

One of the most appealing angles of scale-model building is that you do not have to stick to the latest in plane designs. In fact, most scale modelers prefer to go back in time considerably to produce and fly types that can no longer be seen in full size. World War I planes are particularly popular today and are flown with rubber and glow engines in free flight and with the most powerful engines in radio control. Radio equipment has become so reliable and versatile that scale builders in this category now feel they can successfully fly a scale copy of just about *any* plane of the past. This is far different from earlier years when scale radio builders would carefully compare drawings of dozens of old-timers, to find those few which had considerable dihedral, large-area tail surfaces, a fairly long tail moment, and so on. All these characteristics were mandatory if the plane was to fly at all. Now it makes little difference. However, modern jet planes with their very small wing areas still are not considered good subjects for radio control, though beautiful Dynajet-powered control-line models have been successful.

Such World War II fighters as the Mustang, Corsair, Spitfire, and many others have made fine radio fliers, and in fact you can obtain kits for many of them. Multiengine bombers have been flown with radio, but this becomes tricky, as the thrust varies so widely as different engines run out of fuel. Of course, this makes little difference on control-line, and six-engine bombers have been highly successful. The main problem here is not in flying; it's in getting all the engines going at once.

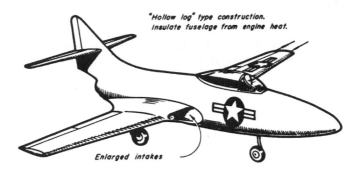

"Hollow log" type construction.
Insulate fuselage from engine heat.

Enlarged intakes

Fig. 16-5.   Control-Line Scale Model Jet

The manufacturers have produced a variety of realistic plastic copies of wartime and other planes for control-line flying, most of them fairly small, to take the .049 size of engine. Many of these come completely assembled and ready to fly. The box even may have fuel, starting battery, control lines, and a handle—every last item you need to fly the model. You can have it in the air a few minutes after you open the box, if you are an experienced modeler and flier. Otherwise, take much more time and carefully study the instructions.

Free-flying scale models are a bit tricky on balance, particularly the rubber types with their very large propellers. It is best to select high-wing cabin types, if you are not expert, as these will be much more stable. It is usual when drawing model plans from the plans of full-size planes to increase the dihedral considerably and to enlarge the tail surfaces, especially the horizontal tail. Such deviations take you away from true scale, of course, but they produce much more successful flying models generally. If you wish to model a plane for glow-engine power, pick a type with a fairly short nose, since long-nosed types will often require weight at the tail to balance; but for rubber power, you *want* a long nose, to balance the weight of the rubber motor which runs to the rear of the wing.

Most model magazines (listed in appendix II) carry scale 3-views of big planes from which you can draw your own model plans. If some avid scale modelers cannot find a plan of a desired airplane, they often purchase a plastic model of it and take the dimensions from that. As we've noted, these plastic kit jobs are often very accurate. With the great variety of scale kits for flying models in every category available today, the would-be flying-scale-model builder should certainly be able to find pretty much what he wants. Again, the model magazines often run scale-model construction articles, and though the magazine plans

197

are generally much smaller than the plane will be, full-size plans are usually available, upon request, from these publications.

17

MODEL ROCKETRY*

Readers of this volume may wonder what model rocketry is doing in a book devoted to model aviation. Actually there are a number of similarities between the two fields, including the fact that many model-plane fliers are active in model rocketry, and vice versa. Materials used by the two groups are similar, as are fabrication techniques. The materials and kits for both are often stocked in the same hobby shops, and model-plane fliers who belong to the Academy of Model Aeronautics and model-rocketry fliers in the National Association of Rocketry are covered by the same insurance policy. Moreover, certain problems of aerodynamic flight and stability apply to both planes and rockets.

Model rocketry is a rather young hobby; it really started around 1957. Now, some readers will tell us that hobbyists have been building small rockets for years—since long before World War II, in fact. This is true, but these builders have been dabbling in a dangerous field that is generally termed *amateur* rocketry. It is vastly different in every respect from *model* rocketry. The amateur builders try to make their rockets of metal tube, pipe, and such components and fill them with chemical concoctions they mix themselves. This results in the very likely possibility of premature explosions, serious injuries, and so on; in fact, a number of fatal injuries have occurred in this field.

Model rocketry is based and conducted on one main premise—*SAFETY*. All model rockets are propelled by commercial engines,

* See note on page 206.

which are manufactured under closely controlled conditions. There is *no* mixing of dangerous chemicals in this field. Engines are used just once and discarded. They are ignited *only* by electrical means; no fuses are allowed. The rockets are fairly small—the average is probably around 1 foot long—and care is always taken to insure that the spent rocket returns to earth in a controlled and gentle fashion. Model rocketry has had no fatal or even serious accidents, and none are foreseen. The engines are so safe that the Post Office allows them to go through the mails with no special precautions. They are *not* considered fireworks nor classified in this category. Despite the great safety of this hobby, it has taken a lot of persuasion to win over some states and municipalities, many of which have had (and some still have) highly restrictive regulations and laws on anything that pertains in the slightest to rockets. Quite a bit of this adverse legislation was set up following serious or fatal accidents among amateur rocketeers. It has been difficult to get such laws amended to allow model rocketry. Through coordinated efforts of the National Association of Rocketry, Connecticut was the first to amend its laws in favor of model rocketry. Other states and municipalities soon followed.

While many youngsters engage in model rocketry, an amazing number of adults are also very active. It should be no surprise that a significant number of the latter are professionals, engaged in research, design, and launching of full-size rockets. Many model-rocket contests have been held at Air Force and other Service facilities; NASA has been a strong booster of "modrocs," as these modelers call themselves.

We stress the safety angle, since most people who hear of rockets immediately think of something streaming aloft followed by a long fiery tail (if it doesn't explode first!), with the remains crashing to ground entirely out of control. This concept is absolutely unlike what we have in model rocketry.

What are its aims? Some would immediately think the principal idea would be to get a model rocket as high as possible. Wrong again! This would have little purpose; you couldn't *see* the models more than 1,000 feet high or so without special tracking equipment. No, the model builders test many different aerodynamic designs, experiment with fin size and shape and model-rocket balance, see what "pay load" they can lift and how gently such a load can be brought back to the ground. A "fragile" standard pay load is a regular egg, which must be protected against the tremendous acceleration of the model rockets and against the shock of landing. These rockets carry cameras aloft, or radio transmitters that send back signals for altitude and to help find the spent rocket. "Boost gliders" are very popular now; these are somewhat like hand-launched gliders, but are powered by model-rocket engines, which are generally ejected and lowered by parachute, while the glider should soar for a time before again touching down. With the tiny radio-control equipment now available, some of these gliders have been equipped for radio steering on the way down.

Many local model-rocket meets are held around this country and in other countries as well. There is a Rocket Nationals every year in the United States, and international model-rocket competition, like the very popular international model-airplane competition, takes place under the auspices of the Fédération Aéronautique Internationale.

The NAR has offices with the AMA (see address in appendix I) and co-operates closely with the plane model group. It is through the AMA that the NAR has entered the international arena.

Here is the Safety Code of the NAR, which gives considerable insight into the aims of model-rocket builders.

I am a model rocketeer and do not engage in any other form of non-professional rocketry. As a member of the National Association of Rocketry, it is my responsibility to keep model rocketry safe. Because safety is my watchword, I will obey this NAR Model Rocket Safety Code:

1. I will use only pre-loaded factory-made commercial model rocket engines that do not require my mixing of chemicals.
2. I will make model rockets of paper, wood, plastic, and other non-metallic materials.
3. I will always use a recovery device in my model rockets that will return them safely to the ground so that they may be flown again.
4. My model rockets will weigh less than 500 grams and will contain less than 125 grams of propellant in their engines.
5. My model rockets will contain no explosive warheads.
6. I will fly model rockets in open areas away from buildings and power lines.
7. I will check the stability of my model rockets before flying them so that their flight paths will be predictable.
8. I will use a remotely-operated electrical firing system to ignite and launch my model rockets.
9. I will use a launching device that is pointed within 30 degrees of the vertical.
10. My model rockets will not be flown as weapons against targets.
11. I will fly model rockets in good weather conditions only.
12. I know that model rockets share the air with other objects and must present no hazard to such objects.

Needless to say, application for membership in the NAR requires that the applicant agree to abide by this code.

Now, what of the model rockets themselves? Bodies are usually made of tough but light cardboard tubes, sometimes of sheet-balsa tube. Nose cones are usually turned of balsa or other light wood. Diameter averages about 1 inch, but some are smaller, others considerably larger. The engines come in a rather bewildering variety of sizes and designs. However, *all* are one-use units, all have solid fuel, and all are electrically ignited. Most weigh only a few ounces loaded.

It is quite possible to send a rocket aloft with a cluster of engines, that is, with several engines grouped together at the tail end and ignited simultaneously. Also, many multistage rockets have been flown successfully; in these, the engines ignite successively. As one engine burns out, this one and its section drop off to return slowly earthward, while another engine in the next stage is ignited to continue the flight.

Unlike many full-scale rockets seen at Cape Kennedy and other launching areas, model rockets always have fins to assure stability—and often relatively large fins. These fins are usually of balsa, though stiff card is also utilized.

The engines are made to standardized outer diameters, and the rocket-body tubes sold in hobby shops have a controlled inside diameter. Thus, engines are usually held in place by a push fit. If they are loose, a bit of sticky tape will make them snug. Most engines have several burning mixtures within. The main body of fuel is ignited to lift the rocket skyward; when this has burned out, a "delay" fuel burns for a few seconds; this has no thrust, but does emit smoke which enables the modeler to spot his rocket high in the sky. Then comes an ejection charge. The purpose of this latter is to pop out a recovery parachute which lowers the entire rocket slowly and safely to the ground, so that it may be used again. The nose cone is blown off by this charge; at the same

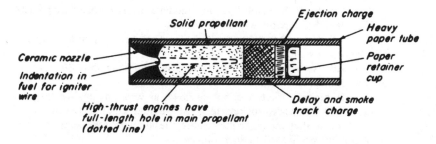

Fig. 17-1.   Model Rocket Engine Cross Section

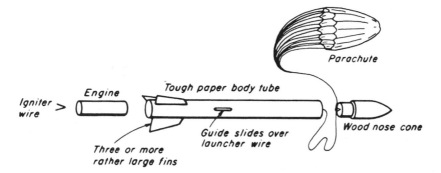

Fig. 17-2.   Model Rocket Components

time the parachute pops, but the cone is attached to the rocket body by a rubber band or cord, so it does not drop free or become lost.

Rockets recovered by parachute must have a fairly long body, but some modelers may wish to fly shorter rockets; in this case the parachute is omitted, but a slow descent is obtained in another way. When the ejection charge goes off, it blows off the nose cone, which upsets the aerodynamic balance of the rocket, and with the cone still tied by cord to the body, it tumbles to earth end over end. It thus lands safely and can usually be used again.

As noted previously, model rockets are *always* ignited by electrical means. Fuses, matches, or fire of any sort have no place on a model-rocket launching area. The igniter is usually a short length of electrical resistance wire, bent in hairpin shape and pushed into the end of the engine; all engines have a slight depression in the fuel for this purpose. The wire is not inserted until just before launching, and inserting it is the last task before take-off. Wires with clips on their ends run from the launch pad to a spot some distance away (at least 16 feet), where the starting battery and switch are situated. The clips are attached to the two hairpin ends, care being taken that they do not touch each other.

A 6-volt battery is generally used for ignition, and a small storage battery is ideal. A plain switch will do the job, but often rather complex switching is used to insure absolute safety. A key switch (auto ignition switches do nicely) is sometimes in the circuit, the key being carried by the modeler who last leaves the launching pad, so that premature switch-throwing and ignition are not possible.

The term "launching pad" sounds complex, especially when we think of the immensely complicated and expensive arrangements seen at Cape Kennedy. But for model rockets it can be very simple; a 3-foot length

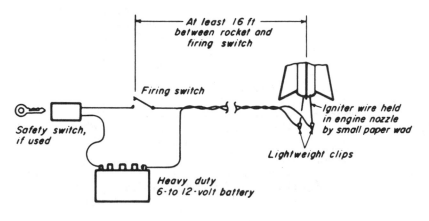

Fig. 17-3.   Firing Circuit

of ⅛-inch-diameter music wire does fine! It must be firmly attached to a sturdy base that will assure launching the rocket straight up. The rocket body has guides cemented to its side to fit over the wire; sections of soda straws are often used as guides. Rockets are generally launched as nearly vertical as possible; this assures that they will come down close to the launch area and not be lost. The wire is sometimes inclined slightly to compensate for wind, but this is a variation for the experienced modrocs to determine.

Just as in model aviation, there is a large variety of engines for model rockets, broken up into groups depending on internal engine construction and on size. There are three main categories. Series I engines are called "end-burning," which means the solid fuel burns only across the ignition end (after a slight burst due to the hole for the ignition wire, which serves to get the rocket off the pad quickly), and they burn moderately slowly. Series II engines have a hole through the center of the solid fuel endwise and burn rapidly and with high thrust, since the fuel burns from the hole outward and the entire length of the fuel charge is burning at once. Series III engines are of small size and are all end-burning. The ¼A and ½A engines in the table are of this style. If a rocket designation has a "0" on the end, it means there is no delay or ejection charge; these are used in the boosters of multistage rockets.

Actual size of engines goes according to the NAR classification in the accompanying table.

Letter Code	Total Impulses (lb/sec)
¼ A	0–0.14
½ A	0.15–0.28
A	0.29–0.56
B	0.57–1.12
C	1.13–2.24
D	2.25–4.48
E	4.49–8.96
F	8.97–17.92

Most engines used today are in the A to C sizes. Model rocketeers are getting into the same problems as model-plane fliers—not enough areas to fly the larger rockets—and hence rockets in the smaller sizes are favored. A representative engine might be labeled "B 3–5"; this would indicate a unit of from .57- to 1.12-pound-per-second total impulse or thrust, about 3 pounds of average thrust, and a 5-second delay time before the ejection charge fires. If there were a 0 instead of the 5, it would mean no ejection charge at all.

Besides designing his own model rockets from the many components available, the aspiring model rocketeer has other choices; he can build a proved design from the countless kits available or from plans that appear in hobby magazines. The kit route is doubtless the best for the novice in this field. After successfully constructing and firing a few kits, he is ready to branch out on his own.

Payloads consist of plain weight carried near the rocket nose or such objects as the egg already mentioned. Still cameras have been lofted, taking fine pictures of the area under the rocket. Light movie cameras have also been sent aloft. Some more advanced modrocs have fitted a very light transmitter in the rocket nose; this can be arranged to record altitude, with a suitable barometric measuring and switching device.

Boost gliders generally have drop-off engine pods, which are wafted to ground by a parachute, thus removing a considerable weight from the glider and allowing a long shallow flight downward. Some boost gliders have been fitted with folding wings, which pop out at the end of the power phase, but most wings are fixed. Since tiny radio equipment is now available that will allow proportional steering for a total weight of ¾ ounce (and still lighter equipment is imminent), the boost glider can be successfully steered earthward.

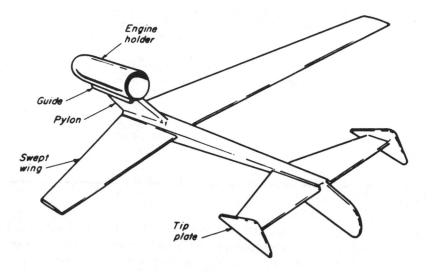

Fig. 17-4.   Simple Boost Glider

With all the possibilities open to them, model rocketeers are increasing in numbers, and competitions are becoming more numerous. There have already been meets overseas with many participating countries, with United States rocketeers attending some of them. Having really started only in 1957, this is a rapidly growing field and one expected to attract many more modelers in the near future.

NOTE

Although illegal under the terms of the Explosives Act of 1892 Model Rocketry commands wide interest in the United Kingdom and efforts are being made to obtain exemption for solid propellant commercial limits as described here and used in the U.S.A.

GLOSSARY

ACTUATOR—A device used to move the controls of a plane by radio; usually found in simple pulse proportional systems.

AERODYNAMICS—The science or study of the forces acting on an airplane in motion.

AIRFOIL—The cross-section shape of a wing taken at right angles to the wing span; also known as the wing section or rib section.

AIRSCREW—The airplane propeller.

ANGLE OF INCIDENCE—Angle of the wing in relation to an arbitrary line fore and aft in the fuselage.

ANTENNA—Vertical rod for emitting signals from a transmitter; also, a wire used to receive signals in the model.

ASPECT RATIO—The relationship of the wing span to the wing chord, expressed numerically by the number of times the span can be divided by the chord.

ATTACK, ANGLE OF—The angle at which a wing strikes the air stream.

AUTOGIRO—An airplane that flies by virtue of freewheeling rotating wings, set "windmill" fashion above the fuselage.

BAFFLE—A kind of wall or partition, as inside a fuel tank, to prevent the sloshing or surging of the fuel; or on top of a piston, to prevent the incoming fuel mixture from going out the exhaust port.

BALLOON TANK—May be common toy balloon used as fuel tank in some U-control planes, or special tank made for the same purpose.

BANK—A turn made in flight with one wing tip lower than the other.

BAR SCALE—Reduced scale, usually showing twelve inches, included in a drawing of less than full size, to indicate degree of reduction.

BEARING—A tubular fitting in a wood wheel to prevent wear of the axle hole; or a washer or metal plate used between the propeller and the plane nose to reduce friction; the part of an engine that holds the crankshaft.

BELLCRANK—The pivoted wood, metal, or plastic arm which converts the motion of the control lines to up-and-down movement of the elevators.

BOOM—A wood tube or strip that extends rearward from the wings or from a short fuselage to support the tail surfaces.

BOOSTER—Holdover term from spark-ignition days; refers to the battery that heats the glow plug.

BOOST GLIDER—A form of model rocket much like a hand-launched glider but propelled aloft by a rocket engine, which drops off when expended.

BORE—The internal diameter of the engine cylinder.

BULKHEAD—A wood former cut from sheet balsa or ply. Used as internal support for longerons, sheet sides, stringers, and so on.

BUSHING—A hat-shaped tubular fitting used in wood wheels to prevent elongation of the axle hole.

CAMBER—The curvature of the wing or horizontal tail, from the leading edge to the trailing edge.

CAP STRIP—A thin flat strip of wood cemented to the upper and lower surfaces of ribs, to support the covering.

CARBURETOR—A device for mixing, metering, and feeding vaporized fuel and air to an engine.

CENTER OF GRAVITY, OR WEIGHT (CG)—The spot where the mass or weight of an airplane may be said to center.

CENTER OF LIFT (CL)—The spot where the lift of a wing (or wings) is said to center.

CENTER OF PRESSURE (CP)—The point on the upper surface of a wing, relative to the chord, where the lift can be said to center.

CHASSIS—Landing gear.

CHOKE—To block the air intake of an engine in order to admit raw fuel for starting purposes, rather than a mixture of fuel and air.

CONSTANT-CHORD WING—One that has parallel leading and trailing edges, with no taper.

CONTRA PISTON—A second piston, adjustable by a screw on the cylinder head, to vary the compression ratio of a model compression-ignition engine.

CONTROL HANDLE—Device held in the hand, to which control lines are attached; rocking movements of handle are carried via lines to the model-plane elevators.

CONTROL-LINE (CL) FLYING—A method for tethering a model to fly in circles around the pilot, who can vary elevator position.

COWLING—A specially shaped nose to enclose the engine.

CRANKCASE—The lower section of an engine, in which is housed the crankshaft.

CRUTCH—Main structural assembly of a model-plane fuselage, consisting of two flat longerons with crosspieces.

CRYSTAL CONTROL—A method of assuring that the frequency of a transmitter or receiver does not vary from the desired spot.

CUBIC-INCH DISPLACEMENT—Volume of a cylinder, calculated between the top of the piston in the up position and its top in the down position.

CYLINDER—The upper part of an engine which houses the piston.

DÉCALAGE—Angular difference between the wing and stabilizer.

DETHERMALIZER—A timer-operated device that functions after a set interval to cause the model to descend rapidly groundward.

DIAMETER, PROPELLER—The size of a propeller measured from tip to tip.

DIHEDRAL—The uptilt of wing panels toward the tips, for purposes of stability.

DOLLY—Wheeled wire assembly used to launch U-control speed models.

DOUBLER—A second sheet of wood cemented inside the main fuselage side sheets on each side, for added strength.

DOUBLE-SURFACE WING—A wing which is covered on both top and bottom with paper, cloth, or other material.

DOWEL—A round hardwood strip.

DOWNTHRUST—The tilting down of the propeller, hence the thrust line, to exert a slight downward pull and offset stalling tendencies.

DRAG—Resistance of the plane to movement through the air.

D-SPAR, or SECTION—A very strong and rigid wing construction utilized widely in radio and control-line stunt planes; wing usually has top and bottom spars at about 30 per cent back from leading edge, balsa sheeting back to these spars, and webs of vertical-grain sheet balsa between each two ribs which are cemented to the two main spars. Cross-section view of the webs and top and bottom sheeting is somewhat D-shaped.

DUCTED FAN—A small-diameter, multibladed rotor, used as a substitute for a propeller in jet-type models in which both fan and engine are mounted inside the fuselage.

DUMMY MOTOR—A nonworking copy of a radial airplane engine used to enhance the appearance of a scale model.

DUTCH ROLL—A side-to-side wallowing motion of a model, often caused by insufficient fin area.

EJECTION CHARGE—A small powder charge which ejects the nose cone and usually a parachute, after the main rocket propulsion charge has burned out.

ELEVATOR—The hinged control section of the horizontal tail or stabilizer.

ENTERING EDGE—The front edge of a wing; also called leading edge.

ESCAPEMENT—An electromechanical ratchet device that applies the power of twisted rubber bands to the controls of a radio model plane.

EXHIBITION MODEL—A nonflying model that is built for appearance only.

FALSE RIB—Short wing rib used between main ribs at the leading edge.

FF—Free flight.

FILLER—A substance used to fill the pores in wood before covering or finishing.

FILLET—A rounded contour used at the junction of vertical and horizontal surfaces on a plane, to reduce wind resistance.

FIN—The fixed forward portion of the vertical tail surfaces.

FIREWALL—A ply bulkhead immediately behind the engine.

FLAPS—Hinged surfaces attached to the trailing edge of a wing, either to increase maneuverability (as on a U-control stunter) or to increase drag (as on radio-control planes).

FLASH—Rough edges on parts of plastic models.

FLIGHT TIMER—A mechanical device that stops the engine after a desired interval; similar device may be used to actuate dethermalizer.

FLOAT (or PONTOON)—A boatlike part that supports a model in water.

FLOOD (or FLOODED)—An engine which has excess fuel in the crankcase that prevents it from starting.

FLYING BOAT—An airplane with a fuselage shaped like a boat, for operation on water.

FLYING SCALE MODEL—A flyable miniature of a real airplane.

FLYWHEEL—Small heavy wheel attached to an engine crankshaft, to smooth operation.

FORMER—See Bulkhead.

FOUR CYCLE—An engine that requires two revolutions of the crankshaft to achieve one power pulse.

FREEWHEELER—A propeller with a special device that allows it to windmill after the rubber motor is unwound.

FUEL-PROOFER—A liquid applied to a painted surface to render it impervious to the damaging effects of glow fuel.

FULL-HOUSE MULTI—A control system for radio planes that includes (at least) variable rudder, elevator, ailerons, and throttle.

FUSELAGE—The body of an airplane.

GALLOPING GHOST—Simplified pulse-proportional radio system that allows simultaneous operation of rudder, elevator, and throttle.

GASSIE—Term applied to any model plane driven by an internal-combustion engine (originated with spark-ignition-engined planes that utilized gasoline fuel).

GEODETIC—A latticework or basket-weave construction.

G-LINE—A form of control-line flying in which the model is tethered by a single line to the tip of a short pole held in the flier's hand.

GLOW PLUG—A device that looks like a spark plug, but has a heated wire element to ignite the fuel in the cylinder.

GUIDE PLATE—A piece of ply, sheet metal, or formed wire with two holes through which pass the leadouts to the control lines; usually external to the wing.

GUSSET—Small strengtheners, often of ply, cemented at points of heavy stress.

HAND-LAUNCH (HL)—To start a model in flight by releasing it or throwing it from the hand.

HAND WINDER—A hand drill or other rotary device equipped with a hook, and used to speed winding of the rubber motor.

HELICOPTER—An aircraft that can rise or descend vertically, by means of large overhead power-driven rotor or rotors.

HYDRO—A model that can take off and land on water.

IDLE BLEED—An adjustment on an engine intake that compensates for an overly rich fuel mixture at slow speeds.

IDLING CURRENT—Current drawn by a receiver when it is tuned to a transmitter but with no tone coming in.

IGNITER—A resistance wire used to fire the fuel charge in a rocket.

INCIDENCE, ANGLE OF—The angular setting of the wing chord relative to the thrust line (or some other arbitrary line through the fuselage).

INDUCED DRAG—Resistance of a wing to forward movement due to disturbance of the surrounding air.

INTERNAL COMBUSTION (IC)—An engine in which fuel is burned inside the cylinder, as opposed to one where it is burned outside (as in a steam engine).

JIG—A fixture or form for holding parts together for assembly.

KEEL—A wide precut piece of sheet balsa used as the backbone of bulkheaded fuselages.

KIT—A boxed assembly of parts for a model.

LANDING GEAR—The wheel and strut assembly that supports a plane at rest on the ground and during take-off and landing.

LAPPED—A precision machining process for obtaining a very close fit between piston and cylinder, or other moving parts.

LEADING EDGE—The front or entering edge of a wing or tail.

LEADOUT—The heavy wires that are attached to the bellcrank and which extend out past the wing tip, to fasten to the control wires.

LEAN—A condition of improper engine adjustment wherein there is too little fuel in the fuel-air mixture.

LIFT COEFFICIENT—An indication of the relative lift of an airfoil.

LIFT-DRAG RATIO—The relation of total lift to total drag of an airfoil, expressed as a mathematical proportion, as 6 to 1, 15 to 1, and so on.

LINKAGE—Mechanical connections between servos (also escapement and actuators) and the controls of a radio plane.

LONGERONS—The main fore-and-aft strips in a fuselage.

LUBRICANT—A liquid mixture rubbed into the strands of a rubber motor to increase turn capacity and life.

MASTER STRINGER—A wide flat strip of balsa sheet, used like a keel piece, but on the sides of an oval fuselage as well as on the bottom.

MICROFILM—A very thin transparent covering for indoor models made by pouring a special liquid on water.

MODROC—Name given to model rocketeers.

MODULATION—The application of a tone to a radio-frequency signal.

MOMENT ARM—The distance from the center of gravity at which a force is applied. Distance between the CG and nose, or CG and tail, for example.

MONOCOQUE—A form of fuselage construction with rounded exterior and very little internal structure in which the skin carries virtually all stresses.

MONO-LINE—A form of control-line flying, in which the elevators are actuated by a single wire between control handle and plane.

MOTOR BEARER—Hardwood strip mount for glow engines.

MOTOR STICK—A heavy strip used to support the rubber motor; the body of stick-type models.

MUSH—A nose-high, slow-speed flight attitude resulting from a slightly tail-heavy trim.

NEEDLE VALVE—An adjustable screw that varies the fuel intake of an engine.

NEOPRENE—Synthetic-rubber fuel tubing that is more or less impervious to the deteriorating action of glow fuels.

NOSE PLUG—A shaped wooden block used to support the propeller bearing.

ORNITHOPTER—A freak-type airplane that flies by flapping its wings like a bird.

PARASITIC DRAG—Resistance to forward plane movement caused by any nonlifting components of the plane.

PARASOL—An airplane in which the wing is mounted above the fuselage on struts.

PISTON—The close-fitting part which moves up and down in an engine cylinder.

PITCH—The distance forward theoretically traveled by a propeller in one revolution, assuming no slippage.

PITCH-DIAMETER RATIO—The relation between the propeller pitch and diameter, expressed as a mathematical proportion, as $1\frac{1}{2}:1$, and so on.

PITCH STABILITY—Stability of a model in climb and dive.

PLANFORM—The outline of wing or stabilizer when viewed from above.

PLANKING—Sheet-wood covering accomplished by cementing thin flat balsa strips side by side on a fuselage.

PLASTICIZE—Addition of materials to dope that prevent it from drying to a hard, brittle finish.

PLUG CLIP—Connector to glow-plug terminals, attached to wires from starting battery.

PLYWOOD—Sheet wood made by gluing together two or more very thin layers of wood with the grain of adjacent layers at right angles.

POD—A short streamlined fuselage fitted with a boom to support the tail surfaces.

POD-AND-BOOM—A model that derives its name from the appearance of its short fuselage and tail-support boom.

POLYHEDRAL—A modification of dihedral, wherein the different panels of a wing are tilted upward at varying angles.

PONTOON—A float or boatlike device that supports a plane on the water.

PORT—An opening in an engine to admit or exhaust gases.

PREFAB—Short for prefabrication, which includes die-cutting and shaping of wood and other parts in a model-plane kit, to facilitate rapid and accurate construction.

PRIME—To squirt unvaporized fuel into the exhaust or intake of an engine, to facilitate cold starting.

PROPELLER—An airscrew that bores its way through the air, pushing or pulling the airplane.

PROPELLER HANGER—A metal fitting used to hold the propeller shaft on a motor stick.

PROPORTIONAL—A form of radio control wherein the surfaces on the model closely follow the movement of a stick or sticks on the transmitter.

PTERODACTYL—A tailless airplane; a flying wing.

PULL-TEST—A controlled strain placed on the control wires and mechanism of a control-line plane to insure its meeting safety requirements before being flown in competition.

PULSE-OMISSION DETECTOR (POD)—Radio-control-plane circuitry that senses lack of pulse modulation and actuates a control device.

PULSE PROPORTIONAL—A simplified form of proportional in which the control surfaces can be seen to have slight continuous movement.

PULSER—The keying circuitry at a transmitter which forms the desired proportional pulses, in response to control-stick movement.

PUSHER—A plane in which the engine is mounted ahead of the propeller, so that the propeller pushes instead of pulls.

PYLON—A fin-type mount for the wing.

QUARTER GRAIN—A wood cut which results in nonbendable sheet, across the grain; also known as C-cut wood.

RADIAL MOUNT—Attachment of an engine directly to the firewall, by means of screws at the rear of the crankcase.

RC—Radio control.

REEL—A storage unit for holding control lines; also for holding glider towline.

RELAY—A device used in radio-control receivers to convert a small current change to a current large enough to operate servos and other control units. Being replaced today by transistor circuitry.

RESISTANCE—Air drag, or the opposition of the air to being displaced by the forward movement of a plane.

REYNOLDS NUMBER—An expression of the difference in performance of small wings (such as model size) from those of full-size planes.

RIB SECTION—The cross-section shape of a wing, from leading to trailing edge.

RICH—A mixture that has too much fuel for the amount of air being drawn into an engine.

RISE-OFF-GROUND (ROG)—A model that will take off under its own power.

RISE-OFF-WATER (ROW)—A model that will take off from water.

RISER—A thermal, or upward-moving column of air.

RUDDER—The vertical tail surface of a plane. Actually, only the rearmost movable portion of the vertical tail on a full-size plane.

SAILPLANE—A highly efficient glider, capable of flying for long periods in gently rising air currents.

SERVO—A motor-driven device for moving controls of a radio plane.

SHEET BALSA—Thin, flat slices of balsa wood.

S-HOOK—A wire fitting that allows quick rubber detachment from a rear hook, for purposes of winding or replacement.

SHUT-OFF—A timed device for cutting the flow of fuel to a model engine, to limit the duration of powered flight.

SIDE THRUST—Offsetting the propeller thrust line, so there is a slight sideways pull.

SINGLE-SURFACE WING—A wing formed from a single sheet of balsa, or one that has a framework covered only on the top.

SLIP STREAM—The column of air pushed rearward by a rotating propeller; it always moves faster than the plane itself.

SOLID MODEL—A nonflying model formed from solid pieces of wood or plastic.

SPARS—Spanwise load-carrying members of a wing or tail.

SPECIFIC IMPULSE—A figure expressing the power output of a model rocket engine.

SPEED PAN—Light cast-metal lower fuselage shell for a speed control-line model, usually of magnesium.

SPIRAL DIVE—An ever-tightening downward corkscrew flying path.

SPIRAL STABILITY—The characteristic of a model that permits high-speed banked turns without diving to the ground.

SPONSON—Stubby, winglike projections on either side of a hull that prevent a model from tipping over on the water; a "sea wing."

SPRAY BAR—A fuel-inlet tube in which the needle valve rotates.

SQUIRT GUN—A fuel can of the pump type.

STABILITY—The tendency of a model to return to level flight, after having been disturbed by any upsetting force.

STABILIZER—The fixed horizontal tail surface.

STALL—The complete loss of lift resulting from too steep an angle of attack.

STALLING POINT—The particular angle at which a wing abruptly loses lift; usually expressed in degrees.

STEP—An abrupt crosswise break in the bottom surface of a pontoon or flying-boat hull, to assist in breaking water suction on take-off.

STICK—A type of model having a plain motor stick as a fuselage.

STOOGE—A device attached to the ground which restrains a U-control plane from take-off until a release cord is operated.

STREAMLINE—To shape the exposed contours of a plane for the least possible air drag; usually rounded in front, pointed at the rear.

STRINGER—Light, lengthwise fuselage strips intended more to give the desired shape than to add strength.

STROKE—The distance that a piston moves up and down in a cylinder.

STUNTED—Said of a plane which has been flown through acrobatic maneuvers (that is, "stunts"). Such a plane is sometimes termed a "stunter."

SUPERHETERODYNE—A form of receiver of considerable complexity, that affords ample sensitivity and very sharp tuning. Also called "superhet."

SUPERREGENERATIVE—A form of receiver characterized by reasonable simplicity, high sensitivity, but very broad tuning. Also called "super-regen" or just "regen."

SWEEPBACK—The angling back of the wings from the center, to increase directional stability.

TAB—A small adjustable surface on wing or tail surfaces, used to make small trim changes.

TAIL—The surfaces at the rear of a conventional plane fuselage.

TAIL SKID—A wire or wood extension downward from the fuselage tail, to support the model on the ground and to prevent damage to the tail parts in take-offs and landings.

TANGENT CUT—A form of balsa cut that produces a very bendable sheet. Also known as A-cut.

TEAM RACER—Special type of U-control plane flown simultaneously with similar planes over a specified number of laps.

TEMPLATE—A stiff pattern for marking the outlines of pieces to be cut from sheet wood or metal.

TENSIONER—A device for keeping rubber motors moderately taut after they have almost unwound.

THERMAL—A rising column of relatively warm air.

THINNER—A liquid used to dilute dope or cement.

THRUST—The propulsive force developed by a whirling propeller.

THRUST BEARING—A washer, tube, or metal plate attached to the nose of a model to hold the propeller shaft; another form of propeller hanger; a bearing holding against thrust.

THRUST LINE—An imaginary line drawn along the propeller shaft and extending rearward through the model.

TIP LOSS—Reduction in lift near the tips of wings due to the leakage of the high-pressure air from beneath to the low-pressure area above.

TORQUE—The reactive force generated by a revolving propeller that tends to rotate the model in a direction counter to the direction of propeller rotation.

TOWLINE—The launching cord used for pulling aloft a glider or sailplane.

TRACTOR—A puller propeller, or a model equipped with such a propeller.

TRAILING EDGE—The rear edge of a wing or tail surface.

TRANSMITTER—Radio device used to generate signals to steer a radio-control plane.

TRICYCLE—A three-wheeled landing gear, with nose wheel, plus two main wheels to the rear.

TRIMMABLE SERVO—A control-surface (or throttle) mover that may be moved to any position, but that is not proportional.

TRUE PITCH—A type of propeller so carved that all points along the blade theoretically travel the same distance forward during a revolution.

TUNGSTEN WIRE—Extremely thin but strong wire used to brace components of featherweight indoor models.

TWO CYCLE—A type of engine that requires one revolution of the crankshaft for each power impulse.

U-CONTROL (UC)—Another term for control-line model flying.

UNDERCAMBER—The concave curve on the underside of some airfoils.

VENEER—A form of extremely thin hardwood or plywood.

VENTURI—The air-intake passage of a model-plane engine.

VORTICES—Twisting air disturbances resulting from the movement of a wing through the air.

WASHIN—Twist incorporated in wing tips to raise the leading edge.

WASHOUT—Twist incorporated in wing tips to raise the trailing edge.

WEDGE TANK—A control-line stunt tank of wedge-shaped cross section that insures steady engine running throughout stunt maneuvers.

WING—The principal supporting surface of a plane.

WING SECTION—AIRFOIL—RIB SECTION—The chordwise cross section of a wing.

ZOOM—An abrupt and steep climb.

APPENDIX 1
Useful Association Addresses

SMAE   Society of Model Aeronautical Engineers.
Sec. R. Nudds, Kimberley House, Vaughan Way, Leicester.

BARCS   British Association of Radio Control Soarers.
Sec. J. Whitaker, 29 Ferriby Road, Hessle, N. Humberside.

CLAPA   Control Line Aerobatic Pilots Association.
Sec. Ted Fowler, 36 Wimblestraw Road, Berinsfield, Oxford.

IPMS   International Plastic Modellers Society.
Sec. G. Hogg, 49 Fountains Garth, Wild Ridings, Bracknell, Berks, RG12 4RH.

SAA   Scottish Aeromodellers Association.
Sec. Ian Glen, 5 Brownhill View, Bonkle, Wishaw, Lanarkshire, Scotland.

MACI   Model Aeronautical Council of Ireland.
Sec. J. McCarthy, Bellvue, Winsord Hill, Glounthane, Co. Cork, N. Ireland.

BMPRA   British Miniature Pylon Racing Association.
Sec. I. King, The Forge Bakery, 50 Silver Street, Dursley, Gloucester GL11 4ND.

CTA   Club Twenty Association.
Sec. A. Rathbone, 1 Hillyard Road, Southam, Warwickshire.

BRCHA   British Radio Control Helicopter Association.
Sec. P. Ashford, 5 Olympic Way, Greenford, Middlesex.

CFA   Combat Flyers Association.
Sec. Jim Carolan, 261 Daniells, Welwyn Garden City, Herts.

RAFMAA   Royal Air Force Model Aircraft Association.
Sec. Flt. Lt. Tom Whittle, 25 Balmoral Road, Oakham, Rutland LR15 6RT.

LSMA   Large Scale Model Association. *Sec.* T. Yates, 45 Cowley Road, Littlemore, Oxford.

APPENDIX 11
Publications

AEROMODELLING MAGAZINES OF THE WORLD

Aerosplai, Aragon 331-1°, Barcelona 9, SPAIN.
Adepte, 16 rue de l'Evangile, 75018 Paris, FRANCE.
Aeromodeller, 13/35 Bridge Street, Hemel Hempstead, Herts., HP1 1EE, ENGLAND.
Aero Revue, Lidostrasse 5, 6006 Lucerne 15, SWITZERLAND.
Airborne, 11 Cornwall Close, Gladstone Park 3043, AUSTRALIA.
Aviation News, High St., Berkhamstead, Herts., ENGLAND.
Control Line Technique, Kinokuni Bldgs., 1-4-2- Ebesu-Minami, Shibuya-Ku, P.P. Codel, 150, JAPAN.
El Aeromodelo, San Antonio Maria Claret 47, Zaragoza, SPAIN.
Flaps, Zuniga 16, Valladolid, SPAIN.
Flug + Model Technik, Fremersbergstrasse 5, 7570 Baden-Baden, WEST GERMANY.
Flying Models, PO Box 700, Newton, New Jersey 0786, U.S.A.
Flyv, Romersgade 19, Copenhagen 1362, DENMARK.
Hobby, Skolgrand 8A, PO Box 9185, 102 73 Stockholm 9, SWEDEN.
Hobby Bulletin, PO Box 10, Bussum, NETHERLANDS.
Indoor News and Views, Box 545, Richardson, Texas 75081, U.S.A.
Indian Modeller, 15 Shakespeare Sarassi, Calcutta 16, INDIA.
Ilmailu, Malmin Lentoasema 1, Helsinki, 70 FINLAND 00700.
La Conquette de l'Air, 53 Avenue des Arts, Brussels 4, BELGIUM.
Le Modele Reduit d'Avion, 12 rue Mulet, 69001 Lyon, FRANCE.
Model Aviation, Academy Model Aeronautics, 815 Fifteenth Street N.W., Washington DC. 20005, U.S.A.
Model Airplane News, 837 Post Road, Darien, Connecticut 06820, U.S.A.
Modelar, Jungmannova 24, 11000 Praha 1, CZECHOSLOVAKIA.
Modelarz, ul Chocimska 14, Warsaw, POLAND.
Modell Bau Heute, Sterkower Strasse 158, 1053, Berlin, D.D.R.

Model Builder, 621 West Nineteenth Street, Costa Mesa, CA. 92627, U.S.A.
Modelflygnytt, Alborggsde 17, 4th, København, DENMARK.
Modellflygnytt, Box 8044, 421-08 V Frolunda, SWEDEN.
Modele Magazine, 15-17 Quai de l'Oise 75019, Paris, FRANCE.
Modell, Postfach 1820, Klosterring 1, 733 Villingen, W. GERMANY.
Modellezes, H-1093 Budapest 1X, Szamuely, U44, HUNGARY.
Modellistica, Borgo Pinti 99r., (Vincino via Giusti) 50121 Firenze, ITALY.
National Free Flight Digest, 654 India Street, San Diego, Ca. 92101, U.S.A.
Playmodel, Via Nemorense 90A, Rome, ITALY.
Radio Control Modeler, Box 487, Sierra Madre, California, U.S.A.
R/C Sportsman, PO Box 11247, Reno, Nevada 89510, U.S.A.
Radio Control Technique, Kinokuni Buildings, 1-4-2 Ebesu-Minami, Shibuya-Ku, Japan.
Radio Modeller, 13/35 Bridge Street, Hemel Hempstead, Herts., HP1 1EE, ENGLAND.
Radio Modelisme, 12 rue des Jeuneurs, Paris 2e, FRANCE.
R/C Scale Modeler, Challenge Publications Inc., 7950 Deering Ave., Canoga Park, Ca. 91304, U.S.A.
R/C Modelle, Ernstmeystrasse 8, 7022 Leinfelden, Echterdingen 1, Postfach 1380, WEST GERMANY.
R.C.M.&E., 13-35 Bridge Street, Hemel Hempstead, Herts., HP1 1EE, ENGLAND.
Scale Aircraft Modelling, High Street, Berkhamstead, Herts, ENGLAND.
Scale Models, 13/35 Bridge Street, Hemel Hempstead, Herts, HP1 1EE, ENGLAND.
Skrzydlata Polska, ul Widok 8, Warsaw 10, POLAND.
Sport Modelismo, Rua Lidia Coelho 5, CX Postal 12235, Sao Paulo, BRAZIL.
Sea & Sky, Patrio Planning 1-22 Yothuya, Shin Jukuku, Tokyo, JAPAN.
Wings of Fatherland, Moscow B66, New Riadanskia 26, U.S.S.R.
Young Modeller, Moscow A39, Suczewskaya U1, 21, U.S.S.R.

BOOKS

All About Model Aircraft by Peter Chinn (Model and Allied Publications Ltd.). 160 pages illustrated, a detailed book for the novice, hard cover.

Aeromodeller Pocket Data Book (Model and Allied Publications Ltd.). Compilation of 61 pages, detailed explanatory sketch instructions on every branch of the hobby.

Aircraft in Miniature by W. O. Doylend (Model and Allied Publications Ltd.). A 130-page book on the art of making solid scale models.

Aeromodeller Annual a compilation (Model and Allied Publications Ltd.). 128 pages produced 1948-1979 with 50 designs, leading articles of note and references.

Aerofoils for Aeromodellers by Martyn Pressnell (Pitman). 208 pages A/4 format, reference to wide range of useful wing sections.

Control-line Manual by R. G. Moulton (Model and Allied Publications Ltd.). 216 pages complete course on Control-line models with historical background.

Flying Scale Models by R. G. Moulton (Model and Allied Publications Ltd.). 128-page standard reference book, acknowledged as the authority for all scale model data.

Know Your Model Aero Engines by R. H. Warring (Model and Allied Publications Ltd.). Covering glow and diesel, plus brief insight into CO_2 engines. 110 pages.

Multi Channel Radio Control by R. H. Warring (Model and Allied Publications Ltd.). 112 pages excellent guide to sophisticated radio equipment explained in simple terms.

Modern Aeromodelling by R. G. Moulton (Faber and Faber). 160-page introduction in simple terms to all kinds of models.

Model Aircraft Aerodynamics by Martin Simons (Model and Allied Publications Ltd.). A detailed work on aerodynamics as applied to flying models, by a professional specialist. Covers the theory of flight in relation to model aircraft, tables of optimum airfoil sections and dimensions, scores of diagrams and pictures. 271 pages.

Radio Control Helicopter Models by J. Drake (Model and Allied Publications Ltd.). Design and construction of radio-control helicopter models. John Drake has specialised in model helicopter design and development for a number of years, and as a computer engineer has made a scientific approach to the subject. 144 pages.

Solarbo Book of Balsa Models by R. H. Warring (Model and Allied Publications Ltd.). 112 pages large format constructional plans compiled with instructions for all forms of elementary model making, including aeromodelling.

INDEX